Evil Men

Evil Men

James Dawes

Harvard University Press

Cambridge, Massachusetts / London, England / 2013

Library of Congress Cataloging-in-Publication Data

Dawes, James, 1969–
    Evil men / James Dawes.
       pages cm
    Includes bibliographical references and index.
    ISBN 978-0-674-07265-7 (alk. paper)
    1. Sino-Japanese War, 1937–1945—Atrocities—Psychological aspects.
    2. Sino-Japanese War, 1937–1945—Personal narratives, Japanese.
    3. War criminals—Japan—Interviews.   4. War criminals—Psychology.
    5. War crimes—Psychological aspects. I. Title.
    DS777.533.A86D38   2013
    940.54'050951—dc23   2012038236

Book design by Dean Bornstein

For my family

CONTENTS

Teachers in our high schools pound it into us that "historia" is "magistra vitae." But when history crashed down upon us in all its brutal glory, I understood, in the very real glow of the flames above my home city, that she was a strange teacher. She gave to the people who consciously survived her, and to all who followed her, more material for thought than all the old chronicles put together. A dense and dark material. It will require the work of many consciences to shed light on it.

—Zbigniew Herbert

PREFACE

This book is about atrocity: what it looks like, what it feels like, what causes it, and how we might stop it. The story began when I traveled with the photographer Adam Nadel to Japan to interview a group of war criminals from the Second Sino-Japanese War. Aging and frail when I met them, many in their eighties, they had done the worst things imaginable as young men. All of them had eventually been captured and held for a decade in prison camps. They showed me pictures of themselves from the war years, faded black-and-white snapshots of young men in uniform, faces proud or scared, fierce or boyish. Looking at their younger selves, they told me they saw emptiness; they saw demons.

I have been involved in the human rights community for many years but before this had never worked with perpetrators. I wasn't ready for how disorienting it would be, how startling to find myself, over time, beginning to see the world through their eyes. The style and structure of this book are designed to share that experience with you. This book isn't just about the things war criminals do; it is about what it is like to befriend them.

In this preface, I develop a cluster of questions about what it means for us today that these evils happened and, perhaps more important, that they continue to happen. The questions are also a conceptual map of the book. The flow of the pages that follow simulates the visual flow of a photographer's searching zoom lens: broadly framing a scene; closing in slowly on a field of visual details; zooming back out again to see the larger setting afresh, the details now lost in the expanding focus but still vivid, like the visual imprint of sunlight gazed upon too long; then zooming back in again on another site of concern.

As I proceed through the book's questions, I will highlight some of the paradoxes inherent to them. The poet John Keats, in a different context, talks about "negative capability": the capacity to experience uncertainty, mystery, and doubt, and to remain *open* to them, to resist the impulse to reduce everything to familiar terms and categories that we can control. Negative capability allows us to experience paradox—and its cousin in the realm of form, juxtaposition—as a way of opening questions, and sometimes meaning, where no words are.

1. To begin: What is at stake ethically in writing and reading this book? How can we look at violently invasive and traumatic events with respect and care rather than sensational curiosity? How do profoundly private injuries fit into our mercilessly public spaces? At the center of the answers to these questions is a single, structuring paradox: the paradox of trauma. *We are morally obligated to represent trauma, but we are also morally obligated not to.*

2. If we are going to move forward together with these shocking stories, what use can we make of them? Can they help us answer questions like this: How do societies turn normal men into monsters? With more focus: What is the individual psychological process and felt experience of becoming a monster? With yet more focus: Given that these monsters are so often men, what role does gender play in genocidal violence? Here, too, the answers revolve around key paradoxes, including the paradox of evil *(Evil is demonic and other; it is also banal and common to us all)* and the paradox of agency and responsibility *(We are free and self-determining; we are also the products of circumstance).*

3. Zooming back out: How does the outrageous suffering we see affect our comprehensive vision of being in the world, our "big picture" beliefs: our hopes for the human future; our final optimism or pessimism; our thoughts on altruism, transcendence, and even the divine? Some of the familiar paradoxes here include the paradox of altruism *(Altruism involves the sacrifice of our interests to benefit others; it also involves the satisfaction of our interests through benefiting others)*, the paradox of nihilism *(To find our meaning we must face our meaninglessness)*, and the characteristically Christian version of the paradox of evil *(How could God be both omnipotent and good and still permit evil?)*.

4. After such cruelty—cruelty that not only shocks our consciences but also destabilizes our understanding of the world—is apology possible? How can individuals or nations expect forgiveness for crimes beyond thinking? And how can they confess truthfully when memory is frail, self-protective, and self-serving, when history itself is tissued with lies? Indeed, what place is there for truth at all in war, torture, and confession? Thinking through this range of related questions will require continually returning to the paradox of confession. *Confession is a healing cultural form that we need; it is also a potentially damaging one.*

5. Finally, to end where we began. Confessions like these are stories, with their own particular ethics. What are the ethics of storytelling more generally? It is here, for me, that the most personally difficult paradox presses: the paradox of writing. *To write about other people's private lives, you must develop respectful, intimate relations with them; but to write about other people's private lives, you must also treat them impersonally, as characters to be constructed, manipulated, and displayed.* Many

people do the difficult work of writing and reading stories of suffering because they believe that it promotes human dignity to do so. Storytelling is not only the most basic work of human rights advocacy, it is also the most basic work of human empathy. But do the stories we tell make a difference? What kind of difference? When we look at violently invasive and traumatic events, is it really possible to do so with respect and care rather than sensational curiosity? What will happen when you read this book?

Evil Men

Do you miss your old war buddies—the people you were with until the end of the war?

Oh, yeah. I miss them. Most of them were, you know, like brothers. Really. They were really like your family.

I'd imagine so . . .

Yeah, we've been through life-or-death struggles together. You know? It's more than what you've been through with your own brothers. I do miss those guys, of course.

———

Each time, I hand the interviewee a small sachet of wild rice from Minnesota. Each time, I begin with awkward, repetitive half-bows, and the same joke about how I cannot properly pronounce "I'm glad to meet you" or even "Thank you." They smile, and I can tell they are surprised to be smiling, and I think it is good that I start each time from weakness.

In the morning, the photographer and I get coffee and pastries outside our hotel. In the evening, the interpreter takes us out for fun: to kabuki, to a martial arts exhibition, to the best inexpensive sushi, to her favorite old bar. The three of us talk about everything but the men.

———

Why was I able to do those sorts of things? Even I don't understand that . . . I'm a farming man after all, I thought—a man from a farming family. I thought that afterwards. That's how you feel in the end, you know. Ah, I'm not a man who would do something like that.

I have never seen a professional fight until tonight. Some of the martial arts displays have been gentle, liquid dances, but this one is a fight. It will be over soon. One man is winning now. He is holding the other man down on the mat and keeps hitting him very hard on the head, over and over. The audience collectively groans with each soft thud. It must hurt, badly, but the man being hit hasn't got any sort of look on his face at all—he looks only like empty waiting. The man hitting him, though, his face is so alive with expression, so wrenched, it looks like he must be angry or afraid, but I cannot tell which.

I stay after long enough, talking with the photographer and interpreter, that I end up in an elevator with the fighters going home. I see then that they are not men, they are boys really. I am surprised to find I am taller than them. In fact, it is almost shocking to stand next to them, to see them there together, smiling and talking. Up close I can see abrasions on the loser's cheek and I think: he has rug burn. For some reason this makes me feel tender toward him. I want to lean close to him and ask: How do you go back, after that, to what's normal?

"You little shits! Asshole!"—that sort of thing. However, we didn't break them down. We tried to pull them up. Because if something happened—if we screwed something up—they'd go to war and die quickly. It was meant to push them forward, to motivate them to act quickly. That's why we scolded them. They get trained to act properly, right? If they become like that, they can avoid the bullet when they get shot. That's why we did that.

I feel uncomfortable that we are going out for entertainment together in the evenings. It feels so discordant. Now I am a tourist at a shrine, now I am asking a dying man to tell me how he learned to torture, now I am discussing aesthetics over drinks with an award-winning photographer. I don't understand how to put these things next to each other. It is like somebody has taken a crowbar and pried open the seams of the everyday, so that the evils we cover over, block out, are now suddenly there, implacably next to us, next to everything.

In fact, that is how I think of the time the three of us spend together, the mornings and nights. They are the "next to" times: what happens next to the interviews. This makes them sound unimportant, and at first I think they are, but over time I begin to change my mind. It matters so much that there is a "next to," whatever it is.

I keep thinking about what it means to be next to something, about what fits together. Once, driving to work, I skidded on the ice and very nearly killed somebody. In the end, nothing happened, it was only being scared. But it was strange just going to work afterward.

It seems to me that I have until now organized my life to be seamless.

And people who could not do that would be shamed after all?
There was no "can't do it" . . . We forced, we forced them to stab.

Over steamy coffee in a Minnesota winter, my friend Anne asks me: Why didn't they kill themselves? She is a quietly indomitable woman, a physician used to asking difficult questions. She flicks her copper-red hair away from her eyes and fixes me with her gaze. Why didn't you ask?

I have no experience working with perpetrators. Spending time with these men, I sometimes felt like I was receiving a guided tour of hell. It was a feeling of intimacy and of vertigo at the same time, of being directed and, simultaneously, being lost. So I processed it the way most professors process new things: I controlled it by trying to make it scholarly. I have looked for help in many places. Much of it has come from the traditions of the arts and humanities. How have great works of literature attempted to give meaning to the carnage of history? How have different religious and philosophical traditions approached the problem of atrocity, reconciling the world's relentless cruelties with belief in higher purposes, existential meaning, or the divine? I have also received a great deal of help from important formulations in the social sciences. What are the political and cultural features common to genocides? What are the organizational and psychological processes for turning men into monsters? And how might these processes be reversed?

These are important questions, and I'm going to share with you the answers I have found to them. But if there is one question at the heart of this book, it is something very different. It is this: What does it mean for me to tell you these stories, and for you to listen to them? That is still the question that troubles me the most. It is the question that determines how these pages follow, how things go next to each other. I'm going to ask and answer it in many different ways as we proceed.

Here is the first story.

Sakakura-san

But then, suddenly, from the village, a group of fifteen, sixteen people jumped out. And at that time I had never even seen the Eighth Route Army [the primary military force of the Communist Party of China], what our enemies looked like before. And I didn't know what sort of people these were, so I quickly dropped down on my stomach. Because lots of people had come out. And then the general said: "Fire!" He said, "Shoot them all!" And so I—I shot too. The bullet I fired hit. "It actually hit," I thought. And most of the people, they dropped like flies, you know?

After they went down, then—there was a sorghum field, it was right in the middle of June, so it was big. The sorghum had grown, grown up to here. [He gestures] And everyone fell into that, or ran into it, all sorts of things. I ran right off after them. And where I went, in that sorghum field, there was a collapsed person. I looked, and it was a housewife. The housewife, she had fallen over dead. And I thought, "Okay, a housewife. Nothing I can do about that," I thought. I started to go, and from under the housewife's arm, there was a small baby, you see. A small baby stuck his head out. And his hand—[silent] well, he was touching the woman's breasts, you know, looking for them, touched them, you know. And then he looked at my face, and he smiled at me. And this really shocked me. After that, I found I couldn't really walk, you know? And then, uh, more than scared, it was . . . I felt a shiver up my spine. And then, although I tried to go, I couldn't walk. And really, the older soldiers came in from behind, came in; we were being chased—"Run away!" they said. And then I left it just like that. We ran away, and then, so, after that, I thought about it, that child, with nobody around, would just die like that, I thought, and that was the most—of the war—my actions, for the first time—that sort of, to me, disgusting sort of feeling—that feeling really hit me, you know? So that's one thing that happened.

———

That is the middle of Sakakura-san's story. When it begins he is a civilian; when it ends he is a perpetrator.

At the time Sakakura-san told me about the baby, he was near death, and he was trying to make sense of his life. He had spent many years in prison camp—and many more years in social exile—examining the things he had done and the things done to him. He had committed atrocities, caused incalculable suffering, but he had also experienced trauma. Indeed, he had experienced his own crimes as trauma. He felt the closeness of death now, he said, like a kind of "pressure." "I don't have a future . . . If I don't hurry up and talk now—if I die, there'll be nobody to tell these stories."

Sakakura-san and the other veterans I interviewed constituted a distinct group. They were all former members of the Chukiren, an association of antiwar veterans that had worked for forty-five years to draw attention to Imperial Japanese war crimes and to promote friendship between Japan and China. They represented a group of approximately 1,100 Japanese soldiers who had been imprisoned by the Soviet Union after the war and then extradited years later to Fushun Prison in China. The Siberian prisons were inhumanly brutal. Fushun Prison was disorienting in its near complete contrast. Chinese staff there were instructed to receive their prisoners like guests, treating them with respect, feeding them well, attending to their medical needs, and organizing sporting and cultural activities for them. The prisoners also underwent thought reform: after a time, they experienced something like a religious conversion. They repudiated the values of their pasts—indeed, repudiated their past selves—and committed themselves to lives of almost evangelical pacifism. The veterans now describe this transformation as "The Miracle at Fushun." In 1956, military tribunals were finally held for the men. Forty-five were indicted. All were eventually freed.

In 1957, these returnees established a formal organization in Japan to support each other in their efforts to end the silence about Imperial Japanese war crimes. Largely scorned or ignored by the public and mainstream media, they nonetheless continued their activism until 2002, when age-related health problems made it impossible for most members to carry on. The Chukiren Peace Memorial Museum was established in Saitama Prefecture shortly after by a new generation of activists. Housing over 20,000 books, with related videos and photographs, it is a warren of bookshelves and seminar tables, more of a resource center and library than a museum. It was here that we were first introduced to the soldiers.

From the start, it seemed to me that the men saw themselves as products of history. They embraced blame, but as part of a context that exceeded them. After World War I, Japan emerged as the dominant military force in Asia. The increasingly militarized country, organized under the rule of the divine emperor, was anxious to assert its power and to resist the pressures of Western imperialism. But to secure its regional hegemony, Japan needed to control resources in China. The result was a catastrophic race "between Chinese reunification and Japanese expansion in China."[1] In 1931, Japan invaded Manchuria and set up the puppet state Manchukuo. Full-scale war began six years later, after a minor military engagement at Marco Polo Bridge. Japan narrated the ensuing conflicts, and all of its war crimes, as a matter of racial glory and destiny. A government report compiled in 1943 presented Japanese territorial ambitions as proto-humanitarian interventions: "We, the Yamato race, are presently spilling our 'blood' to realize our mission in world history of establishing a Greater East Asia Co-Prosperity. In order to liberate the billion people of Asia, and also to maintain our position of leadership over the Greater East Asia Co-Prosperity Sphere forever, we must plant the 'blood' of the Yamato race in this 'soil.'"[2]

Religious justifications echoed imperial ones. Even Zen scholars joined in, publishing arguments that China had failed as a nation in its understanding of Buddhism and needed to be saved from itself. Through Japan's superior spiritual understanding, China would find "its unreasonableness corrected." "Through a compassionate war, the warring nations are able to improve themselves, and war is able to exterminate itself."[3]

This context is what the Chukiren wanted to emphasize to me, as an American. U.S. forces were occupying Iraq as we spoke. There is always a context.

———

Atrocity both requires and resists representation. The argument that we must bear witness to atrocity, that we must tell the stories, is the core of the catechism of the human rights movement. We gather testimony, we investigate and detail war crimes, because we are morally bound to do so. Our obligation is acutely urgent in cases where legal prosecution is a realistic possibility, but it is also powerful long after the call for trials has faded into history—especially when there is a robust practice of denial and historical revision, as there is in Japan. We are creating a collective moral archive of our time for future generations. We are making public history intelligible to survivors who have seen their deepest personal truths denied daily. And sometimes, as the soldiers I spoke to believed, we are using the safe-to-imagine past as a way of making visible what we are doing in the present.

In recent decades, Japanese government officials, scholars, and former military officers of all ranks have denied and downplayed the atrocities committed by Imperial Japan. In 1994, Minister of Justice Shigeto Nagano described the 1937 Nanking Massacre—in which an estimated 300,000 civilians were murdered—as a "fabrication." In the carefully worded apology that followed, he continually referred to the "Nanking Incident."[4] In 2007, Prime Minister Shinzo Abe denied that Korean women were coerced into becoming military sex slaves.[5] In 2001, the Ministry of Education approved for use a revisionist school history textbook that glossed over war crimes, including the Nanking Massacre, the widespread use of sex slaves, and experimentation with germ warfare on Chinese civilians.[6] In 2005, a book by a Japanese scholar was translated into English (and personally sent to me by the publisher) that lambasted the late author Iris Chang for perpetuating "the myth of a massacre's having been perpetrated in Nanking."[7] The list could go on. If Elie Wiesel is right in saying that to forget is to kill twice, then the Second Sino-Japanese War never ended. It just shifted to the landscape of memory.

So all of us—the photographer, the interpreter, and I—began this project with the same assumption: bearing witness to atrocity, in this case and in general, is a good unto itself. Whether it's telling the story of the crime as it's happening or collecting and sharing the testimony years later as we were doing, the struggle for human rights and the battle of memory requires a single clear moral position: either speak out or be silent, either resist or be complicit.

I am not so sure anymore.

There is a paradox to representing suffering. To stop people from being injured, we have to tell the story of what's happening; but in telling the story, we can injure people in unexpected ways. We hope to shame perpetrators into moral obedience, but sometimes incite them to further violence. We hope to elicit compassion from spectators, but sometimes further their desensitization or even generate disgust. We hope to give therapeutic voice to survivors, but sometimes retraumatize them. We hope to turn distant strangers into vivid, intimately felt persons, but sometimes only trap them in the abstract, two-dimensional identity of "victim."

I see now that there is a corollary for belated testimony, for representing suffering distant not only in place but also in time. Gathering evidence is an act of respect to survivors and to the dead, and it is a small but real verbal bulwark against the repetition of mass atrocity. And so we will again and again say "never again." But gathering and sharing evidence triggers chains of consequences we cannot control. It, too, causes harm. Over the course of this project, I began to believe that the work of collecting perpetrator testimony requires moral myopia, perhaps even arrogance. To me, there seemed to be no other way to make it through the thicket of questions the work poses. What is at stake in telling the perpetrators' stories when the victims cannot tell theirs? When does listening to and recording a plea for forgiveness become a silent promise of forgiveness, a forgiveness you have no right to bestow or deny? And what is your motivation for doing the work: the call of responsibility to the other, the narcissism of moral righteousness, or the writer's desire for sensational material? Is showing the most vicious and crude details an exercise in the pornography of evil? Or is failing to do so moral cowardice? If you self-censor, are you protecting trauma from representation—from invasive staring, simplification, dissection? Or are you ignoring trauma's cry for representation and reenacting the bystander avoidance that makes such cruelties possible in the first place?[8]

Emmanuel Dongala is the author of *Johnny Mad Dog,* a novel about a child soldier in the Congolese Civil War. Dongala was himself a refugee from the war, saved from likely death by a group of humanitarian workers. Dongala knew the only reason the humanitarian workers had been able to reach him was because they had been able to raise money and gain access by revealing dramatic stories like his about suffering in Congo. He knew, in the moment of his rescue, that he was trading his story for his life. But when we spoke about it he told me he was also painfully aware of the dehumanizing quality of such storytelling, aware that the price of each such rescue was a solidification of the image of the suffering African, the African whose natural state is suffering. It wasn't only that such images contributed to the racist logic manifest in, for instance, François Mitterrand's infamous comment about Rwanda: "In countries like that, a genocide is not very important."[9] It was also that such storytelling involved a kind of theft not unlike the theft of war looting itself. As a young African woman insists in Dongala's novel, in response to a plea from a Western journalist to film her dying mother: "Mama's stumps were *our* suffering, *our* pain . . . We had the right to keep it private."[10]

Susan Sontag has written extensively about the ethical problems of atrocity photography, about our desire to take pictures of the dying and our desire, later, to gaze upon the images. She concludes:

One can feel obliged to look at photographs that record great cruelties and crimes. One should feel obliged to think about what it means to look at them, about the capacity actually to assimilate what they show. Not all reactions to these pictures are under the supervision of reason and conscience. Most depictions of tormented, mutilated bodies do arouse a prurient interest . . . All images that display the violation of an attractive body are, to a certain degree, pornographic. But images of the repulsive can also allure. Everyone knows that what slows down highway traffic going past a horrendous car crash is not only curiosity. It is also, for many, the wish to see something gruesome. Calling such wishes "morbid" suggests a rare aberration, but the attraction to such sites is not rare, and is a perennial source of inner torment.[11]

Our enjoyment—or rather, the fear of our capacity for enjoyment—is indeed a torment. But what about the problem of enjoyment on the other side of the camera? What about perpetrators who are not hiding from the cameras, but performing for them? Human rights workers who use "exposure" as an intervention technique face difficult questions about its effectiveness. What is the point of seeing if we cannot act on what we see? What if seeing promotes "story fatigue" rather than action? More troubling, they also face questions about whether exposure-as-intervention might be a service to perpetrators. As Thomas Keenan writes, mobilizing shame in a shameless world could just be a kind of perverse publicity work.[12]

Such problems may be insoluble. But we have no other choice than to live in the possibility of their solution.

———

In his novel *The Wind-Up Bird Chronicle*, a magisterial account of atrocity and memory in the Second Sino-Japanese War, Haruki Murakami presents a poignant model of personal narration as counterspell to meaninglessness through the character Lieutenant Mamiya. Mamiya witnesses and suffers intolerable cruelty in the war; it leaves him emptied of personhood. He continues to exist for decades after, but he is profoundly affectless, seeing little point in living, and little difference in it from dying. In his last days, however, he has the chance to talk about the war with a sympathetic listener. Making bundles of meaning out of his memories feels like purpose to him, and remembering what it feels like when there's a point to living makes it easier—or rather, more fitting—for him to die.

In telling their stories, the Chukiren were seeking not so much a chance for a meaningful life as a chance for a life that wasn't, finally, meaningless. Avoiding meaninglessness meant, for most, achieving a sense of coherence: that is, conceptualizing their lives as tellable and purposeful stories, moving out of the isolation of incommunicable memory into the reciprocity of shared narrative. There had to be a way to make comprehensible stories out of their incomprehensible evils. Their lives had to be more than a pointlessly intersecting series of events to no purpose. If experiencing the events of our lives as causeless, as essentially nonnarrative in form, is a basic, existential human trauma, then creating a personal history that can be shared with another is a basic form of rescue. To do so is to imagine the life arc as a linear narration, as a series of events with causes, with joys that are not accidental and suffering that is not reasonless. And to be the author of such linear narration is to control events that were once frighteningly out of control.

For the men I met, there were many paths to coherence and meaning. For some, it was apology. "I am, without argument, truly wrong, and I know this—I am sorry. There's nothing I could say but that," Sakakura-san said. "By telling these stories, I seek atonement." For others, it was grieving, a use of narrative to give enclosing shape to the otherwise open wound of melancholia. For still others, it was intervention; it was warning. *This is what you are becoming, perhaps have already become.* It mattered to the veterans that I was a U.S. writer. Americans, they believed, must not be allowed to continue averting their gaze from the filthy details of their wars. And for most of them, it was pro-Communism, anti-militarism, and anti-imperialism. As Kubotera-san said, reeducation in Communist prison camp had helped them to see that they had become "devils"; it therefore also "revived" them "as human beings." Now, their lives had a clear mission. Their end days had purpose. "We should come together now and ask today's young people never to repeat our mistakes," Koyama-san said. "We must say this consistently until we die."

But there is always a remainder, something unshareable that endures. This exchange between my interpreter and another veteran, Kaneko-san, is typical:

KANEKO-SAN. Make sure the professors understand.

INTERPRETER. Right. I'll be sure to tell them.

KANEKO-SAN. Please do . . . I want to say that, I say it everywhere I go. Anything and everything is pinned on us soldiers . . . What's being worshipped at Yasukuni [a shrine to the war dead]—it's just a bunch of names on paper. That's what's left there. Where do you think the remains are? The bones? In the Siberian dirt. In Chinese dirt. In the southern islands. There—everybody's still buried in the ocean. The bones. Isn't that right? The dead—the—[mumbling], we saw the bodies. It was wretched.

INTERPRETER. You've been—

KANEKO-SAN. Please. I'm counting on you.

INTERPRETER. [Translating to me] "I'm counting on you to repeat it—"

KANEKO-SAN. Do you think they understood?

INTERPRETER. Right, no problem.

KANEKO-SAN. Do you think they understand?

INTERPRETER. I just—I just said it all properly.

Cathy Caruth has argued that the problem of putting trauma into words isn't so much a problem of description as it is a problem of experience. "In trauma," she writes, "the greatest confrontation with reality may also occur as an absolute numbing to it."[13] Trauma represents an impossibility in language because it is primarily an assault on meaning rather than a kind of meaning. There is no final understanding. There is no transcendence. There are only momentary stays against confusion.

———

I try not to sound frustrated when I whisper to her. *You can stop writing, please. Ask him what it felt like the first time.* The man I'm interviewing, Kaneko-san, has recently returned from the hospital for intestinal blockage. He is eighty-eight years old. The skin hangs from his arms like draping sheets. He is getting tired and will want to stop before we're finished—I know it. We do not have much time.

My interpreter is writing down a shorthand outline of every answer the man gives as he gives it. Sometimes, after he has finished speaking, I wait a full minute or two while she continues to write. *Please stop writing,* I tell her, *let's just move to the next question. I don't need the outline; we will translate it all later.* Her head twitches and her eyes dart back and forth between me and the man and she's still writing, jerkily. *Wait,* she says, *I'm almost done.* She's not a professional. She volunteered to do this for free. The photographer and I truly had to force money on her. She's a graduate student; she cares about the project, feels some personal connection to it. The work is stressing her out.

What was it like the first time you raped someone—how did you feel?
There—isn't really a feeling for that, you know? It was just, "I want to try that out"—that's all.

At night we drink and laugh a lot, the interpreter, the photographer, and I. The interpreter is hilarious; the photographer is hilarious on purpose. After a day of interviews, we're all jittery and confused, but the photographer is never rattled. He buys us sake and makes us laugh. Being together for so long in such strange circumstances, we sometimes tell each other things we wouldn't otherwise tell people. They slip out between jokes because we need to say them and because we know—however much we may be the whole world to each other now—that our lives will separate soon and that there will be no uncomfortable consequences to the sharing. You can always tell when the interpreter is about to say something. She tenses her body into a preparatory coil, like she is about to physically hand something to us, and then she announces things about herself. At one point it occurs to me, very suddenly, that she is beautiful.

During the day, dehydrated on subways, we talk about the frustrations she is having interpreting, simultaneously as she shapes my posture with impatient, untouching hands so that I take up less space and seem less disorderly. *There are no matching words,* she glares at me, waving my arm to my side and my feet together. How long it takes us to come to a shared understanding of the word "razzing"! (The photographer fits in easily everywhere—no glares for him—but one time he elbows a businesswoman's forehead while getting off the subway, and everybody stares, and I feel happier. "Gaijin," our interpreter apologizes.)

But the complexities we have are not just about words or about the way I hold my body. I think of studies I've read that say interpreters can become more focused on pleasing the person who hired them than on serving the people they are giving voice to. Or that in their role as cultural mediators, they are always involved in the tricky tangle of saving face for themselves and for others—and that even though this is just as important as their work as "language converters" and can radically change what kind of information you end up getting, it isn't ever intelligently planned for.[14] I learn later, when reading transcripts, that our interpreter doesn't always ask the questions the photographer and I ask her to ask. And sometimes I ask a short, direct question, hoping to have a bracing conversational effect, which she then interprets in a way that takes an inexplicably long time. The photographer and I look at each other then with question-mark eyebrows, befuddled. Reading the translations later, I see she is sometimes apologizing for, or softening, the question. (Thank you, I am whispering to her.)

The problem of being lost in translation carried over into the transcription of testimony. I hired secondary interpreters to double-check all the work of my primary interpreters. They didn't always agree. One insisted another was translating too formally, like a "prude." For instance, she wanted to change "I was mad" to "I got pissed off"; "No, the jerk at NHK didn't air me" to "No, the fricking NHK didn't air me"; and "There was none of that, of course, just things like 'Come on, pick up pace, you bum!'" to "Hell no! No fuckin' way! Sure—well . . . we said things like 'Come on, pick up the pace, you asshole!'" Another insisted the language of the men was just too old-fashioned, hard to understand both on tape and on the page. Also, two of the interpreters I hired quit. In both cases, they interviewed successfully and I gave them materials to work on. They began their work, and then I didn't hear from them again for a long time, despite repeated attempts to contact them. They finally admitted they had quit, indicating symptoms of depression. One of them got in trouble with family members when they discovered what the work was about. In that case—an error of judgment only a college professor could make—I had prepaid for several months' worth of work. I couldn't bring myself to ask for it back. When the photographer organized our travel, he made sure we had a Japanese "fixer" to structure professional and institutional interactions. Photographers know how to do things.

Those comfort stations cost money, right? And rape doesn't cost a penny, right? . . . We didn't have money, so we didn't really go to the comfort stations. And since rape is free—so when we went to the front, we definitely did rape. "How many'd you do?" This sort of thing. "I did two," or "I did three." With this, too, a sort of competitive mood would spring up.

But, one thing I can say, that one time, all sorts of—it's a disgusting story, though—whether pregnant women felt good or not—I'd hear that sort of thing. And we, you know, we'd actually go and search out women who looked like they were pregnant. That sort of thing happened, you know? And then, after we'd done her, we wouldn't kill her. Yeah. Sometimes we'd kill her, however—if she resisted, we'd kill her. Three, five, six soldiers would come together, drag out a woman, pin her hands and legs down, and again spread them out, then shove a rod inside. Shove in a rod. And then we'd kill her. That sort of thing happened, you know?

And the people over there—the women, they thought they'd be ra, rap, raped by Japanese soldiers—troops, right? And in the kitchens over there they have these large stoves. And in these stoves, black ash. They would rub it on their faces, like this . . . And when they did that, they thought Japanese soldiers wouldn't rape them, so they rubbed it on their faces like this. But we thought: "These idiots . . . This kind of thing, we're going to do it anyway." And we raped them; we went and did it anyway. 'Cause it just didn't matter, right? However, then the women thought of a different strategy. What do you think they thought of?

What, I wonder? [The interpreter's laugh conveys confusion]

Feces! . . . They would take feces, right? And rub it here. And sure enough, we didn't go after them like that. And so, we'd go to a place, to a village, right? And they'd take crap, maybe kids' crap, and rub it all over themselves. It really smelled awful, and we couldn't get close. And then we thought, "This bitch, mocking us," and then beat her. We'd look for another woman—as to be expected.

My interpreter is a buffer between me and the men—but one, I think, that makes them feel safe, less directly challenged, more willing to open up. Sometimes when the men are talking my interpreter doesn't translate, so I sit and listen with open, passive attention, as if to music. My mind wanders sometimes. I listen to the sound of the monk chanting in the next room. I think about what I'm going to do with this material. I wonder why I am here: responsibility or curiosity? I feel horrible that I can't stay focused on the moment, that I'm thinking about how to write about this, that I'm thinking of it as material at all. The photographer is like a natural force when he works, entirely present, radiating concentration. The interpreter kneels before each interviewee, tight-wired with focus but at the same time deferential, gentle, eyes wide. She knows why she is there. I watch her. When the interviews start the men don't look at her when they're answering questions, they look at me and the photographer. They think we can do something. More than one has said they are counting on us. They have told their stories before in Japan, but only so many are willing to listen. They believe we can get their message out more effectively to the rest of the world.

When we first arrived in Tokyo, we were taken on an off-hours tour of a local peace museum by the staff. At the end, they asked us to use our power in the media to help them resist censorship pressures from the local government and the nationalists. I was too embarrassed to be honest and admit that it was preposterous to think I could do something; but I also couldn't bring myself to lie to them outright and say I would help. So I repeated their request and earnestly affirmed their need—a cowardly move, because I knew they would interpret my response, wrongly, as an implicit promise that I would do something. Why else would I be there?

This is a question from Dr. Dawes. You've talked to me about this . . . um . . . many things so honestly. What he's wondering is how you feel talking about things like rape to someone like me, a woman of the younger generation . . .

I hated it at first . . . The conversations get dirty . . . But if I don't talk about it—people wouldn't know how the position of women was really miserable, you know? If I just say the words "comfort women," nobody would understand it, you know? They would just think if you only get men and money—they would just think those women did it with men for money. You wouldn't know the reality, right? If they don't know the story behind—they wouldn't understand what it was like inside comfort stations. That's why I talk about it. I hated it at first. Yeah. Of course. Even our buddies, if they get asked things like, "Didja go to a comfort station?"—they would hem and haw around saying, "Well . . ." "Didja rape anybody?" And we'd say, "Well . . . rape, huh . . . Well, I heard that they certainly did that . . ." They'd dodge the question. Everybody was like that at the beginning. It's only recently, everybody has started talking about it. Things started changing little by little, you know? At the beginning, even I hated it . . . But because this was something I had to do, I talked about it . . .

When there's a war, the ones who cry the most—are women. Their husbands—the fathers of their children are dragged into the army. And basically, if their husbands die, what do you think happens? They live hand to mouth crying—right? And then eventually they end up turning into comfort women . . . How are they supposed to make a living with their kids? It's the same as with [unclear]. As long as you have things, you can sell them. After you skin everything, all that's left is your body, at the end, you know? So, eventually—they sell their body, make money and get

by. It is the women who suffer the most. And so I always, everywhere I go,
I always say—women should be the ones who oppose war the most . . .
It's our responsibility to do this sort of thing, you know. This is
something we don't want to bring on young people again. That's our
conviction . . . That's why I'm telling this story to you—up front. I hated
it at first. My wife, too—everybody hated it. My kids hated it. You know?
My kids said, "Dad . . . don't bullshit . . ." Everybody was like that, see?
The issue with comfort women—everybody—wives didn't like it. Wives
would even say, "Divorce me!" They would say that, you know? And that's
why they didn't talk about it, but I thought I had to . . . everybody . . .
[Mumbling] Did Mr. Y——— talk about it? Did he?

———

If there is a dominant image or model for helping us think about
war criminals today, it is likely to be found in the Nazi bureaucrat
Adolf Eichmann, who played a major organizational role in the
deportation of European Jews to extermination centers. Eichmann
as an example offers a way of seeing; he is a type, so to speak, that
prepares us to understand other types of his sort, types we otherwise can't or don't want to understand. During the Iraq War, for
instance, Eichmann was the shadow behind Lynddie England, who
tortured and abused prisoners at Abu Ghraib prison in Baghdad.
Evil as represented in these figures is *thoughtless,* in both senses of
the word: not only unthinking of others but also incapable of thinking. Eichmann, Hannah Arendt explains, was most notable not for
diabolic villainy but for his "remoteness from reality," a remoteness identifiable through the symptoms of his language: he spoke
in clichés, used stock phrases, seldom varied his words. "The longer
one listened to him," Arendt writes, "the more obvious it became
that his inability to speak was closely connected with an inability
to *think,* namely, to think from the standpoint of somebody else.

No communication was possible with him, not because he lied but because he was surrounded by the most reliable of all safeguards against the words and the presence of others, and hence against reality as such." Eichmann, insists Arendt, simply *"never realized what he was doing."*[15] This is what evil looks like. It is unimaginative, banal. It is the Lynddie England we have constructed in our media. It is the Lynddie England of Judith Thompson's play *Palace of the End,* who delivers monologues composed of language used before: clichés, snippets of songs, advertising jingles, movie lines—prepackaged language as a safeguard against thought.

There were moments in my conversations with these veterans when I felt them retreating behind the protection of packaged narratives. Over the years they had found a way to describe to themselves what they had done, stories they had told over and over again, stories with beginnings and endings and involuntarily memorized phrases. At one point I became frustrated with this. The stories were honest, but they felt like a barrier, a defense against the possibility of engaging sincerely in the moment. When Kaneko-san started doing this in one of our conversations, I asked him what I thought would be an unexpected question, something that would force him to think past the protective, rote narrative. He was an old man, very traditional. It was easy to surprise him. He was not used to being asked about his feelings; people just wanted to hear about his crimes.

Did you ever tell your mom?

The conversation stumbled when I asked this. He wasn't ready for it; he became agitated. My interpreter had to ask the question twice, to explain the shift in conversational gears. Kaneko-san explained that his mother died shortly after he came home. In fact, he believed she had waited for him to return before she died. *When I came back home,* Kaneko-san said, *my mom made me dinner. Do you know one of my favorites, azuki?* [Clicks his tongue] *Sort of a—a home-*

town bean soup, she had made that. And I said, "Ma, I'm home!" And at
the time, she was sick, and—she had lost an eye; it was gone. And so with
one eye, she stared me firmly in the face. She stared me firmly in the face
and . . . she touched my legs.

At this point in the conversation, Kaneko-san starts to cry. My
interpreter turns to me and whispers: *In Japan, we believe ghosts don't*
have legs. If you fear somebody is a ghost, you touch their legs.

(Kaneko-san lived alone with his wife until 2009, when they built a
duplex to live in with his older daughter's family. One year later, on
November 25, 2010, he passed away. He was born in Urayasu in 1920
and went to Jinjo Elementary School. Before being drafted he
worked at a scrap iron company in Tokyo.)

———

In the winter of 1960, Stanley Milgram began pilot experiments for
a study on obedience, using as subjects male adults between twenty
and fifty years old. They all lived in the New Haven and Bridge-
port, Connecticut, areas and worked in a variety of occupations.
Subjects were given the role of "teacher" in a rigged "teacher-
learner" experiment on memory. They were told by a fake doctor
in a lab coat to shock a "learner" every time he gave a wrong answer. The shocks were to increase in intensity with each wrong
answer, up to 450 volts (which read "Danger: Severe Shock—XXX").
As the experiment proceeded, the fake learner made increasingly
desperate pleas to stop; the fake experimenter insisted each time
that the teacher must continue.

Milgram asked forty psychiatrists from a prominent medical
school to predict the performance of subjects in the experiment.
They predicted that most subjects wouldn't go past 150 volts, that
nearly 96 percent of subjects would defy the experimenter at 300

volts, and that at 450 volts only one-tenth of one percent would obey. Astonishingly, 62 percent of subjects continued to deliver shocks until the bitter end of the experiment.

When the teachers delivered the shocks, they did so with evident distress, stuttering, trembling, giggling nervously, sweating. Some gave lower than the required level of shock when the experimenter was not present. In versions of the study where the learner was visible, teachers averted their gaze when delivering shocks. Here's Milgram's account of one of the exchanges with a teacher who continued delivering shocks all the way up to 450 volts.

150 volts delivered. You want me to keep going?

165 volts delivered. That guy is hollering in there. There's a lot of them here [referring to the questions that remained to be asked]. He's liable to have heart condition. You want me to go?

180 volts delivered. He can't stand it! I'm not going to kill that man in there! You hear him hollering? He's hollering. He can't stand it. What if something happens to him?...I'm not going to get that man sick in there. He's hollering in there. You know what I mean? I mean I refuse to take responsibility. He's getting hurt in there. He's in there hollering. Too many left here. Geez, if he gets them wrong. There's too many of them left. I mean who is going to take responsibility if anything happens to that gentleman?

[*The experimenter accepts responsibility.*] All right.

195 volts delivered. You see he's hollering. Hear that. Gee, I don't know. [*The experimenter says: "The experiment requires that you go on."*]—I know it does, sir, but I mean—hugh—he don't know what he's in for. He's up to 195 volts.

210 volts delivered

225 volts delivered

240 volts delivered. Aw, no. You mean I've got to keep going up with the scale? No sir. I'm not going to kill that man! I'm not going to give him 450 volts!

[*The experimenter says: "The experiment requires that you go on."*]—I know it does, but that man is hollering in there, sir . . . [16]

Throughout this process, the learner's shrieks of pain can be heard through the walls of the laboratory. "Let me out!" "You have no right to hold me here!" "My heart's bothering me!" Eventually, the learner stops responding altogether. In the video record of the experiment, you can see the teacher covering his face with his hand as he delivers each shock, calling out to the learner: "Answer please! Are you all right?" He tells the experimenter he believes something has happened to the man, and asks to look in upon him. "He might be dead in there!" The experimenter refuses, and the teacher continues delivering shocks, very upset. "You accept all responsibility?" he asks. The experimenter does. The teacher continues to deliver 450 volt shocks until the experimenter finally stops the experiment.

In the debriefing immediately after the experiment, the experimenter asks the teacher if the learner could have said anything to make the teacher stop shocking him. The teacher seems confused, pauses, tries to redirect the conversation, but finally, as the experimenter presses, answers "No." When the experimenter asks why, the teacher says: "He wouldn't let me. I wanted to stop." The teacher comments repeatedly that he was *just* about to walk out.

Remarking in amazement that an anonymous experimenter with no real authority could force adults to repeatedly inflict extreme pain on people shrieking in agony, Milgram wrote: "One can only wonder what government, with its vastly greater authority and prestige, can command of its subjects. There is, of course, the extremely important question of whether malevolent political institutions could or would arise in American society."[17]

———

Yuasa-san

When they got there, they were placed opposite four Chinese, and then the jailer, right before our eyes, fired two shots into the stomach of each of the Chinese. And then, ten of us to each Chinese wailing in pain, we went to different rooms and practiced surgery. We practiced removing bullets from the bodies. Our orders were to keep them alive until the bullets were removed. But because we were not very good, everyone died in the middle of the surgery. I think perhaps they fainted in agony, and had painful deaths.

And then, I came over to the farmer. Our [unclear] pushed that farmer up to the operating table, but he retreated, stepped back. I was in a tough situation. He was pushing and struggling in front of me. Normally, I would give off the aura of an officer, so I tried to show that dignity, the majesty of an officer—but, sadly, I didn't really succeed. But I tried to show everyone a good part of me, and pushed him—I pushed him out. The farmer gave in, and with his head down, went over to the operating table—and—and he put his hands—his hands on the top of the table. I remember I had done something to impress everyone—showed them a good part of me—I remember I was proud of myself . . . When the farmer walked over there—you know, this was something I was proud of. I'd done something impressive, and I was proud. But this farmer didn't try to get onto the operating table; it fell to the nurse to put him on there. And the nurse said, "I'm going to give you some drugs, administer some drugs—it won't hurt; just lie down," she said. The farmer, with his head lowered, didn't have much choice, so he lay down on the table. That young nurse then stuck her tongue out at fresh-faced-novice me, as if to say, "How do you like that?"

After the farmer lay down on the table—I was the [unclear] of that unit's doctors' training session, ehh, we administered a general anesthesia, and put him to sleep. Then [coughs], the ten or so military doctors who'd come were split into groups of five—and it was surgery practice. At the start we did appendix surgery, and then intestinal sutures—surgery on the bowels—and limb amputation—we practiced all of these things. I watched all of this, and I [coughs]—was driven by these urges. There was living material right in front of me. And there were machines, as well. So to open that man's [coughs] throat, there was a thing called a "field mach—surgery machine"—a machine for slicing open [organs], and we used that. But when we pu—put it into the throat, blood—*whoosh,* all of this RED [emphasized] blood spurted out—it came out with the air. I remember that. And soon, after an hour and a half, we ended the surgery, and the troop doctors went back to the troop. Later, the sturdy-looking man who looked like a soldier was still breathing his last breaths—*haa, haa* [imitates the breaths]—inside the room. I would have felt uncomfortable putting this thing [the man] into a hole like that, so I used the general anesthetic, took it in a syringe, and injected it into that big arm. [Coughs harshly for effect] He coughed violently, and then his breath stopped. This is proof that I, two months after separating from my mother and father, had already become a full-fledged adult militarist.

This sort of surgery practice was conducted four, five [coughs] times. At first, despite that, I felt disgusting—I was timid. The second time, I—the second time, I felt just fine. Around the third time, I took the initiative and planned everything out. One time, completely by my own idea, I trained twenty men this way, and I called the military police—called the military police, took one and showed him the surgery practice—I've done that, too. I did this with new soldiers straight from Japan who hadn't adjusted to conditions on the front, in order to imbue them with the right spirit—for study, or—together with a lesson in anatomy, to give them bravery. I planned it out. We had illustrations—dissection illustrations, and, you know—what're they called? Models, dummies. But I chose vivisection, and of my own volition performed them. [Coughs] And this happened four or five times—and, uh—and I remember we performed vivisections on ten individuals.

So, did you, doctor, at the time, take pleasure in your art—feel good about it, or perhaps take joy in it or that sort of thing . . . did you feel anything like that at the time?

Ah, yes, yes. It was a feeling like, "I did it!" Yes. I was never really conscious of the wrongness of the fact that I was killing people.

———

The problem of human rights pornography—Sontag's horrendous car crash—is only one of the worries I have about this book. In this section I'm going to talk about four others. Each has the structure of a paradox. They include the paradox of trauma, the paradox of evil, the paradox of narcissism, and the paradox of writing.

First, the paradox of trauma: it is unspeakable, but must be spoken. What makes a traumatic event traumatic is, in part, the impossibility of making it comprehensible. "Whatever pain achieves," writes Elaine Scarry, "it achieves in part through its unsharability, and it ensures this unsharability through its resistance to language."[18] Describing her experience as a child of Holocaust survivors, Eva Hoffman explains that nothing so clear as "memories" were passed on to her. It was "something both more potent and less lucid; something closer to enactment of experience, to emanations or sometimes nearly embodiments of psychic matter—of material too awful to be processed and assimilated into the stream of consciousness, or memory, or intelligible feeling."[19] Her parents' chaos of emotion, she writes, shattered language, "erupting in flashes of imagery; in abrupt, fragmented phrases; in repetitious, broken refrains."[20]

Medical research on post-traumatic stress disorder (PTSD) connects such difficulties in memory and communication to heightened amygdala activity and decreased activation of the hippocampus and Broca's area (areas involved in emotional regulation, cognitive mapping, and speech production). Caruth tracks this problem of intelligibility back to the nature of the traumatic event itself. She calls the core of trauma "the delay or incompletion in knowing, or even in seeing, an overwhelming occurrence that then remains, in its insistent return, absolutely *true* to the event."[21] In other words, the event is such a deep shock, so impossible to process with our habitual categories of perception and interpretation, that it is in a sense never experienced by the person to whom it happens. The event overwhelms the act of experiencing. And because the event thereby permanently escapes understanding, because it resists incorporation into the map of memory that makes up personality, the survivor must continually return to it. The event demands perpetual replay. The psyche recursively attempts (and fails) to gain control over trauma through the varieties of repetition, through the returns of nightmare, flashback, hallucination, and displaced anxiety, returns that are testament to the impossibility of ever fully understanding and thus closing the trauma.

If trauma is in this sense not simply cognition resistant but noncognitive, then there are serious costs to putting trauma into words. Caruth writes: "Beyond the loss of precision there is another, more profound, disappearance: the loss, precisely, of the event's essential incomprehensibility, the force of its *affront to understanding*."[22] Writer and teacher Patricia Hampl recalls one of her students, Mr. Henle, an elderly man from a creative writing class she taught at the Jewish Community Center in St. Paul, Minnesota. "He did not like the word Holocaust," she writes. "He did not approve of the package, the tidiness the word made of chaos, bundling up so much in its furious sound."[23] Hampl's friend, human rights lawyer Barbara Frey, commented to me that this kind of falsity is precisely why trial narratives do not aim for understanding in any deep sense, "but rather for a certain type of justice for certain selected victims." "Paradoxically," Frey speculates, "only fictional accounts can come close (though still inadequately) to creating an understanding of trauma."

So how can you tell the story that must and cannot be told? Hoffman describes the difficulty: "To make a sequential narrative of what happened would have been to make indecently rational what had been obscenely irrational. It would have been to normalize through familiar form an utterly aberrant content. One was not to make a nice story out of loathsome cruelty and piercing, causeless hurt."[24] Converting deep shock into coherent life narrative, making comprehensible stories out of incomprehensible atrocities, is a belittlement. Atrocity gets turned into something else, something lesser, when put into words. Filmmaker Claude Lanzmann, director of the documentary *Shoah*, puts it bluntly: "There is an absolute obscenity in the very project of understanding."[25]

Discussing the Armenian genocide, David Eng and David Kazanjian explain the problem this way: the world now has a genre for genocide, a genre with rules about what counts as genocide talk, and these rules are a painful match for personal trauma. The discourse of "Genocide," they claim, is a discourse of evidence, archives, and proof. Indeed, it is a discourse that transforms genocide *into* archive, that converts eye-witness accounts "into so many pieces of evidence." "By claiming to represent the totality of such an event" through quantifiable data, they argue, "the discourse of 'Genocide' paradoxically replicates the very calculable logic by which Ottoman authorities organized the deportations and killings of Armenians."[26] The demands of genocide discourse, Marc Nichanian explains, are forever "dispossessing the victim of his own memory."[27] "The executioner that we bear in the depths of ourselves always exhorts us: Speak, say the truth, prove if you can! And we obey him incessantly."[28]

Recounting the Eichmann trial, Shoshana Felman offers as an illuminating extreme the testimony of Ka-Zetnik, who survived Auschwitz. Physically sick with anxiety on the witness stand, Ka-Zetnik began "rambling" in a manner deemed inappropriate to courtroom protocols. When the judge admonished him, calling him to order, he collapsed and lost consciousness. He never finished his testimony. Felman summarizes the incident: "The law is a straightjacket to tame history."[29]

This "juridical" genre may sound pitiless, but according to many critics the "therapy" genre is little better. The work of human rights involves creating narratives for trauma, narratives that sometimes follow a predictable pattern: crisis and confusion proceeds to clarity; clarity produces action and rescue; rescue is followed by redress through sharing, healing, and justice. Sometimes, Allen Feldman charges, this pattern transforms the victim of political terror into a "commodity artifact for a marketplace of public emotion." That is, the survivor's trauma is publicly renarrated in a way that is sufficiently general to be accessible to a mass-market audience; and it is then processed according to generic conventions that help achieve therapeutic closure, a "cathartic 'break' with the past" that allows community, national, and international movement forward. But, warns Feldman, citing the Argentinian Plaza de Mayo mothers "who refuse a final state-sponsored memorial for their disappeared children," collective remembrance of the general can feel like private forgetting of the individual, and memorialization can also feel like final deletion.[30]

One way of responding to these and other concerns about the terrible difficulties of representing trauma is to call for silence. The call for silence after catastrophe can be a way of respecting, even hallowing. To treat the disaster as unspeakable is to treat it as beyond, as transcendent; the lexicon of such accounts often shadows the divine. For children of Holocaust survivors, Hoffman writes, the rhetoric of the unfathomable and the unspeakable "echoes a childhood sense of an incomprehensible cosmos, of sacred or demonic forces."[31] It is, finally, a "rhetoric of awe," an "unintentional sacralization."[32] Maurice Blanchot, who lived in France during the Nazi occupation, writes of the disaster: "But the danger (here) of words in their rhetorical insignificance is perhaps that they claim to evoke the annihilation where all sinks always, without hearing the 'be silent' addressed to those who have known only partially, or from a distance the interruption of history."[33]

For some, however, this rhetoric of mystery is not only, or not always, a way of hallowing. It can also be a way of ignoring. Yehuda Bauer critiques this approach to the Holocaust as an "elegant form of escapism."[34] Dominick LaCapra warns that the impulse toward "sacralization" is also an impulse toward "silent awe"[35]; and Alvin Rosenfeld declares: "If it is a blasphemy, then, to attempt to write about the Holocaust, and an injustice against the victims, how much greater the injustice and more terrible the blasphemy to remain silent."[36] Discussing Rwanda, Philip Gourevitch explains:

"The language that's used most frequently in the popular response to something like Rwanda are words like unspeakable, unthinkable, unimaginable. And [in the case of Rwanda] those all struck me as words that ultimately were telling you not to speak, think, or understand, that they basically are words that get you off the hook and then in a sense give you license for both kinds of ignorance—literal ignorance, not knowing, and ignoring."[37]

Those who favor the idea of trauma's unspeakability despite such critiques often do so because they have an implicit ethical commitment to the idea that the survivor's experience is unutterably unique. If the trauma is literally untranslatable, then it can belong only to the individual. It is irreducibly personal; it cannot be converted to a version of the common. To adopt such a stance is to adopt a stance of care toward the survivor. But as many critics have pointed out, in the more extreme versions of such theoretical models, unspeakability and untranslatability can begin to function like undifferentiated and impersonal universals. Trauma increasingly seems less like a singular event in an individual life than a *concept* of event that transcends individual life. Trauma becomes a common pathological structure of experience. It is what it is independently of political context, cultural history, family background, life experiences, and individual psychic makeup and therapeutic labor. Trauma is external to the individual, impenetrable by the individual. It therefore belongs to no one, and can be transmitted across individuals and even generations. As one concerned critic writes: this way of thinking about trauma presents as a value "the unknowable particularity of the traumatic experience" but in the end "makes particularity meaningless and makes trauma available to anyone, not just without recourse to painful experience but without recourse to experience as such."[38] That which is intended to preserve only diminishes.

This brings me to the second difficulty I've had writing this book. Trying to understand traumatic events is much like trying to understand the perpetrators of traumatic events; that is, to understand them as real humans rather than mystified monsters. There is a similar paradox, what might be called the paradox of evil. Conceptualizing perpetrators as people we can understand is a moral affront, and refusing to conceptualize perpetrators as people we can understand is a moral affront. In other words, we must and must not demonize them.

We must not demonize because to demonize is to adopt a stance that shares features with the demonic: namely, a dismissal of the other's full humanity. This is no mere theoretical concern. When moral outrage becomes, at its extreme, moral rejection of the other, it can become difficult to distinguish from hate, just as the cry for justice can become difficult to distinguish from the cry for retribution. This has consequences that are not only dangerously political but also deeply interior. When we demonize we are committing ourselves to an idea about who the other is *and* to an idea about who we are.

To demonize, moreover, is to promote a vision of the otherness of evil that shuts down not just the possibility of reconciliation but also the possibility of prevention. If we allow ourselves to imagine that evil is somehow extraordinary, somehow beyond the human, then we can never identify and address the very ordinary situational and organizational features that regularly produce it. And finally, othering the evil leads to eviling the other. Over time, as Charles Mathewes characterizes the view, a culture's overly close association of the terms promotes a conflation, "so that we fear otherness and label it evil, and see in 'the other' only things that we fear." Ultimately, "all externality, all that is strange, is evil to us."[39]

If we do not maintain our sense of the otherness of evil, however, we lose our capacity for making crucial philosophical distinctions. Our feeling that some acts defy comprehension, that they are alien to our nature, isn't a "mere" feeling; it's an indicator of categorical distinctions. Our moral language is impoverished if it cannot account for those acts that shock our conscience, acts whose enormity cannot be encompassed by the language of the wrong, bad, or even wicked. We need to conceptually distinguish such acts both as a matter of respect for the truth value in our emotions and as a matter of respect for the survivors and the dead.

On top of that, when we lose our sense of the otherness of evil we also lose our hate—and this *is* a loss. Hatred is a matter of "profound rejection," argues Claudia Card, and "rejection can be good." To reject is to clarify and solidify one's sense of self and one's moral commitments. When we call something evil we are not only denying that we could have anything in common with it, we are also committing ourselves to act consistently with this denial. The hatred that evil calls out in us can, in this way, be "energizing" to our sense of moral purpose.[40] Finally, when we lose our sense of the otherness of evil, when we turn it into something common, or seek to understand its situational and organizational causes, we come perilously close to excusing or accepting it. Jean-Jacques Rousseau sees this problem as intrinsic to narrative identification: "I suspect that any man, to whom the crimes of Phaedra or Medea were told beforehand, would hate them more at the beginning of the play than at the end."[41]

Nothing in our own time has dramatized the risks of demystifying evil more furiously than the controversy surrounding Hannah Arendt's "banality of evil" thesis. "The trouble with Eichmann," Arendt wrote, "was precisely that so many were like him, and that the many were neither perverted nor sadistic, that they were, and still are, terribly and terrifyingly normal."[42] And again elsewhere: "The sad truth of the matter is that most evil is done by people who never made up their minds to be or do either evil or good."[43] Many reading Arendt for the first time in 1963 felt that in helping us to understand Eichmann as somebody like us, Arendt had taken something from us; that with Eichmann's unriddling something important had been lost, much in the same way that you lose the cognitive affront of trauma when you seek to put it into language, make it understandable, or try to explain it in a way that people can relate to. Denying Eichmann's unique monstrosity in the way Arendt did felt like an insult to the survivors and the dead. "No banality of a man," Norman Podhoretz protested, "could have done so hugely evil a job so well."[44]

Perhaps it is true, admits Harold Rosenberg, that aging war criminals do look "just like other people." And perhaps it is true that, to some degree, "punishment is always meted out to a stranger who bears the criminal's name." The real criminals, he writes, "have been carried off by history and will never return. In their place has been left a group of aging stand-ins, sick and trembling with fear. Judgment will be pronounced on a round-up of impersonators, a collection of dummies borrowed from the waxworks museum." But to commiserate with these old men "as human beings," Rosenberg insists, is "intellectually degrading and morally degenerate": "'But, ah!' cried a voice from the balcony at the Eichmann trial in Jerusalem, 'you should have seen him in his colonel's uniform.' Yes, the trial is about that other, the creature empowered to dispatch millions to destruction, not this pathetic organism anxiously following the proceedings through his earphones. That fabulous malefactor, though locked forever into an interval of his past, and no longer accessible to the living, cannot be allowed to rest in his perfect refuge."[45]

Saul Bellow expresses a representative contempt for Arendt through his character Artur Sammler: "The idea of making the century's greatest crime look dull is not banal . . . Intellectuals do not understand." He continues: "Everybody (except certain blue-stockings) knows what murder is. That is very old human knowl-edge. The best and purest human beings, from the beginning of time, have understood that life is sacred. To defy that old under-standing is not banality. There was a conspiracy against the sacred-ness of life. Banality is the adopted disguise of a very powerful will to abolish conscience. Is such a project trivial? Only if human life is trivial."[46] For Bellow as for others, the effort to understand assaults on our moral world can feel like an assault on our moral world.

In *The Reader*, Bernhard Schlink characterizes what might be called the Eichmann problem as a matter of our competing public and private selves. "I wanted simultaneously to understand Han-na's crime and to condemn it," his protagonist explains of the woman he loved after he discovers she is a Nazi war criminal, re-sponsible for the deaths of hundreds of Jewish women locked in a burning church. "But it was too terrible for that. When I tried to understand it, I had the feeling I was failing to condemn it as it must be condemned. When I condemned it as it must be con-demned, there was no room for understanding . . . I wanted to pose myself both tasks—understanding and condemnation. But it was impossible to do both."[47]

This difficulty of sorting out the public and private is central to the third worry I have about this book: the paradox of narcissism. I first publicly shared material from these confessions in a reading I gave at a university in South Korea. There had been talk that rep-resentatives from a survivors' group would be in the audience. I was anxious. A friend in the audience, Ben, teased me afterward, saying I spent almost all my time apologizing for what I was doing:

apologizing for trying to understand the perpetrators as humans rather than monsters, for presuming to put atrocity and trauma into words, for the human rights pornography of it. And then, in what approached neurotic comedy, I spent time apologizing for apologizing—because, it seemed to me, apologizing is a way of putting the self and its motivations at center stage, and it felt wrong to put my little internal dramas at center stage amid such epochal horrors.

I gave versions of this talk many times afterward, and thought of Ben each time. I always wanted to disappear, but finally I couldn't. The scale of atrocity is unselfing, and self-examination as a response is a natural protective reflex, a way of restoring one's own emotional reactions to their familiar, central place. It is also narcissistic, and it is luxury morality. But avoidance—refusing to interrogate one's own relationship to the desire to see, to make something see-able—is no better, perhaps worse. Why do you do this kind of work? What personal dramas are you playing out, and what blind spots might that leave you with?[48] Atrocity work requires an appropriate drawing of the gaze toward the self that is inappropriate. So the "I" remains here in this book, as do the apologies—even if now they are disguised as analysis.

As I look back on it, I realize there is one thing I forgot to apologize for in that talk in South Korea. It also has to do with Schlink's moral collision of public and private. The collision is especially intimate to the writer, or rather, is the result of the intimacy of writing. This is my fourth problem, and like the others it has the structure of a paradox: writing of this kind is simultaneously personal and impersonal, connected and alienated. When you interview somebody for their story, you are not extracting data, you are entering into a relationship. Sometimes, when they invite you into their homes and into their most vulnerable memories, there comes a moment when you *see* each other. It is as delicate and trusting a moment as humans can share. When you part after this happens, you believe you must meet one another again; you say so to each other, you plan. But in most cases, you never do.

And then time passes, and the moment is forgotten, and then the people aren't people anymore, really. They're material. That's when you can write about them, when you're mentally and emotionally far away. The best writers can achieve that state quickly. It takes me a while, and it was especially hard this time. These men were *great* material. They were also individuals, tragically real individuals, who each had urgent internal visions of the story I would tell about them. What would they think about what I finally wrote? Some might have been disappointed by a version of their story that did not put at center stage the moral clarity provided by their Communist reeducation in Chinese prison camp. Some might have been disappointed by a book that treated them as instances of psychological patterns, rather than fully exploring their individual paths toward reconciliation and forgiveness. Some might have been disappointed by an analysis that failed to treat these crimes as uniquely Japanese, the special burden of their history, guilt, and responsibility. And most would have been disappointed by a book that wasn't explicitly organized around anti-nationalist, anti-imperialist, anti-militarist values.

Those would not be small disappointments. Those messages are the very meaning of their lives now—for the ones that remain. But a writer must not care about what other people want. A writer says: my first responsibility is to my project.

———

X—— was a member of Unit 731, a now-notorious military unit that conducted research in biological and chemical warfare on human subjects at a secret military installation in Ping Fan, an outlying district of Harbin in northeast China. Scientists in Section I of the unit worked with a range of diseases, including but not limited to cholera, typhoid, dysentery, anthrax, glanders, tetanus, gas gangrene, scarlet fever, tick encephalitis, epidemic hemorrhagic fever, whooping cough, diphtheria, pneumonia, salmonella, venereal diseases, and epidemic cerebrospinal meningitis. Working at full capacity, they were able to produce 300 kilograms of plague bacteria each month.[49] Over 10,000 prisoners were used in such experiments.[50] X—— explained that to cultivate the necessary bacteria at highest toxicity, they needed to use living bodies. It was important to begin dissecting people while they were still alive. He also noted that he and his colleagues did not refer to the prisoners as human beings. They referred to them as "logs."

In Section II, scientists and technicians tested bombs, maintained airplanes, and bred fleas. Over the years of Unit 731's operations, members experimented with various dispersal mechanisms in the "field," dropping bombs, crop dusting with lethal pathogens, releasing infected rats into densely populated areas, lacing wells with germs, stashing infected sweet cakes in areas where they would look like supplies accidentally left behind by soldiers, and giving chocolates to POWs who were then released so that they would return home and unwittingly distribute them among children.[51] Sheldon Harris estimates that at least 250,000 civilians were killed in field tests.[52] During the Zhejiang campaign, more than 10,000 soldiers were killed, but they were accidentally Japanese soldiers (such weapons are difficult to control).[53] Recent estimates put total deaths near 600,000.[54]

Casualties mounted well after the war ended. Plague epidemics continued to break out in the region over the years, claiming tens of thousands of lives. Many believe that this was caused by infected animals deliberately released into the population by members of Unit 731 when they evacuated in 1945. Some mice and rats today still test positive for Unit 731 pathogens.[55] And as late as 1992, Chinese officials estimated that "approximately 2 million pieces" of chemical weapons remained buried in China, with "approximately 100 tons" of chemicals.[56]

Unit 731's human subjects included captured Soviet prisoners, Chinese and Korean civilians accused of crimes ranging from vagrancy to spying, and the mentally handicapped. Many were simply kidnapped off the streets or from their homes; some were abducted after innocently showing up at city offices for fake jobs advertised by Japanese authorities.[57]

Prisoners were shackled and stripped of personal possessions, assigned numbers to replace their names, and then fed with "the loving attention that Kobe cattle raisers lavished on their herds."[58] They were strapped down and injected with pathogens, sprayed with droplets, and forced to ingest contaminated foods and liquids. Experiments involved hanging people upside down until they died, dehydrating people to death, injecting horse urine into their kidneys, freezing various body parts to investigate methods of healing frostbite, researching high-altitude flying by locking subjects into special pressure chambers and filming them while they died in convulsions, spreading syphilis through forced sex and then vivisecting the patients to see the effects upon various internal organs at different stages, and infecting children with tuberculosis (a disease far too slow for utility as a biological weapon, Harris asserts, and therefore likely studied "for purely academic purposes").[59] The youngest test subject was a three-day-old infant.[60]

All told, more than 20,000 personnel were involved in the biological warfare program.[61] Why did they do it? Members of Unit 731, it appears, were normal men. They did it because they believed the ends of advanced research justified the means; their first responsibility was to the project. As General Ishii confessed in an inaugural speech: this work "may cause us some anguish as doctors" with a "god-given mission" to fight disease. "Nevertheless," he continued, "I beseech you to pursue this research" in the thrilling spirit of "a scientist to exert efforts to probing for the truth in natural science and research into, and discovery of, the unknown world."[62] They also did it because it would advance their professional lives. Hundreds of the researchers later acquired leadership positions in Japanese universities and hospitals; seven became directors and five vice-directors of Japan's postwar National Institute of Health; three became founders of the Japanese pharmaceutical giant Midori Juchi ("Green Cross").[63] And finally, they did it because the experimental subjects were "prisoners." Unit 731 researchers reasoned that, since the prisoners were going to be executed anyway, it would be better to acquire useful information rather than simply waste it.[64]

As did the U.S. military, which granted immunity from war crimes prosecution to members of Unit 731—and paid them—in exchange for the information they gathered in their experiments.[65] "Naturally," wrote Lieutenant Colonel Robert McQuail of Army Intelligence, "the results of these experiments are of the highest intelligence value."[66]

The Soviets might have acquired the information, after all. That was a worry. Another worry was embarrassment. Edwin Hill, a chief U.S. scientist investigating Japanese biological weapons research, wrote of Unit 731 members: "It is hoped that individuals who voluntarily contributed this information will be spared embarrassment."[67] Another military officer, who fervently supported an immunity deal, nonetheless did emphasize "the risk of subsequent embarrassment" for the U.S. government.[68]

But despite such worries over embarrassment, the data was considered too important, and the deal too good, to pass up. As Hill explained: "Such information could not be obtained in our laboratories because of scruples attached to human experimentation. These data were secured with a total outlay of ¥250,000 ($695) today, a mere pittance by comparison with the actual cost of the studies."[69]

———

While I was writing this book, I met with a delegation of Chinese researchers from Harbin. They worked in the very shadow of Unit 731's haunting urban ruins, but they needed to come here, to the United States, to fully understand what had happened there. We still have so many of the once secret documents.

One of the researchers told me this story about their work. A woman had been trying for many years to find out what happened to her father during the war. He had been arrested, and then he vanished. When she came to the institute, they were able to determine through the archives that he had been a prisoner at Unit 731. The woman knew what this meant, knew, then, that her father had died as a human guinea pig. She was devastated.

Was it worth it, telling her? I asked. They believed so. Surviving families needed answers to be able to get on with their lives.

———

How can people do these things?

Some people believe this is the wrong question. We shouldn't be shocked that these things happen as often as they do. We should be shocked that they don't happen more. And we shouldn't be shocked that, deep down, we are really interested in knowing the ghastly details. Yes, we experience revulsion when witnessing pain.

But we *want* that experience. The only reason revulsion happens inside us in such moments is because we've trained ourselves to react that way. It isn't instinctive or natural. Why *wouldn't* we be drawn to representations of our inescapable human fate, pain?

But it's more than that, insists Sigmund Freud. We are essentially violent creatures, by nature; our voyeuristic interest is actually aggressive. The truth, he writes,

> is that men are not gentle, friendly creatures wishing for love, who simply defend themselves if they are attacked, but that a powerful measure of desire for aggression has to be reckoned as part of their instinctual endowment. The result is that their neighbor is to them not only a possible helper or sexual object, but also a temptation to them to gratify their aggressiveness on him, to exploit his capacity for work without recompense, to use him sexually without his consent, to seize his possessions, to humiliate him, to cause him pain, to torture and to kill him. *Homo homini lupus;* who has the courage to dispute it in the face of all the evidence in his own life and history? This aggressive cruelty usually lies in wait for some provocation, or else it steps into the service of some other purpose, the aim of which might as well have been achieved by milder measures. In circumstances that favour it, when those forces in the mind which ordinarily inhibit it cease to operate, it also manifests itself spontaneously and reveals men as savage beasts to whom the thought of sparing their own kind is alien.[70]

But despite our easily summoned ferocity, Barbara Ehrenreich counters, we are not really natural predators; we are, rather, natural prey who succeeded too well. We are drawn to gladiatorial spectacle, for instance, not by bloodlust but by "the thrill of defensive solidarity," an evolutionary holdover that continues to give us "fear-dissolving strength." Therefore, Ehrenreich writes, "We will not find the roots of the human attraction to war by searching the human psyche for some innate flaw that condemns us to harass and kill our fellows. In war we act as if the only enemies we have are human ones, but I am proposing that the emotions we bring to war are derived, in an evolutionary sense, from a primal battle that the entire human species might easily have lost. We are not alone on this planet, and we were once decisively outnumbered by creatures far stronger and more vicious than ourselves."[71]

Because we are sociable creatures that form communities and bond intensely with each other, we are also vicious. Fierce xenophobia is a by-product of our ardent in-group identification. We hate because we love. We are aggressive because we have things we care about protecting. Some believe the civilizing process and the domestic and international laws of the modern world of nation-states set limits to and curb our atavistic aggression. It is in anomic conditions—quintessentially, in the civilization-unmaking space of the battlefield—that we revert to our more animal selves. But others believe that, on the contrary, the civilizing process has succeeded, as Zygmunt Bauman writes, "in substituting artificial and flexible patterns of human conduct for natural drives, and hence made possible a scale of inhumanity and destruction which had remained inconceivable as long as natural predispositions guided human action."[72] The small practices we used in our deep past to limit intraspecific violence—for instance, exogamy (the practice of marrying outside a social unit to promote intergroup harmony)—don't stand a chance in a world of massive nation-states characterized by strong historical narratives and ideological commitments.[73] And when these states experience significant economic problems or dramatic social changes—particularly when combined with a collective memory of injury at the hands of others (what Ervin Staub calls "unhealed wounds")—feelings of collective disorganization and helplessness can lead to scapegoating at the level of whole peoples.[74]

Genocide is not a modern invention. The Athenian slaughter of all men captured in the invasion of Melos and Rome's sack of Carthage, for instance, have both been described as genocide.[75] But widespread acceptance of the word itself (which was coined by Raphael Lemkin in 1944) and the intensive study of the phenomenon are both post-Holocaust.[76] After those horrors, scholars searched feverishly and exhaustively for "predisposing characteristics"[77] to genocide, in the hope that understanding causes could give us clues about prevention. Initially, teams of researchers looked for commonalities in the personalities of perpetrators. It would be comforting to believe that there is something broken, or at least different, in evil people—that we could spot them, even if only with hindsight. Is there an authoritarian personality, a type predisposed to prejudice and hate? Are they insane? Do they have split or "doubled" identities? Are they sensation seekers? Do they tend to rely upon others to cope with problems? Do they have difficulty dealing with stress? Do they suffer from depression? Do they have tendencies toward self-condemnation, or all-or-none thinking? Do they have low self-esteem? High self-esteem? Did they have domineering fathers and punitive mothers? Were their basic needs frustrated in early life? Are they submissive to authority? Are they unimaginative or rigid in their thinking? Superstitious? Preoccupied with toughness and sex? James Waller lucidly summarizes a range of such studies conducted over the decades and concludes bluntly: the features purportedly common to evil people "are also common to millions of other individuals who may have done nothing more criminal in their lives than commit a parking meter violation."[78] The evil are, in Christopher Browning's phrase, "ordinary men."[79]

Today most scholars trace genocidal behavior to organizational identity, social context, and national ideologies, rather than to individual personalities. In other words, you're not so much who you are as where you are. Ben Kiernan makes a persuasive argument for these commonalities to genocide: "racism, religious prejudices, revivalist cults of antiquity, territorial expansionism, an obsession with contesting and cultivating land, and the idealization of social classes such as the peasantry."[80] Staub emphasizes nationalism, difficult life conditions, cultural self-concepts that combine a sense of entitlement with underlying insecurity, monolithic rather than pluralistic value systems, a history of devaluing the groups that would become victims, and authoritarian or hierarchical social structures.[81] Waller blames ethnocentrism, xenophobia, and the desire for social dominance (as part of evolutionarily programmed human nature), and also rational self-interest, moral disengagement, and an orientation toward authority (as predictable patterns in organizational behavior).[82] And Browning lists "wartime brutalization, racism, segmentation and routinization of the task, special selection of the perpetrators, careerism, obedience to orders, deference to authority, ideological indoctrination, and conformity."[83]

Many emphasize that the capacity for genocidal violence involves cultural training that starts young. Prewar public education in Japan, for instance, involved "systematic inculcation of militarism and emperor worship," including arithmetic lessons "based on battlefield situations," and science classes that included "general information about searchlights, wireless communication, land mines and torpedoes."[84] An emblematic story from a Japanese primary school textbook goes like this. During the First Sino-Japanese War of 1894–1895, an officer sees a sailor weeping over a letter from home. The officer chastises the sailor for this shameful display of weakness, assuming that the letter is from a lover begging for his safe return and that the young man is crying over their separation. But the young man reveals instead that the letter is from his mother, and that she has written to say she is ashamed of him for not distinguishing himself in battle or gloriously dying for the emperor. The officer is surprised, and pleased.[85]

Emiko Ohnuki-Tierney finds this "blatant 'die for the emperor' ideology" throughout prewar Japanese society: in a kindergarten counting song, an elementary school song about locomotives, a prize offered in a box of candy (a military songbook).[86] Ohnuki-Tierney also notes how the evocative symbolism of cherry blossoms in Japanese culture was manipulated across a range of social fields to naturalize the emperor system and aestheticize militarism. To the list of things that prepare us for violence, then, we might also add beauty. Nationalist wars, after all, are always magnificent (songs, parades, uniforms, flags, lovely metaphors glorifying death).

Kaneko-san described to me a number of the formative books he was required to read as part of his compulsory education. One book had a moment in it that was particularly memorable for Kaneko-san as a young boy. As the young hero takes leave of his mother to go to war, she tells him: "When you go to the front, for His Majesty the Emperor—fight hard for our country, boy!" When it came time for Kaneko-san to be deployed, he remembered that moment, and said to his mother: "Mama, when I go to the front, I'm definitely gonna do something honorable."

"I intended to be praised by my mom," he said, "to make her happy, so I said that. And then my mom, very still, silently listened. And then she stared hard at my face, and said, 'You idiot. Your mama, she doesn't need any goddamn [unclear word, likely a reference to rewards]! Just survive and come home!' And at the time, I thought, 'Wow, what's wrong with my mom?'"

At the front, Kaneko-san dreamed about being honored. "This was what you might call arrogance. You'd go back to your town, and they'd say, 'Ahh, that guy, Kaneko, he went to the front and killed so many people. That's a big deal.' They'd say that sort of thing. 'Ahh, this guy called Kaneko is amazing! Amazing!' The village people would all say that sort of thing, wouldn't they? It'd become something to be proud of."

It was different when people died, Kaneko-san said. "When we soldiers die, we were taught to always say, 'Long live His Majesty the Emperor!' But not a single person said, 'Long live His Majesty the Emperor!' Yeah. Everyone yelled, 'Maaa, Maaa,' right? Everyone said that. And that was the end."

Unfortunately, when our illusions are shattered on the battlefield, we are not rendered less dangerous, less vicious. Easy heroism, personal immortality, the moral righteousness of one's leaders, the glory of sacrifice—when the illusions that inspired us to pick up weapons fail, we can become, paradoxically, more likely to use those weapons with reckless frenzy.

Ebato-san

You know, public education, they drove loyalty and patriotism, that sort of ideology home. In other words, what does that mean? It means that the country of Japan is, well, the country of God. It is the absolute best country in the world—that idea was thoroughly planted into us . . . If you turn it over, it means to despise other races. That is the sort of ideology it is. And from the time we were small, we called Chinese people *dirty chinks*—made fun of them. We called Russians *Russkie pigs*. We called Westerners *hairy barbarians,* you know? And so this meant that when the people of Japan joined the army and went to the front, no matter how many Chinese they killed, they didn't think of it as being much different from killing a dog or a cat.

Another reason is, like I said before, to give your life to the leader, His Majesty the Emperor, of what is absolutely the greatest country in the world, Japan, is a sacred duty and the highest honor. There's that ideology, you know. And this ideology, when you go into the military, is strengthened more and more, and your personality is taken away . . . When it's time to go to battle—at those times, when you were ordered by a superior, you couldn't resist. So the humanitarian ideology I learned about in college just couldn't win out over the ideology of "loyalty and patriotism" that had been drilled into me from the time I was small. In my mind, there's nothing as important as primary and middle-school public education.

So what else must political movements do to make the monsters they need?

For the sake of argument, let's take as a starting point the idea that this question makes sense. Let's assume that we are not inherently evil creatures, that it takes *work* to make us do such things. This is not obvious, and in fact runs counter to a common assumption about wartime behavior: that brutality is released when socializing constraints are absent; that once men are released into battle their primal impulses to cruelty will emerge. In fact, it doesn't take a battle at all. All it takes is a little bit of permission. All it takes is a doctor's gown (as we saw in the Milgram experiment) or a prison guard uniform (as we will see in the Stanford prison experiment) to make us hurt each other gratuitously.

But we do not have to accept this grim view of what it is to be human. Cicero's maxim, "In time of war the law is silent,"[87] is often taken as a truism both about what happens in war (we abandon moral rules) and about what we believe about war's interior structure: namely, that it is a rule-free event; that it tends toward maximum violence because that is its nature. But the International Committee of the Red Cross's *People on War Report,* an unprecedented survey of civilians *and* combatants all across the globe, reveals a robust international consensus to the contrary. Only 4 percent of respondents and interviewees believed that in war "everything is allowed"; 59 percent believed wars have rules and that violators should be punished afterward; 64 percent insisted combatants are morally obligated to *"leave civilians alone."*[88]

Such beliefs do not dissolve under gunfire. In fact, after World War II, Army Brigadier General S. L. A. Marshall released a (now controversial) study claiming that, on average, only fifteen to twenty men out of a hundred used their weapons at all during combat action. Lieutenant Colonel David Grossman, a professor and former Army Ranger, goes on to argue that this ratio seems relatively stable across time and cultures. The human resistance to killing other humans is so strong, he writes, that "in many circumstances, soldiers on the battlefield will die before they can overcome it."[89]

William Faulkner's allegorical novel *A Fable,* in which Jesus Christ returns as a soldier in World War I to organize pacifist resistance, commemorated a very real anxiety among that war's military leaders: namely, that despite the brutalizing effect of uncountable, mutually inflicted casualties, alarming outbursts of nonviolence continued to recur along the front. Violent regimes over the centuries have always understood this truth: we are not wolves needing only to be unleashed. Tyrants and war makers need to be deliberate, thoughtful, thorough, and unresting. They need to do a great number of things over a long period of time to create and sustain their killers, to overcome, as Hannah Arendt wrote, "the animal pity by which all normal men are affected in the presence of physical suffering."[90]

So what do political movements need to do to make the monsters they need?

First, everybody agrees, you must put them in a group. From French psychologist Gustave Le Bon to American theologian Reinhold Niebuhr, thinkers have theorized the dangers of crowd and group behavior. In *Moral Man and Immoral Society,* Niebuhr sharply condemned the "moral obtuseness of human collectives." He argued that "the frustrations of the average man, who can never realise the power and the glory which his imagination sets as the ideal," make him a willing implement of the groups—inevitably driven by "lusts" and "ambitions"—that can provide, finally, a taste of power.[91] Group identity is not only a protective shell for those made insecure by social disruption; it is also a kind of abandon. Group behavior, Niebuhr and others have argued, hews to the moral lowest common denominator.

The anonymity of group action is one of its primary moral hazards. In a seminal study on anonymity and aggression, Philip Zimbardo had female college students administer what they believed to be painful electric shocks to other women. The students concealed by hoods and loose coats delivered twice as much shock as those who remained physically recognizable. Zimbardo concluded from this experiment that we are more likely to engage in reckless behavior when we enter a state of "deindividuation"—that is, a state in which a person loses sense of herself as a separate individual, in which self-focused attention or self-consciousness is reduced. Further studies have revealed that almost anything that makes people feel deindividuated—including crowds, cover of night, face paint, masks, and sunglasses—increases the possibility of antisocial behavior.[92]

Group membership can promote not only deindividuation, in which the moral self is psychically submerged, but also what might be called intra-individuation, in which the moral self is psychically subdivided.[93] In intra-individuation, your identity does not expand, diffuse, and dissolve into the generalized aspect of the crowd. Instead, it shrinks, rigidifies, and compartmentalizes into self-contained units, into narrow, noncommunicating, and even incompatible functions. If in deindividuation the self is no longer a particular, in intra-individuation the *other* is no longer a particular. In other words, with deindividuation your relationship to yourself is mediated through your collectivized identity; with intra-individuation your relationship to others is mediated through your specialized social role. The other becomes an *abstraction*. Where deindividuation promotes impulsive cruelty, intra-individuation promotes calculated cruelty—or rather, it promotes behavior that is sufficiently rationalized so as not to feel like cruelty.

Consider Eichmann, the bureaucrat of the Holocaust. Better yet, argues Arthur Applbaum, consider Charles-Henri Sanson, the executioner of Paris during the Terror. Some saw him as a ghoulish monster, others as a "tragic figure caught between duty and sentiment." But the executioner saw himself, and Applbaum wryly suggests we might too, as just another professional, no different from a lawyer or doctor. If the collective determines it is necessary to have executioners, then there will be executioners. And if you are that executioner, you really ought to be a good executioner. Being good at your job is, after all, part of what it means to be a good human: part of your responsibility to others (do your share) and also your responsibility to yourself (transcend mediocrity). Your job may require actions that are not typically a component of human goodness. "[But] you would not describe what a surgeon does as stabbing, what a lawyer does as robbing, or what a prosecutor does as kidnapping, would you?" an imagined Sanson asks in Applbaum's philosophical dialogue. Yes, good executioners murder, good doctors ignore pain, and good lawyers lie, but when we do these things as occupiers of roles rather than as individuals, we are not murdering, ignoring pain, or lying. We are executing, triaging, and offering alternative theories. So even though lawyers regularly and "intentionally induce false belief," they aren't deceiving; they are only (in scare quotes) "deceiving."

Socially authorized specialization allows lawyers in their special capacity and us in our various special capacities (citizen, father, soldier, etc.) to substitute the circumscribed morality of a role for our full human morality. The pilot of the Enola Gay denied moral discomfort over bombing Hiroshima. But we all deny, in one way or another, as easily as we slip into water. So who are we to criticize the executioners we rely upon? Our discomfort with them isn't driven by authentic moral force—it's driven by personal squeamishness. "I act *for* the people in every sense of the word: in their name, for their benefit, and upon their direction," declares Applbaum's executioner. "Every time I cut off a head, every citizen—or at least every citizen who approves of the death penalty—does so as well. If they are blameless, so am I. If I am blameworthy, so are they."[94]

The existence of roles demanding antisocial behavior, of course, is not enough. Such roles are usually self-limiting. Law provides minimal authorization, and personality provides maximal resistance. Both say: Go only this far. To make war criminals—demons and devils, as the men I talked to described themselves—you need the opposite combination: maximal authorization and minimal personality.

You must erode the identity of those you need to do the killing, whether soldiers or torturers, by systematically humiliating them and stripping them of their normal domestic identity. Collectivize their sense of self by shaving their heads; making them wear identical uniforms; controlling their language through in-group slang and chants; and forcing them to eat, sleep, and march as one. Control access to information; isolate them from their family and friends and the regular world. Subject them to systematic physical stress and sleep deprivation, and to a rule system that combines harsh and arbitrary penalties with occasional rewards. Nearly every former soldier I talked to emphasized the tremendous effects of peer pressure, describing incidents of bullying and shaming, especially being slapped or hit. And everybody emphasized the importance of the regime's willingness to take responsibility for their actions. To make people like this, regimes must exploit the normal human impulses to obedience and conformity—the very same impulses that can generate group altruism and morality—but instead orient them toward violence. As one British soldier describes the procedure: "Take a young man, desperate to establish an identity in the adult world, make him believe military prowess is the epitome of masculinity, teach him to accept absolutely the authority of those in command, give him an exaggerated sense of self-worth by making him part of an elite, teach him to value aggression and to dehumanize those who are not part of his group and give him permission to use any level of violence without the moral restraints which govern him elsewhere."[95]

But making monsters isn't only a matter of conditioning; it's also a matter of narrative. Commonly among unrepentant war criminals, you will see a grandiose self-pity that helps them to preserve a sense of self: *I bore the burden of having to do these things.* Robert Jay Lifton saw this narrative template in the Nazi doctors at Auschwitz, who perceived their terrible but necessary work of killing as an "ordeal" of self-sacrifice for "the immortal Germanic people."[96] Such self-absolution, in Germany and elsewhere, is made possible by the stories of historical mission and utopian possibility provided by charismatic leaders. It is a psychological entry into an abstract, even mythic time that blurs the individuality of conduct.[97]

So perhaps the best way to think about violence and social roles is this. The problem isn't that we reduce people to specific roles that permit violence; the problem is that the roles aren't specific enough. In war, everything is weird. The landscape is foreign, seemingly unreal; we are separated from all the reference groups we have grown to rely upon for moral judgment; nothing is familiar; there are no reality checks. War confuses us. In that confusion we begin to create new moral realities. Veteran Tim O'Brien writes: "For the common soldier, at least, war has the feel—the spiritual texture—of a great ghostly fog, thick and permanent. There is no clarity. Everything swirls. The old rules are no longer binding, the old truths no longer true. Right spills over into wrong. Order blends into chaos, love into hate, ugliness into beauty, law into anarchy, civility into savagery. The vapors suck you in. You can't tell where you are, or why you're there, and the only certainty is overwhelming ambiguity."[98]

In what are known as the Asch conformity experiments, subjects are shown simple lines and asked to match their lengths. Volunteers in the experiment have no trouble identifying correct line length. But when volunteers are surrounded by actors posing as volunteers and these actors then select the incorrect lengths, volunteers begin to conform and also misidentify the clearly identifiable lines. They typically resist in the beginning, displaying confusion and discomfort, but with repeated trials they begin to acquiesce to the group judgment, often with visibly defeated apathy. In these experiments, psychologists distinguish informational conformity (volunteers begin to distrust their own judgment) from normative conformity (volunteers know the group is wrong, but do not wish to appear deviant by disagreeing). Either way, the important thing these experiments show is how easy it is to get people to repudiate the basics of their world.

This sad truth is the great revelation of twentieth-century totalitarianism. Drawing upon the work of Arendt, one scholar writes: "We may desperately want to believe that there is something about human beings that cannot be transformed, something deep about the human self, the voice of conscience or sense of responsibility that cannot be obliterated. But after totalitarianism, we can no longer hold onto these beliefs. This is the specter that now haunts us."[99]

Perhaps more frightening, however, is that totalitarianism is not required. Take a group of poorly trained young people, put them in a strange and frightening environment, and give them unclear roles with light or no regulation. Each small hurtful act they commit in the course of making their confused way will make the next act seem more normal. Give them time, and they will eventually shed their moral identities. But not because they are inhuman. They will do it because they are human.

In 1971, Philip Zimbardo recruited college students for a mock prison experiment at Stanford University. Subjects were randomly assigned the position of "prisoner" or "guard" and were then asked to role-play their positions. Zimbardo planned for the students to live together in a simulated prison in the basement of the Stanford psychology building for several weeks so that he and his student research associates could study group dynamics. Zimbardo quickly lost control of the experiment, however, and had to cancel it after a handful of days.

The experiment began on a Sunday. Zimbardo convinced the local police to stage surprise arrests of the would-be prisoners.

Some public witnesses, including at least one family member, believed the arrests were real. Once everybody was gathered in the basement, behaviors degenerated quickly. Here is Zimbardo's account of Tuesday: "Our prisoners are looking raggedy and bleary-eyed, and our little prison is beginning to smell like a men's toilet in a New York subway station. Seems that some guards have made toilet visits a privilege to be awarded infrequently and never after lights out. During the night, prisoners have to urinate and defecate in buckets in their cells, and some guards refuse to allow them to be emptied till morning."[100]

By that point, even Zimbardo found himself succumbing to the pressures of the simulated role-playing, thinking and acting strangely. He was behaving less and less like a psychologist and more and more like a prison warden, obsessing over the possibility of a rumored assault upon his prison and working to hide signs of distress from visiting parents.

On Wednesday, Zimbardo arranged for a priest to visit with the prisoners. He describes the meeting:

> Prisoner Stew-819 is looking terrible, to say the least: dark circles under his eyes, uncombed hair going in every direction but down. This morning, Stew-819 did a bad thing: In a rage, he messed up his cell, tearing open the pillow and throwing the feathers everywhere. He was put in the Hole and his cellmates had to clean up the mess. He has been depressed following his parents' visit last night...
>
> Priest: "I wonder if you discussed the idea that your family might get a lawyer for you."
>
> 819: "They knew I was a prisoner. I told them what I was doing here, about the numbers, the regulations, the hassles."
>
> Priest: "How do you feel now?"

819: "I have a bad headache; I need a doctor."

I intervene, trying to discover the basis of his headache. I ask him whether it was a typical migraine; or maybe had been caused by exhaustion, hunger, heat, stress, constipation, or vision problems.

819: "I just feel kind of drained. Nervous."

Then he breaks down and starts to cry. Tears, big heaving sighs. The priest calmly gives him his handkerchief to wipe the tears away.

"Now there, it can't be all that bad. How long have you been in this place?"

"Only three days!"

"You're going to have to be less emotional."[101]

By Thursday, guards were sexually humiliating prisoners.

"Okay, now pay attention. You three are going to be female camels. Get over here and bend over touching your hands to the floor." (When they do, their naked butts are exposed since they are wearing no underwear beneath their smock-dresses.) Hellman continues with obvious glee, "Now you two, you're male camels. Stand behind the female camels and *hump* them."

Burdan giggles at this double entendre. Although their bodies never touch, the helpless prisoners are simulating sodomy by making thrusting motions of humping.

The next day, Friday, Zimbardo closed the experiment.

Afterward, students were asked to reflect on their remarkable experiences. Recalling a violent scuffle he had with a prisoner, one guard explained it this way: "I realized then that I was as much a prisoner as they were. I was just a reaction to their feelings. They had more of a choice in their actions. I don't think we did. We were both crushed by the situation of oppressiveness, but we guards had the illusion of freedom . . . I realized later that we were all slaves to something in this environment."[102]

———◆———

Ebato-san

Right, right, right. Yes, the recruitment training in the Japanese army was extremely, well, in a word, you could say it was barbaric. So what did they do? Well, the older soldiers—the new recruits would be put inside this one room with the old soldiers. And then the old soldiers would call it education—but what they called the education of the recruits was, in fact, [unclear phrase] boredom, you see. The old soldiers, who were already sick of the army, would deal out corporal punishment on the recruits day and night. [Laughs a bit] Do you understand that, corporal punishment? You know, they'd hit our cheeks . . . slaps . . .

Slaps?

Right here, yeah. At all hours of the day, again and again. And so—if you're wondering what kind of thing brought that on—if you were called on and your response was bad, say. Or if you answer—if you acted big. [Laughs] Like if you were—you were swaggering around. Or if you didn't maintain your shoes, or you didn't maintain your weapons. Due to those things, day or night, the slaps would come. As a result, if you're wondering—that, day or night, we'd be slapped—the result of that was, in short, that the feeling and reason that we humans have was completely destroyed by this corporal punishment. That when you heard a superior or an old soldier say something you could respond instinctively—like, well, a robot, I suppose. And so, the character that each individual human being has, they killed it—destroyed it, you could say, I suppose. But they'll make it so you respond reflexively to the orders of those above you, like a robot or a slave . . .

———

Kaneko-san, like the others, spoke of being trained to revere authority. Many people have made the argument that Japan at that time was uniquely extreme in this way. But the fact is, all regimes train their subjects in obedience (if in different ways and to different degrees), and war and genocide are possible because we *want* to be obedient. We desire to surrender our responsibility for our choices to another, to escape what existentialist Simone de Beauvoir calls the "anguish of freedom."[103] We let ourselves believe a leader can create our meanings for us, and we delight in surrendering the terrible weight of our individual agency. John Glenn Gray, a U.S. veteran of World War II, writes of the "satisfaction" soldiers experience in "sloughing off responsibility": "Becoming a soldier was like escaping from one's own shadow." Frequently, he claims, he heard people remark of the army oath: "When I raised my right hand and took that oath, I freed myself of the consequences for what I do. I'll do what they tell me and nobody can blame me."[104] The mass violence of humans is complex and perplexing, but in most cases it can be traced back to this simple moment, when a man (often, but not always, a man) permitted himself to surrender his agency to another.

There is an attractive simplicity to obedience, an intelligibility to be found in the doctrine of superior orders. But we seek a still more comprehensive simplicity than that: not just simplicity of choices in confusing moments, but also simplicity in our world view. We have a need to retreat from the complexity and indeterminacy that defines existence into a comforting clarity. As a prominent Nazi once said: "I was full of gratitude to the SS for the intellectual guidance it gave me. We were all thankful. Many of us had been so bewildered before joining the organization. We did not understand what was happening around us, everything was so mixed up. The SS offered us a series of simple ideas that we could understand, and we believed in them."[105]

Fanaticism clarifies meaning, gives strength and structure to identity, enables confident action in a bewildering world. It provides a frame of meaning for suffering and thereby ameliorates it. It promises purpose where we most need it, turning even the most difficult experiences into opportunities to embody our deepest values, turning trauma into tragedy.[106] Indeed, fanaticism is a necessary aspect of human identity, and a prerequisite for social order—although when people are fanatical about things that fit in with social norms or our own values, we don't call it fanaticism. We call it "belief." (I find myself flinching when the Chukiren's anti-nationalist pacifism is characterized as fanaticism, for instance, but not their youthful devotion to the emperor, even though both seem to me the products of the same emotional structure: namely, a dogged capacity for commitment, once capable of transcending the belief-shattering horrors of the battlefield, and now capable of transcending the scorn of their homeland.)

In a world of complex problems and inevitably imperfect fixes, fanaticism promises simple and total solutions. So does violence. Part of the simplifying clarification of the Chukiren's midcentury world involved identifying and demoting out-groups—specifically, preparing to injure Korean and Chinese people. As in other cases of genocide, what you need to do is to make the victim seem an appropriate target. Emphasize through a comprehensive propaganda program, through media and education, that those you want to target are different, that they do not belong. Emphasize their alienness, their exclusion from the real human community that would otherwise deserve and indeed naturally command our respect. This work is crucial. To overcome the strong, possibly innate, human inhibition against intraspecific violence, we must form what Erik Erikson calls "pseudo-species": in-groups established through ritual that embody *the* human identity." Killing is facilitated by the collective reconceptualization of the enemy group as less than fully human, and the consequent determination that any individual member of that group of "inimical identities" is a suitable target of lethal violence.[107]

Purity is an especially useful concept here. If a culture can successfully cultivate all-or-nothing, polar thinking, it can divide the world into the pure and impure. The impure deserve injury not only because their impurity is inherently disgusting, but also because it threatens to contaminate the community of the pure. In what is truly a vicious circle, the pure merit violence too because they can never embody the total demands of polar purity—which means that their secret guilt and self-disgust is then projected onto the impure as amplified contempt. This is the stuff, writes Lifton, of "mass hatreds, purges of heretics, and political and religious holy wars."[108]

The deadly racism in the Second Sino-Japanese War, like the racism deployed in other violent and nonviolent conflicts, was the product of shifting historical tensions and manipulative cultural renarration. Michael Weiner tracks racial tensions between Japan and China back to the end of the Tokugawa period, when scholars of the Kokugaku (School of National Learning) upended the centuries-old tradition of relying upon Chinese Confucianism "as the primary source of civilisation and morality." In rejecting sinocentrism, scholars "sought to establish the innate superiority of Japanese culture over that of China and all other nations, and in this respect foreshadowed the imperial rhetoric of the nineteenth

EVIL MEN | 64

century." According to the new cultural narrative, the ancient purity of the Divine Land "had in fact been corrupted by external agents in the form of Confucianism and Buddhism. Slavish adherence to an alien culture had only served to obscure the true Wakon [Japanese spirit or soul], and thus deprive Japan of its rightful position in the world order."[109]

Meiji Japan's promotion of religious nationalism in the form of state Shinto and its ideology of the family state, united under the divine emperor as father, helped solidify the notion of a distinct and homogenous Japanese people and unique Japanese culture.[110] The pressure of Western imperialism exacerbated this nationalism and racial exceptionalism—as expressed in the newspaper *Nihon:* "If a nation wishes to stand among the great powers and preserve its national independence, it must strive always to foster nationalism . . . if a nation lacks patriotism how can it hope to exist? Patriotism has its origin in the distinction between "we" and "they" which grows out of nationalism, and nationalism is the basic element in preserving and developing a unique culture."[111]

Racism against Koreans blossomed in the first half of the twentieth century with colonial subjugation and an influx of Korean labor into Japan.[112] Colonization both needed and helped foster a view of the colonized as less civilized, as an inferior race in need of guidance from a racially pure Japan.[113] As Takekoshi Yosaburō wrote: "The Koreans can be slowly and gradually led in the direction of progress, but it is against all laws of sociology and biology to make them enter a new life all at once."[114] As with Western colonialism, the benevolent "embrace" of Japanese colonialism included fear of racial mixing and violent fear of violent resistance.[115] After the Great Kantō Earthquake of 1923, for instance, 6,000 Koreans were massacred because of groundless rumors that they had started riots.[116]

This racism remains useful today. In 2005, two manga (Japanese comic books) became runaway best sellers: "Hating the Korean Wave" and "Introduction to China." In the former, readers and protagonist come to understand both that South Korea cheated in the World Cup and that it owes its contemporary successes to Japanese colonialism. The latter denies Imperial war crimes and depicts China as a "prostitution superpower" obsessed with cannibalism. Discussing such cultural phenomena as a symptom of national insecurity, historian Yutaka Yoshida claims of contemporary Japan: "Lacking confidence, they need a story of healing."[117]

———

For the men I talked to, even all of this—the racism, the military training, the commitment to total obedience, the release into stressful combat conditions—even all this was not enough to make them into murderers, to make the atrocities possible. Kaneko-san described some of their first experiences killing unarmed civilians:

> And so our superiors thought, these soldiers have to be trained in killing people. And so, when we would enter a village, they would bring over some villagers. About ten. They would bring ten or fifteen of them. They would tie them all up to trees. Tie them up to trees, and after a while, ten or so of us would stand in front of the trees in a long line. And we were holding our rifles. We held our rifles, and in here we'd stuck bayonets, right? Draw your blade, whip it out, stick it in here, and then stand in front of them, you know. And then, "You guys, kill those Chinese civilians," is the order we received. Then we charged in, and aimed for the left part, where the heart is, but we did not think our first time killing someone would be this scary of an experience. Everyone was trembling with fear. Trembling. If you fight one-on-one, you have to kill your opponent or you yourself will be killed, right? Then we'd do it as

though in a dream. However—you know, our opponents were tied to trees, so although it was easy to kill them, we were actually trembling with fear.

My opponent was bound to a tree, just staring and staring at my face. I aimed at that place, and then I went in and I stabbed in the left part of the chest, but after hitting, my hand slipped! I did it like this, but since it was so terrifying—[My hand] slipped. And when that happened, only this much went into him. When I did this—there was a high-ranking "instructor" soldier who specialized in training us soldiers, you know? And he said, "Are you fighting like a soldier of Japan, dirtbag?!" and raised his hand, and he smacked me. I couldn't do it even once. And, most guys, everybody, they couldn't stick them with their bayonets.

Since they couldn't go in, in the end some old soldier would say, "Alright, you [scum], watch me do it then," and with that, he gave us an example to follow. And when he did that, he did it like so, with this half, see? The blade, he held the blade like this, and just thrust it in. And after that, normally, after you go in, you have your ribs right here, right? If you compare the width of the ribs and the width of the blade, the blade is wider. When you go like that, [the blade] doesn't go in. But, the old soldiers would push until [the blade] was partway in, and then *hut!,* just like that, they'd [turn the blade] like this. When you do that, [the blade] gets thinner, you see. You do that, and [the blade] slips right in. That's the sort of training we received.

Kaneko-san and the others emphasized that you must build toward cruelty patiently. It takes time to take men who tremble at the thought of killing and turn them into people who are eager for it, take men who can't even hold their bayonets without shaking and turn them into men who can calmly and deftly twist the blade to slip it in, just the right way, through the ribcage. You must methodically humiliate the victims until they seem like they deserve humiliation. In other words, the mortification of the enemy during wartime—nonlethal practices like ransacking homes, or beating and verbally abusing people—are not accidents or mistakes or things that somehow get out of hand. They are deliberate parts of the training process.[118] A person who has been shamed, starved, hurt, beaten, or humiliated begins to seem pitiful, begins to seem like she deserves to be shamed, starved, hurt, beaten, or humiliated. It makes it easier to kill her.

Psychologists explain this process through the "just-world" hypothesis. That is, the stress of distrusting our environments is too much to bear over time. Our daily psychic equilibrium depends upon assuming that the world is basically safe and just. When we see outrageous and apparently senseless suffering, this "just-world" assumption is threatened. To deflect the anxiety such moral destabilization causes, we convince ourselves that the sufferer must have done something to deserve her lot. The world, after all, *is* just. Simone de Beauvoir provides a frightful example: "Those who have done it say that it is easy to walk on a corpse and still easier to walk over a pile of corpses . . . in Algeria I have seen any number of colonists appease their conscience by the contempt in which they held the Arabs who were crushed with misery: the more miserable the latter were, the more contemptible they seemed, so much so that there was never any room for remorse."[119] Perpetrator regimes must systematically remove the conditions for remorse.

Brutality, of course, isn't only or always a consequence of indoctrination, training, or intention. It is also situational, a consequence of stress, rage, and fear. It is a consequence of "the now." In a seminal analysis of PTSD in Vietnam, Jonathan Shay describes the shocks that can precipitate a soldier's "berserk state": "betrayal, insult, or humiliation by a leader; death of a friend-in-arms; being wounded; being overrun, surrounded, or trapped; seeing dead comrades who have been mutilated by the enemy."[120] The impulse to violence—and even "berserk" violence—is a natural human response to certain kinds of stressors.

But there is always, also, system and planning. Blame the victim, desensitize, and combine professional incentives with threat and punishment. Atrocity is a plot of incremental escalation. The Chukiren describe the process.

> Sakakura-san: They made us just watch and learn. They would stab at bodies until you couldn't make out the body—the form anymore. Maybe thirty, twenty people would stab, all together. And we would observe. And when we went back to the troop, about half the people didn't eat. And our—me too—we didn't feel great, you know? And when you'd remember that—while you were remembering the sight of the body, you couldn't eat your food. This is the truth. And then, you know, you'd get used to it, the first time, second time, third time—and by then you're used to it, so now you're thinking, "I'll do this and my record will improve."

> Kaneko-san: In the Japanese Army, they don't hit the head. They hit the body. So, just here. Just right here. Even if it swells just a little, just so you can't eat, that's how they did it. They would never hit your head, because then you'd get a bruise on your head . . .
> When we were fresh recruits, we would stab the chest like this, right? One of our fellow soldiers—"You guys, I can't do this!" he'd cried out. However, that soldier, after a year had passed, he was killing without blinking an eye. After a year. When he did it, he'd just cry, "Wah-wah." He couldn't do it. And then he was beaten on the cheek about ten times by an old soldier. Even then, he didn't do it. But after a year had passed, now, on the contrary, he would do it on his own. That's what's so terrible about the army, you know?

If you're not used to [chopping off heads], you'd of course shake, right? Then you can't do more than cut the head off halfway. Then the Chinese person with his head chopped halfway thrashes about with pain. So, in the end, you stab them to death. They make you do that two times, three times. After they make you do it twice and three times, you'd get the knack and toughened up. Then, in one go, *bam!* The head goes rolling off. Completely chopped off. You do it no problem. However, soldiers don't have Japanese swords. So what do you think they use to cut heads off? [*Interpreter: No clue.*] Um, that officer cut off the head. We soldiers don't have Japanese swords, you know. We say, "Aww, we too wanna cut off heads! Let's do it together!" And—do you know the tool to cut straw? The tool for cutting straw. You get—get food for horses, like this. The thing for [unclear]. We'd take one of those, put the head like this, where you tie Chinese [mumbling]. Then five or six of us hold the person down, and then, *bam!* Cut off the head. That's how they'd toughened you up.

Kubotera-san: Ahh, if you disobeyed an order—at any rate, if you disobeyed an order on the battlefield, they said you got the death penalty. And then, well, even if you didn't get the death penalty, you'd be court-martialed, and nobody would consider doing something dishonorable. Well, anyway, ahh, I was greedy to become private first-class, so that was part of it, too . . . [If you disobeyed] your advance to a higher rank would come to a complete stop . . . I wanted to be promoted . . . Human beings are not straightforward, I think. In all sorts of things, complicated feelings come out.

Eventually they did things they couldn't believe.

Kubotera-san: It was this sort of gently rolling countryside. And far off in the distance, there were lots of mountains, and when we went over there, it was because my platoon commander looked at them through binoculars and realized, "Ah! There are people over there!" And so we hurried over. And then, in this pit . . . ah . . . There was a mother and child. And well . . . When I think about it, this was extreme cruelty . . . Because [my platoon commander] shouted, "Private Kubotera! Shoot them!" Ah, I did not expect that. But I could not disobey a platoon commander's orders, so ah . . . well . . . I shot them.

Well, ah, I really could not—I couldn't look at the child I'd shot or anything like that. Yeah, I quickly turned my back to it, and I didn't really know what had happened until others went and checked everything out. This—this was cruel. The mother—finding a mother and child and shooting the child . . . this was very . . . because it was so common, it's unthinkable. However, your platoon commander's order was His Majesty the Emperor's order, and that's how we were taught. Well, ah . . . I obeyed, and I pulled the trigger, but this—when I think about it now, this kind of cruel thing, even if I were to be killed, I wouldn't want to do it.

In his essay "Torture," Auschwitz survivor Jean Améry talks about "the first blow." "The first blow brings home to the prisoner that he is *helpless*, and thus it already contains in the bud everything that is to come." If the "expectation of help, the certainty of help," is one of the "fundamental experiences of human beings," then, Améry continues, "I am certain that with the very first blow that descends on him he loses something we will perhaps temporarily call 'trust in the world.' "[121] I know that there is something very wrong with making this comparison, but it seems to me nonetheless that something similar is true for he who becomes a perpetrator. The first blow he gives is the beginning of the end of his world. "Because I joined the army," Kubotera-san said, "I lost my humanity."

Of course, all kinds of people were needed in the Resistance. There was one German-Jewish student who had taken some art courses in Berlin. She didn't work with us on hiding children, but she was great at falsifying documents. And sometimes doing nothing is doing something. When I was transporting a really Jewish-looking boy or girl, no one on the train said a thing, though they knew exactly what was happening. That was helping with the Resistance too.

Then again, there were people like this one couple—I invited them to join our group and the girl said, "You must look at this in a more astral way. Try to imagine that you are far off in the stars, and that you then look down from there on what goes on here." I had no time to argue. I said, "You can just go burst!" and walked off. Sometimes people would tell me, "The Germans are unstoppable; whatever you do won't matter." I answered, "It will matter to the children that we save."

—HETTY VOÛTE, *THE HEART HAS REASONS*

We, this whole people, have been clamorous
For war and bloodshed; animating sports,
The which we pay for as a thing to talk of,
Spectators and not combatants!

—SAMUEL TAYLOR COLERIDGE, "FEARS IN SOLITUDE"

I've been talking about the perpetrator, his peer group, and the authority structure surrounding him. But for violence to be extensive over space and durable over time, it needs many concentric rings of support. Massacres would not be possible without a massive population of collaborators who are not directly involved. You need the workers and bureaucrats who maintain the institutions that produce the violence. And you need the bystanders—generally the civilian population at large—who do nothing more than wave national flags or antiwar banners, like supporters of competing football teams.

The astonishing passivity of bystanders in the face of outrageous suffering has been the subject of much study. Researchers emphasize diffusion of responsibility (a term used to explain an infamous 1964 incident in which a young woman named Kitty Genovese was murdered while an entire New York neighborhood watched and listened, each person assuming that someone else would take action); confusion (when we cannot conceive of an effective intervention, or information is uncertain or complex, we respond with passivity); expert culture (as Staub writes, "Everywhere people tend to accept a definition of reality provided by 'experts,' their government, or their culture"); and pluralistic ignorance (people hide their reactions and emotions in public, and then look to others to see what an appropriate emotional response is; seeing little or no concern in the public actions of others, who are also hiding their emotions, they decide there may be no reason for concern after all).[122] This last psychological pattern has a parallel at the level of national politics, as Samantha Power explains: "It is in the realm of domestic politics that the battle to stop genocide is lost. American political leaders interpret society-wide silence as an indicator of public indifference."[123]

However, while passivity, distraction, and ignorance can prevent helpful interventions, they are often not sufficient to generate direct aggression. To move your people to kill, or to actively support killing by proxy, you need generalized social anxiety (over economic crises, for instance) to be publicly renarrated as specific fear. Such fear is distressingly easy to manufacture. Thomas Hobbes saw fear as a basic force underlying the social contract. He writes: "And from this diffidence of one another, there is no way for any man to secure himself, so reasonable, as anticipation; that is, by force, or wiles, to master the persons of all men he can, so long, till he see no other power great enough to endanger him."[124] Or, as the Athenian generals declare to justify their destruction of Melos in Thucydides' *Peloponnesian War*: "You and everybody else, having the same power as we have, would do the same as we do."[125] But as Daniel Chirot and Clark McCauley put it in *Why Not Kill Them All?*, fear comes in many forms, and the most excessive violence requires a particular combination: "simple fear" and "fear of pollution." Simple fear—fear that you will be injured as a group—creates a pliable public. Fear of pollution—"the sentiment that a particular group is so polluting that its very presence creates a mortal danger"—creates a potentially genocidal one.[126]

To maintain violence over long stretches of time, distance, euphemism, and censorship are also required. Distance can be in physical space or in the causal chain. With violence support staff, for instance, there are usually several layers separating the actions of the individual from any imaginable injuries. My father was an engineer for the Department of Defense. He is one of the most decent men I have ever known and would certainly never hurt anyone. He managed the personnel who maintained valves on U.S. nuclear submarines. No isolated action he ever performed in his job could be considered morally objectionable. He is now remembered in his community as a wonderful father, a kind and supportive supervisor, and a man who helped maintain a deterrent system that guaranteed U.S. security for a time. Had his submarines used their weapons and started a nuclear holocaust, he would have been remembered differently. He is morally lucky.

Censorship and euphemism (censorship writ small) are just as important as distance. If civilian populations were forced to name accurately all the events of war, the emotional costs would quickly become unbearable. We simply cannot talk every day about burned skin and corpses piled high. Instead, we substitute, we make metaphors. Coleridge writes, "All our dainty terms for fratricide; / Terms which we trundle smoothly o'er our tongues / Like mere abstractions, empty sounds to which / We join no feeling and attach no form!" Coleridge presents a poetic thought experiment to reveal the astonishing psychic power of these trivially familiar, trundling terms. "What if all-avenging Providence, / Strong and retributive, should make us know / The meaning of our words, force us to feel / The desolation and the agony / Of our fierce doings?"[127] The cumulative weight of such agony in sudden revelation would be shattering.

So, daily, we use sanitizing language that allows us to name injury without imagining it or, rather, to imagine it as patiently thoughtful and worklike. The 1946 atomic bomb tests on Bikini Atoll were carefully named "Operation Crossroads"—a largely successful public relations decision that conveyed an appropriate sense of caution, care, and awe. The name also turned gazes away from painful images of radiation casualties toward abstract visions of the development of "humanity itself" (as the namer, Vice Admiral Blandy, put it to a Senate committee).[128] Less subtly, the multiyear campaign of herbicidal warfare in Vietnam, in which millions of gallons of Agent Orange were sprayed over nearly 20 percent of the forested land to destroy crops and cover—causing hundreds of thousands of cancers, birth defects, and stillbirths, along with enduring toxic hotspots and massive refugee flows into urban areas—was given the patiently rugged, earth-tending name "Operation Ranch Hand."

In the U.S. Gulf Wars—the most widely and instantly covered wars in human history—language and image management were at the very center of battle strategy. They provide numerous examples of war imagined as worklike, playful, even healthful. Our "surgical strikes" were not only clean, but sounded like healing. When they "softened up" the enemy, they sounded like acts of gentle persuasion. "Cleaning out pockets of resistance" or "mopping up the resistance" provided both the domestic satisfaction of tidying up and the predatory provocation of imagining the enemy as filth (the "death squads" we cleaned out and mopped up in Iraq sounded like zombies that were already dead anyway). Combat by way of gaming metaphors—"entering the red zone," "rolling the dice," "Operation Flea Flicker," "Operation Triple-Play"—allowed the public to repetitively experience the fantasy that combat is low-stakes, that its injuries are minor, and that it ends with the clarity and finality of a football or baseball game. No blowback, no quagmire. And having reporters "embedded" sounded fantastically democratic and inclusive, promising an access to truth unlike anything we might have gotten from reporters who were, in other wars, simply "assigned."

The names of campaigns are arguments in disguise. Sometimes they work. "Desert Storm," for instance, helped eliminate any lingering doubts and anxieties that could have hindered the war effort. A hesitant president George H. W. Bush, deeply uncertain about what to do with the defiant Saddam Hussein, needed language that carried the force of natural fate, that simultaneously conveyed total conviction and avoided any traces of rash human aggression. The idea of the storm was perfect. A storm chooses you; it is impossible to avoid. But at the same time, if you are safely housed, it can be a thrilling spectacle to passively witness. And a *desert* storm is even better: it is the inevitable working out of the enemy ecosystem.

Sometimes, however, things don't go as planned. George W. Bush's "Shock and Awe" campaign in the Second Gulf War failed as language. It promised something it couldn't deliver. In the gap it left between promise and reality, it commemorated war's true shock: that grand words will always seem cheap next to spilled blood.

In the invasion of Iraq, the early use of language celebrating U.S. military ferocity (helpful in getting soldiers "pumped up," as Brigadier General Sean MacFarland said) over time began to give way to more pacific language designed to win over civilian populations on both sides. Hence the astonishing shift from "Shock and Awe" to, years later, "Operation Glad Tidings of Benevolence" and "Operation Together Forward."[129] This pattern of rhetorical de-escalation recalls a similar shift in the Korean War, in which public revulsion over "Operation Killer" forced a change in naming strategies. Lieutenant General Matthew Ridgway, responsible for the hated nickname (along with "Operation Ripper"), responded to the criticism he received with barely constrained contempt: "I am not convinced that the country should not be told that war means killing. I am by nature opposed to any effort to 'sell' war to people as an only mildly unpleasant business that requires very little in the way of blood." Ridgway's clarifying frankness contrasts sharply to Lyndon Johnson's frustrated reaction during the Vietnam War to the name "Operation Masher," which Johnson felt inappropriately underemphasized "pacification." As General William Westmoreland put it, Johnson was upset that "the connotation of violence provided a focus for carping war critics."[130]

Look back as far as the U.S. Civil War memoirs of Generals Sherman and Grant, and you will see the same sanitizing strategies and distorting verbal reflexes: "our flank was damaged" or "we delivered a message" (not "ten of our young soldiers died" or "we shelled a civilian neighborhood"). But sometimes more severe linguistic coercion is required. Sometimes it is necessary to stop people from talking altogether. Abraham Lincoln's restrictions upon free speech were notoriously unflinching and pervasive. Just so, Japan's twentieth-century wartime political rearrangements included the Newspaper and Publications Control Ordinance, the

Press, Publications, Assembly and Association Special Control Law, and an expansion of the Peace Preservation Law that regulated subversive thought and behavior. Over 70,000 were arrested under this law from 1928 to 1941. "We have strengthened our control," declared Prime Minister Tōjō in 1941, "over those who are anti-war and anti-military, such as communists, rebellious Koreans, certain religious leaders, and others who we fear may be a threat to the public order."[131]

Discussing Argentina's Dirty War, Marguerite Feitlowitz tracks the systemic damage violent regimes inflict on communication: "I have come to believe that, even after the regime has ended, language may be the last system to recover."[132] Jacobo Timerman, a journalist arrested and tortured by the military junta, describes the "great silence" that appears "in every civilized country that passively accepts the inevitability of violence."[133] Discussing Mao Tsetung's China, Lifton epitomizes the social damages of censorship in the idea of "the thought-terminating cliché": language that prepares us for violence because it reduces complex problems to simple "ultimate terms" (god and devil, good and evil, that which must be cultivated and that which must be eliminated).[134] And Arendt, finally, explains that violent regimes must sustain themselves through "language rules." "For whatever other reasons the language rules may have been devised," she writes of the Holocaust, "they proved of enormous help in the maintenance of order and sanity in the various widely diversified services whose cooperation was essential in this matter."[135] In paradigmatic instances of what Arendt later chillingly called "defactualization,"[136] Nazis redescribed "extermination," "liquidation," and "killing" as "evacuation," "change of residence," and "resettlement."[137]

Claude Lanzmann's documentary film of the Holocaust, *Shoah*, reveals the logic of Nazi atrocities: violence starts in secrecy and silence, and it perpetuates such silence as part of its very nature. The film, composed of interviews with witnesses, survivors, and perpetrators, continually points back to the Holocaust's shattering of language as its primary enabling condition and also its legacy:

"No one can describe it."

"And let's not talk about that."

"Anyone who uttered the words 'corpse' or 'victim' was beaten."

"It was impossible to say anything—we were just like stoned."

"We were not allowed to talk to each other or to express our views or our minds to each other."

"Resettlement program. No one ever spoke of killing."

"*You had to take an oath?* No, just sign, promising to shut up about whatever we'd see."

"Well, when the word got around, when it was whispered. It was never said outright. Good God, no! They'd have hauled you off at once!"

"And the key to the entire operation from the psychological standpoint was never to utter the words that would be appropriate to the action being taken. Say nothing; do these things; do not describe them."

"If you lie enough, you believe your own lies."

"I don't think the human tongue can describe the horror we went through in the ghetto."[138]

It's hard to avoid talking about Nazis, but I wish I could. They are such exotic evil, they have nothing to do with us. Nobody reads the paragraph above and says, for instance, Yes, that's what it felt like watching as antiwar voices were stigmatized and marginalized in those first heady days of the Gulf Wars. Or, Yes, that's what it felt like watching television news under the U.S. media coffin ban. Or, Yes, that's what it felt like watching videos of smart bombs blowing up empty bridges and buildings. Or, Yes, that's what it felt like hearing suicide attempts by detainees at Guantánamo described as "manipulative self-injurious behavior." Nobody thinks such things, and nobody should.

At some deep level, Nazis allow for what Albert Bandura calls "exonerating comparison."[139] And perhaps also they prohibit comparison. In the paragraph just above on censorship, for instance, I wanted to talk about the My Lai massacre but wasn't comfortable fitting it in next to the Holocaust. Here's what I wanted to say (My Lai will follow at a distance). Censorship isn't only somebody else stopping you from receiving troubling information. It's you not permitting yourself to understand troubling information you receive. Study after study reveals that we are relatively awful users of information, and that our errors tend to close us off to others. We see our own negative actions as a result of our situation and see the negative actions of others as a result of their nature (actor-observer bias), we like familiar things just because they are familiar (mere-exposure effect), and we perceive diversity in our own communities but think of members of other communities as "all the same" (out-group homogeneity bias).

We think especially poorly when we think together. We tend to adopt more extreme opinions in groups than we would when alone (group polarization), become more competitive with other groups than we would when alone (discontinuity effect), and make riskier decisions than we would when alone (risky-shift effect). In groups we prefer easy solutions to good ones (satisficing); we do things just because everybody else is doing them (information cascade); we focus on the information we all already share at the expense of new information held only by a few (shared information bias); and when listening to each other, we simplify what we hear (reductive coding), exaggerate differences in order to create clear distinctions (enhancement of contrast), focus on beginnings and endings (middle message loss), reinterpret messages so that they match previous ones (assimilation to prior input), and reinterpret messages so that they match what we anticipated hearing (assimilation to expected message).[140]

On top of all that, we pay more attention to negative information than positive information (negativity bias), focusing on threats over signs of safety, remembering bad experiences more intensely than good ones, giving more weight to negative information about strangers than positive information, experiencing our dislike of bad behavior in others more intensely than our liking of their good behavior, and forming negative stereotypes about others more quickly and with less data than we do when forming positive stereotypes.[141] This gets worse when we are anxious or insecure. In those emotional states, we are even more likely to stereotype others; to show in-group favoritism; to judge members of our group as possessing better features than those of other groups; to engage in downward social comparison (focusing on worse-off others to comfort ourselves); and subsequently, to remember negative rather than positive things about those handy worse-off others.[142] Finally, we seek out information that confirms our existing beliefs, while filtering out information that challenges them (confirmation bias); and we seek cognitive consistency at sometimes unbearable costs, denying even the plainest revealed truths if accepting them would require us to give up, with pain, previously cherished beliefs (cognitive dissonance).

At its extreme, we call this cluster of cognitive patterns "denial of reality." In the My Lai massacre, Jonathan Glover notes, U.S. soldiers crouched into defensive firing positions when shooting fleeing children, as if to persuade themselves they were in a combat situation facing armed soldiers. As one soldier described it afterward: "If you're actually thinking in terms of a massacre or murder, going in and shooting a bunch of defenceless people, why crouch? . . . Because your judgment is all screwed up . . . they actually look like the enemy, or what you think is the enemy."[143]

U.S. soldiers in My Lai had reason to be scared of enemies, but not scared just then, with those families. I think the United States is in a similar situation now and has been for some time. We are a culture crouched into a defensive firing position.

———

Ebato-san

But they'll make it so you respond reflexively to the orders of those above you, like a robot or a slave . . . You could say that training those sorts of people was what Japanese recruit-training was. And other than this corporal punishment was this [unclear] bullying. And this was [unclear], endlessly. For instance, there was this punishment we called "young lady." Another one was called "nightingale crossing the valley," and in this you'd crawl through the bed calling out like a nightingale! [Imitates a nightingale] Then the old soldiers would say things like, "Good lord, the nightingales sound awful this year!" and go on and on. They thought out endless punishments and ways to abuse the new guys. That was the recruitment training, and the result of that was, well, uh—the individual personality was completely killed, and you follow *only* your superiors' orders. That kind of robot. The kind that could, on the battlefield, if the order came down from a superior, kill the other races with cool and composure.

Everybody would wind up that way. So, to become a person without ideas—without thoughts—that your body would do in a flash what you're told. You could say we became that sort of person. So we went to the army, and as I said earlier, by things like the new recruit being killed on the battalion commander's orders, the body trained by this recruit training would simply jump over one's reason—and then you commit the crime . . .

In the end, it's like what you ask—it becomes pleasurable. [Unclear] For instance, you'll shut them up in a house, set fire to it, and watch it burn. That sort of unbelievably gruesome, brutal pleasure.

———

Veteran William Broyles Jr. calls war a "terrible ecstasy," explaining that its fundamental allure is the "passion to witness, to see things, what the Bible calls the lust of the eye and the Marines in Vietnam called eye fucking."[144] J. Glenn Gray, veteran of an earlier U.S. war, describes combat as a matter of aesthetic delight and the experience of the sublime. War, again, is "the lust of the eye"; it involves "delight in destruction." For some, it becomes "a consuming lust which swallows up other pleasures," turning men inward upon themselves and making them "inaccessible to more normal satisfactions."[145]

Some psychologists use what is called "opponent-process theory" to account for the development of this kind of sadism. The theory holds that whenever a body is excited out of its normal state, an internal process must follow that returns it to equilibrium. Baumeister and Campbell describe the dramatic effect that repetition has on this cycle: "The initial, departing (the A process) response is often strong at first, whereas the restorative B process is relatively inefficient, but over time (i.e., through many similar experiences), the B process becomes increasingly efficient and powerful, whereas the A process becomes weaker. In effect, the B process comes to dominate."[146]

This description sounds arcane, but it is common sense, and we have all experienced it. As Baumeister and Campbell explain, it is the principle of physical exercise—for instance, the "runner's high." The first time you run to exhaustion you will feel sick, your body will recover only gradually, and the pleasure of escaping from the distressed state will be weak. If you do it more, however, the workout will become less distressing (the A process weakens) and the escape from distress will become more and more pleasurable (the B process dominates). You will eventually crave running.

Christopher Browning describes how the men of Nazi Germany's Reserve Police Battalion 101 were, after their first massacre, "depressed, angered, embittered, and shaken." He writes: "They ate little but drank heavily. Generous quantities of alcohol were provided, and many of the policemen got quite drunk. Major Trapp made the rounds, trying to console and reassure them, and again placing responsibility on higher authorities. But neither the drink nor Trapp's consolation could wash away the sense of shame and horror that pervaded the barracks."[147] However, over time "the horrors of the initial encounter eventually became routine, and the killing became progressively easier. In this sense, brutalization was not the cause but the effect of these men's behavior."[148] Applying opponent-process theory to these kinds of atrocities, Baumeister and Campbell write that "euphoria" would be the body's "most effective antidote to the severe disgust and distress" caused by hurting others.[149]

Acquiring a taste for violence is a gradual process. Discussing the terror of combat in the Sunni triangle (ambushes, roadside bombs, civilian casualties), one U.S. veteran puts it this way: "It was the oddest feeling. The only way to describe that kind of combat is that it is like being raped, but really enjoying it. It scars you, it's horrible, but at the same time, you start to like it."[150] But even though the process of acclimatization to violence is slow, in any given episode—even in first episodes—violence can accelerate quickly once it begins. Those same depressed and reluctant men Browning describes above self-amplified that very first night. As darkness approached, "the shooting became even less organized and more hectic."[151] The emotional arousal of violence is, as Zimbardo writes, "upwards-spiraling." Describing how women in his shock experiment increased the amount of electricity they delivered as the trials continued, he explains: "The agitated behavior becomes self-reinforcing, each action stimulating a stronger, less controlled next reaction."[152]

But this behavior is not evidence of sadism, argues Zimbardo—not exactly. It comes instead, he postulates, from "the energizing sense of one's domination and control over others at that moment in time." Jacobo Timerman, imprisoned by the Argentine military in the 1970s, saw in his torturers a pathological need for such domination. "The torturer," he writes, "needs to be needed by the tortured."[153] He explains further: "The conversion of dirty, dark, gloomy places into a universe of spontaneous innovation and institutional 'beauty' is one of the most arousing pleasures for torturers. It is as if they felt themselves to be masters of the force required to alter reality. And it places them again in the world of omnipotence. This omnipotence in turn they feel assures them of impunity—a sense of immunity to pain, guilt, emotional imbalance."[154]

William Schulz sees this craving for omnipotence, this need for the need of others, as deeply, universally human. A Unitarian Universalist minister and the former executive director of Amnesty International USA, Schulz recalls discovering these cruel pleasures in himself as a child when he abused a dog. "It was fascinating to feel this little creature so entirely under my control," he writes.[155]

Violence is energizing and fascinating. It releases us from feeling the repetition and boredom of life—in this way it is a natural cousin to pranks and thrilling diversions.[156] Violence also makes up for all the awful moments in our lives when we felt small and weak and helpless. Virtue can be satisfying, but it smacks of obedience. Violence, by contrast, is freedom. It liberates us from the restraints and duties that hold us close each moment of our days. In *The Thin Red Line* James Jones describes the thrill Private Doll experiences when he first kills an enemy Japanese soldier—it was like a first sexual encounter, Doll thinks; it makes him feel "vastly superior." "It had to do with guilt. Doll felt guilty. He couldn't help it. He had killed a human being, a man. He had done the most horrible thing a human could do, worse than rape even. And nobody in the whole damned world could say anything to him about it. That was where the pleasure came."[157]

In its extreme, the emancipating moral alienation of violence can be transcendent, even ecstatic. As one Soviet soldier said of his time in Afghanistan: "We will never walk, or make love, or be loved, the way we walked and loved and were loved over there. Everything was heightened by the closeness of death: death hovered everywhere and all the time. Life was full of adventure: I learnt the smell of danger . . . we are homesick for it, some of us; it's called the Afghan syndrome."[158]

"That violence is often associated with ecstatic experiences is seen in our using the same phrases for both," notes psychologist Rollo May. "We say a person is 'beside himself' with rage; he is 'possessed' by power."[159] The combination described in these phrases—simultaneous self-escape and total absorption—is narcotic. It can also be, for many, sexual. All of the soldiers above, like other soldiers over the years, characterize the pleasure of battle in sexual terms. "Sex in war," Christopher Hedges writes, "is another

variant of the drug of war."[160] At the height of war during the breakup
of Yugoslavia, Hedges notes, Belgrade had "seventy escort services,
three adult cinemas, and twenty pornographic magazines"—a radical change from the prewar regime, which had banned pornography.[161] Combat violence is linked together with sexual violence.
Hedges calls rape a "natural outcome" of war.[162]

While men and boys are often victims of sexual violence in war,
women are favored targets. Why do soldiers rape women? In *Fraternity Gang Rape*, Peggy Sanday describes how the rituals of hazing that produce intense bonding in male social groups depend
upon contempt for women. The submersion of the self in the group
is generated, in part, through a two-step process: produce anxiety
in the individual by representing the feminine "as both dirty and as
part of his subjectivity," and then resolve that anxiety by cleansing
the individual "of his supposed feminine identification and promising him a lifelong position in a purified male social order."[163] In a
sense, the cruelty toward women recounted by the Chukiren was
not so much a result of the upward-spiraling nature of violence as
its cause, not so much the climax of accumulating violence as the
originary moment that made it possible.

If you combine a misogynistic hazing, bonding, and initiation
process with the very real need to rely upon and to trust one another to survive, you get a fraternal codependence that is unfath-
omably deep. When that codependence is combined with the
shared alienation of incommunicable trauma, it becomes world-
defining. Siegfried Sassoon, the British poet and veteran of World
War I, writes: "The Man who really endured the War at its worst
was everlastingly differentiated from everyone except his fellow
soldiers."[164] People will do almost anything to avoid expulsion from
this brotherhood. "This is what is most difficult," a French soldier
in Algeria said of his refusal to fight alongside his comrades, "being

cut off from the fraternity, being locked in a monologue, being incomprehensible."[165]

But soldiers don't only kill for each other. They also die for each other. Anybody who looks at war fairly must acknowledge what this means. War works because of what is worst about us—our fear and weakness—and because of what is best about us—our capacity to love something more than we love ourselves. Jonathan Shay, a staff psychiatrist for the Department of Veteran Affairs outpatient clinic in Boston, writes: "Of all groups in America today, military people have the greatest right to, and will benefit most, if they reclaim the word 'love' as part of what they are and what they do."[166] Reflecting on his own experience of war, J. Glenn Gray writes:

> Are we not right in honoring the fighter's impulse to sacrifice himself for a comrade, even though it be done, as it so frequently is, in an evil cause? I think so. It is some kind of world historical pathos that the striving for union and for immortality must again and again be consummated while men are in the service of destruction. I do not doubt for a moment that wars are made many times more deadly because of this striving and this impulse. Yet I would not want to be without the assurance their existence gives me that our species has a different destiny than is granted to other animals. Though we often sink below them, we can at moments rise above them, too.[167]

Despite my discomfort with Gray's words in this passage, I feel myself reaching in sympathy toward the yearning he expresses for lives that transcend petty self-interest. Wars are born in love, and through this love, we find meaning. "Even with its destruction and carnage," Hedges writes, war "can give us what we long for in life. It can give us purpose, meaning, a reason for living."[168]

The first of the three dialogs that follow depicts sexual violence. As with the other sections about sexual violence, I am mindful here of Wendy Hesford's and Wendy Brown's incisive analyses of the way graphic representations of rape in human rights work can place their "readers in the position of voyeur," license "the pornographic gaze," and—by making a spectacle of female victimization and powerlessness—"inadvertently perpetuate the most powerful icon in the violent production of gendered identities," thereby resubordinating the subject "historically subjugated through [that] identity."[169]

I include the passage that immediately follows nonetheless because of two things I want to emphasize about it, things that illuminate both the psychology of the perpetrators and the meaning of the phrase "comfort woman" (a historical reality still denied, distorted, ignored, and euphemized around the world). First, the long line of men participating in what could only be called institutional gang rape was not unusual for this woman. It happened so often that she had developed strategies for minimizing the expected tissue damage. And second, the story is structured to have a certain kind of punch, and the punch is about hygiene. This story is about disgust. There *is* a woman in the story as the veteran tells it. But insofar as this is an anecdote deemed worth repeating (and it is one of the stories I know he told other people before talking to me, that he thought of *as* a story), it is on a certain level not about what war did to this woman, but about what war did to men.

KANEKO-SAN. Soldiers were forming a loooong line. Lined up. And the soldiers . . . the woman, what did she look like? She had her thighs open. Right? She opened her thighs, and in this, this place her thighs were opened. She was lying down, and I was under, under her like this. And then I took off my pants, and, she just rubbed me, and then I was done. And, I was all done. Holding her and having sex—kissing—there was none of that. The woman just left her thighs open. And then a man would go in, and just rub. And that was it. And so we just paid out one yen, fifty sen. For that, soldiers were allll lined up in a row.

Then on the way home, this is what I said. "What the hell, you guys? You just left her like that when you were done? One by one, you didn't even wipe her off?" Normally, after you do it once, you wipe her off, don't you? "You didn't even wipe her off?" [Speaking harshly and quickly] . . . I was angry. And then, the woman apparently said to them, "Mr. Soldier, if I wiped here—how many soldiers do you think there are? It'd just swell up here. It'll swell," she said. "That's why I can't do it!" That, that's what happened, you see.

———

INTERPRETER. Did you yourself ever think something like, "I feel sorry for these women"?
KANEKO-SAN. Well, you . . . I don't really remember about the time . . . No . . .
INTERPRETER. So, this is about the comfort stations . . . Do you believe that you raped the women at—
KANEKO-SAN. Eh?
INTERPRETER. . . . that you sexually assaulted them [interpreter addresses him with honorific language]?
KANEKO-SAN. I don't think so. No. Because I paid money. I think that's pretty obvious.
INTERPRETER. Yes . . . certainly.

———

YUASA-SAN. And when I first went, another doctor, a superior of mine, said everyone should choose whatever they liked, and then disappeared into a room. What was left was—at the time I thought under 30, maybe 26, 27—a woman who looked to me like she was older than me. She was sad and alone. Turns out older people don't—[laughs] they don't sell after all, huh? She looked pretty pitiful, and I took that woman by the hand into a room . . . Anyway, the place where the bed is. And there was a futon there, and then in the corner there was a sort of tool for washing your hands. Presumably she cleaned up there, hm? And so we went in there and I asked her, "Why did you come here? I thought you came here for business . . ." And then, this was a Korean woman, and she said, "My older brother told me to come here." "Ahh, is that so," I said. And so for a long time I thought she had come because her older brother told her to, but that wasn't it! She just couldn't say, to an officer in the Japanese army, that she was tricked by the Japanese to come there! And so, maybe, that's what happened, I think. So what I thought all the time was so-called prostitution—I began to think I was mistaken!

[Returning later to the same questions]

INTERPRETER. After you had gone, did you feel anything in particular about it?

YUASA-SAN. I guess it's to be expected—Americans, when we talk about comfort stations and the sort, they really put a lot of weight on emotion and feelings, don't they?

INTERPRETER. Yes, as expected . . . So, when you think about it now, at the comfort stations, do you think that's rape?

YUASA-SAN. They were ugly. Ugly. You know? As you'd expect, all I felt about them was that they were really disgusting—vile women. They seemed like vile women. Mm. They were sex tools. I didn't feel anything but that.

FEMALE VISITOR. But you were asking whether it was rape or not, weren't you?

INTERPRETER. Yes, that's right.

FEMALE VISITOR. She asked if it was rape!

YUASA-SAN. Wha?

FEMALE VISITOR. Going to the comfort stations—do you think that was rape? That's what she's asking. Was it rape?

YUASA-SAN. Agggghhhhhhh . . . I don't—I don't think the comfort stations [laughs] are rape, noo . . . Nope, as you might expect, I don't think it's rape—I don't feel like I raped them. Mm. Hmm . . .

As a [unclear]—hmm, by the government—maybe it was a sort of a "rape agency" . . . ? I don't really know about that right now . . . Mm . . . You know, maybe it was a kind of rape after all . . . "Rape station" . . . It has a bit of a [laughs a bit] . . . different flavor to it, doesn't it . . . ? I don't know whether it was a rape station, hmm. Well, maybe since they were smiling so much when they serviced us, I just don't know how to answer. But it didn't feel like a rape station, I have to say . . . [Clicks tongue]

FEMALE VISITOR. Doctor, are you okay? Are you okay? Is your body okay?

YUASA-SAN. Ahh, no problem, no problem.

[Long silence]

[Break]

YUASA-SAN. Well, they were smiling and took us in like that, so . . . I just, somehow, don't think it was clearly a "rape station" . . . Mmm . . . they were smiling and, mmm, sweet, you know—using words like "yo" and everything . . .

INTERPRETER. "Yo"?

YUASA-SAN. Ahh, a word for someone you feel close to, you know . . . ?

INTERPRETER. Oh, really? Ohh, right, right, right. Korean—the Koreans say that.

YUASA-SAN. Right. And maybe they had to say that sort of thing, but [unclear] I still—ah—I don't really think it was a "rape station" . . . I don't really know . . . I'm still thinking. Mm.

(Yuasa-san was born to a doctor's family, graduated from Jikei University School of Medicine, and worked as a doctor before, during, and after the war. He passed away November 2, 2010. He is survived by a wife, son, and two daughters.)

———

Kaneko-san claims not to have gone to comfort women often and not to recall many faces. But he remembers one woman vividly. He assumed she was Korean—that was the norm. But her Japanese was too good. When he complimented her language, she confessed to being Japanese. Kaneko-san was stupefied, outraged. How could a Japanese woman be in such a place? He left in disgust.

Yoshiaki Yoshimi estimates that between 50,000 and 200,000 women were forced or tricked into becoming comfort women during the course of the conflict. Some evidence suggests that the Japanese military decided upon comfort stations in order to reduce incidents of unregulated rape. In one document from 1938, the chief of staff of the North China Area Army expressed concern that rape of local women was inflaming anti-Japanese antagonism in occupied areas, and therefore that establishing "facilities for sexual comfort as quickly as possible is of great importance."[170] But at the same time, Yuki Tanaka argues, officers found rape a useful tool "to stimulate aggression" in their soldiers—sometimes providing them with condoms before embarkation. One U.S. intelligence officer recalls finding supplies of condoms "regularly issued" to Japanese soldiers. The wrappers had a picture of a soldier charging with a bayonet above the caption "Totsugeki" (Charge!).[171] A former Korean comfort woman gives this testimony: "I was nearly killed several times during my time as a 'comfort woman.' There were some military men who were drunk and were brandishing swords at me while making demands for perverted sex. They drove their swords into the tatami [woven straw floor matting], then demanded sex from me . . . Afterwards the tatami was full of holes from them driving their swords into it . . . The threat they were making was obvious—if I didn't co-operate they would stab me."[172]

Meanwhile, in the same conflict, Tanaka writes, U.S. soldiers "engaged in the mass rape of Japanese women . . . young girls raped in front of their parents, pregnant women raped in maternity wards, and so on." In one ten-day period in the Kanagawa prefecture, there were 1,336 reported cases.[173]

Is mass rape inevitable in war? "Every time there is a war, there is rape," writes Catherine MacKinnon. However, she continues, while rape does occur "in all wars, both within and between all sides," characterizing rape as an inevitable outcome of war can nonetheless have perverse and devastating global consequences. In Serbia's wars against Croatia and Bosnia-Herzegovina, MacKinnon explains, rape was a weapon of war; it was genocidal. But for some time the world was blinded to this fact because of the quieting effect of "natural rape" theory. "If all men do this all the time, especially in war," MacKinnon asks, "how can one pick a side in this one? And since all men do this all the time, war or no war, why do anything special about this now?"[174] Notably, the Ministry of Education in Japan made just such an argument when deleting references to wartime rape in China from a 1962 textbook: "The violation of women is something that has happened on every battlefield in every era of human history. This is not an issue that needs to be taken up with respect to the Japanese Army in particular."[175]

But what if rape is *not* a natural outcome of war? Elisabeth Jean Wood claims it isn't, pointing to the apparent relative absence of sexual violence on the part of the Tamil Tigers of Sri Lanka. Wood argues that even while the Tamil Tigers inflicted thousands of civilian casualties, they were able to control sexual violence through strict internal discipline and a system of brutal punishment. She speculates that there are other paths to limited sexual violence during wartime.[176] But to find them, we must first believe they exist. We must insist, in other words, that "why" is a serious question with specific answers, and not a rhetorical gesture.

Why do soldiers rape women?

One common answer is the "pressure cooker" theory of rape: soldiers rape because they need sex. Society "acts as a hindrance to male's natural bestial sexual behavior—a hinder which is often removed in the climate of warring."[177] But most scholars reject this idea. Summarizing why rape-as-lust is empirically implausible, Wood writes: the model cannot account for "the frequently observed targeting of particular groups of women, nor the often-extreme violence that frequently accompanies wartime rape, nor the occurrence of nonrape sexual torture. And if this argument were complete, we would not see rape by forces with ample access to prostitutes. This is certainly not always the case."[178]

Most scholars today favor theories of rape that emphasize features like violence, competition, and insecurity instead of desire. Summarizing their interviews with perpetrators from the state military organization of the Democratic Republic of the Congo (DRC), Maria Eriksson Baaz and Maria Stern explain: "The soldiers explicitly linked their rationale for rape with their inabilities (or 'failures') to inhabit certain idealized notions of heterosexual manhood."[179]

In their study of police torturers in Brazil, Martha Huggins, Mika Haritos-Fatouros, and Philip Zimbardo pay special attention to cultural constructions of masculinity. In patriarchal cultures, they explain, masculinity is both a performance and a contest with winners and losers, where identity is at stake. The competitiveness of such masculinity turns quickly to aggression, they write, "because few men are able to successfully demonstrate their masculinity constantly within a system of pervasive competition over scarce and elusive masculinity resources."[180] As a veteran of Vietnam explained of wartime rape: "They only do it when there are a lot of guys around. You know, it makes them feel good. They show each other what they can do—'I can do it,' you know. They won't do it by themselves."[181]

The brutal performance of such manhood extends beyond battlefield violence into the very structuring of an interior self. It is a performance that one does not know one is performing, that one performs for oneself. Sandra Whitworth provides an example:

Male soldiers who experience PTSD discover that they have not successfully obliterated the feminine other and indeed risk becoming "women." As Lisa Vetten writes, the masculinity affirmed by the process of most contemporary military training "is a fragile one, entirely unable to tolerate traces of femininity." When the stoic, tough, emotionless soldier begins to feel and react, when he feels pain, fear, anxiety, guilt, shame and despair as a result of the activities in which he participated as a soldier, he violates the precepts of his military identity and can no longer fulfill the myths of militarized manhood that have shaped him.[182]

A good amount of contemporary academic thinking about masculinity and sexual violence relies on one version or another of this basic model: a masculine (as distinct from male) identity is a fragile construct forever policing itself for signs of the feminine. Late 1970s and 1980s feminist psychoanalytic work on the institution of exclusively female caregiving remains seminal for this field of inquiry. As Nancy Chodorow writes, in patriarchal societies where fathers are distant, an infant's experience of being starts as a total fusion with the mother. Mother is the "external ego," the child's origin and limit. For boys, importantly, it is *against* this original union that a sense of masculinity arises. His emerging social identity must prove itself against his primary, formative relationship. Indeed, while the daughter's gendered self develops in relation to the present mother, the son's gendered self develops in relation to an absent father. Masculinity, Chodorow argues, is therefore "elusive," constructed "largely in negative terms." The self is a matter of *nots:* not dependent upon his mother, not constrained by identification with her, not defined by attachment.[183] Identity conceived thus as dyadic struggle generates, in Freud's words, "the contempt felt by men for a sex which is the lesser"—"What we have come to consider the normal male contempt for women."[184] Writes Jessica Benjamin: "The vulnerability of a masculinity that is forged in the crucible of femininity, the 'great task' of separation that is so seldom completed, lays the groundwork for the later objectification of women."[185]

The psychic work of a male child in patriarchal societies requires internalizing a stable "masculinity" and voiding his "femininity." This, as it turns out, is a lifelong task. While a boy will quickly learn to inhibit "feminine" behaviors in order to avoid punishment, he might, nonetheless, find it impossible to avoid thinking about or wishing to "act feminine." Since for a child it is often difficult to maintain a strong internal sense of the difference between wishing and doing, between fantasizing and enacting, the male child will continue to feel anxiety about gendered behavior patterns long after he has apparently internalized them. He will continue to harbor a secret, unspeakable self-doubt: namely, that he is, deep inside, nothing better than a "dirty girl" after all. Among other things, this is the core logic of pornography (which is, like drugs and alcohol, part of the equipment of war). Susan Griffin argues: "It is the female aspect of the self who is punished in pornography—punished and then blamed for her own punishment. The pornographer's fear of his own sexual feelings is written implicitly into every scene in which a man binds and silences a woman. When the pornographer murders a woman, part of himself dies."[186]

Pornography, male initiation rituals, and hazing and bonding practices serve the important function of killing the girl inside. And they lay the groundwork for killing the girl outside. Pierre Bourdieu writes:

> What is called "courage" is thus often rooted in a kind of cowardice: one has only to think of all the situations in which, to make men kill, torture or rape, the will to dominate, exploit or oppress has relied on the "manly" fear of being excluded from the world of "men" without weakness, those who are sometimes called "tough" because they are tough on their own suffering and more especially on that of others—the assassins, torturers and "hit men" of all dictatorships and all "total institutions," even the most ordinary ones, such as prisons, barracks or boarding schools.[187]

This cluster of related arguments is helpful in making sense of male sexual violence. But collectively they are also subject to three important qualifications. First, such theories have insufficient accounts of paternal love.[188] Second, the widespread effort to understand pathological masculine identity can sometimes verge on treating such identity as a norm. As Kelly Oliver cautions: "We could *diagnose* contemporary marginalization and exclusion *using* theories of identity that are built on abjection [self-creation through exclusion], but this type of identity is not the only type." A better model of identity would emphasize our essential intersubjectivity and healthful interdependence (more on this in the final pages of this book). Applied here, intersubjective theories of identity would reject the traditional psychoanalytic belief "that an infant's relationship with her mother is anti-social and must be broken off," and instead view the mother as "the first cooperative partner in a social relationship that makes subjectivity possible."[189]

The third limitation to these explanations of pathological masculine identity is, precisely, that they are explanations of identity. To explain rape as a behavioral norm in subcultures of war, much more is needed than an individual- or identity-based account. To become a mass practice, rape must have broad organizational functions. It must be widely understood or experienced as serving a range of important purposes—psychological ones certainly, but also military, political, and cultural ones.

In some cases, rape can function as a combat training and unit cohesion ritual. With public rape or gang rape, for instance, new recruits are forced to permanently shed their connections to the known moral world, thereby becoming ever more intensely bonded to those who share their alienation. Rape can also function as an enduring political deconstruction of enemy nationhood. In many cultures, Ruth Seifert explains, the "female body functions as a symbolic representation of the body politic": the territory that nurtures us and that also needs protection is gendered female in art and other public discourse. Because of this, the woman's body is simultaneously a physical, psychological, and cultural target. "Violence inflicted on women is aimed at the physical and personal integrity of the group. This in turn is particularly significant for the construction of the community. Thus the rape of the women in a community can be regarded as the symbolic rape of the body of

this community. Against this background, the mass rapes that ac-
company all wars take on new meaning: by no means acts of senseless brutality, they are rather culture-destroying actions with a
strategic rationale."[190] Susan Brownmiller adds: "In one act of aggression, the collective spirit of women *and* of the nation is broken,
leaving a reminder long after the troops depart. And if she survives
the assault, what does the victim of wartime rape become to her
people? Evidence of the enemy's bestiality. Symbol of her nation's
defeat. A pariah. Damaged property. A pawn in the subtle wars of
international propaganda."[191] As Human Rights Watch concludes:
war rape "is neither incidental nor private," but rather "acts as a
tool for achieving specific military or political objectives."[192]

On the flight home after my final interview, I read Nora Okja
Keller's *Comfort Woman,* which tells the harrowing story of Akiko,
a survivor of the Japanese "recreation camps." In this brutal and
lyrical novel, Keller depicts the trauma of sexual violence as a matter, in part, of broken language. Sex slaves are not permitted to
speak, speak in code, are murdered for speaking out. Survivors are
mute, are given voice, are spoken for, are spoken over. Wives and
mothers keep secrets from their families, their daughters; they
speak with the dead more clearly than with the living. And sex traf-
ficking itself begins in lies—lies about jobs abroad for young Korean girls, in factories, in restaurants.

Against this cascade of violence's language-smothering moments, however, Keller offers powerful images of voices being
raised—often, importantly, in song. Song is, in key ways, an opposite to trauma. If trauma is the human experience that most impov-
erishes language, that reveals language's poverty in translating experience, song is the human mode that most dramatically amplifies

language, that reveals language's capacity to carry meaning beyond what can be translated. Even after her liberation, Akiko finds her daily life invaded by the noise of the camp. Listening to a missionary's sermon, she is unable to make out words over the loud internal echoes of slaps and bullets. But when the congregation rises to hymns:

> What I heard after my ears cracked open was a single song, with notes so rich and varied that it sounded like many songs blended into one. And in that song I heard things that I had almost forgotten: the enduring whisper of women who continued to pass messages under the ears of the soldiers; a defiant Induk bellowing the Korean national anthem even after the soldiers had knocked her teeth out; the symphony of ten thousand frogs; the lullabies my mother hummed as she put her daughters to sleep; the song the river sings when she finds her freedom in the ocean.[193]

At the center of psychic survival, *Comfort Woman* seems to say, is the problem of translation, in the deepest sense of the word.

Kaneko-san

Children I never could do . . . I never could, on my own, target and shoot them. And stabbing kids with a bayonet—I've never done that a single time. I just couldn't do it to kids. But women were no problem.

[Later, when the question is repeated]

Aggggh. [Aggravated noise] There were no children! No kids.

[Pause]

However, one thing I can say, there was just one. It happened when we went into a village . . . and the old soldiers were first set on rape. And so we went to each village. And then, in China, there is something called an *ondoru*—a heater, you know? Inside there, a woman was holding her child, like this. And so the old soldiers and us went inside. "There's a woman here. Kaneko, pull out the kid and go out front. When I'm done, I'll hand her over to you." And I took the kid out front as I was told.

Then there was a woman trembling in the corner. Then what we could hear from the old soldier behind us was the old soldier's noise—his angry voice. His voice. "Make this [inaudible]—Do [inaudible]!" That sort of thing. And then after he did it for a while, we heard the woman's crying voice. And after that, after a while, the old soldier grabbed the woman's hair and came out front. "Kaneko, come with me!" he said. "Yes, sir," I said, and I went with him. And then I forgot that the kid was even there. And then, in a village, there is definitely always—because long ago they didn't have running water—there's always a well. He took her to where the well was. He took her to where the well was, and then the old soldier pushed the woman against the well—did it like this, you know? Like this—he pushed her against it. Her head, her hair. And I—"Kaneko, you hold her legs." I'm holding both of the woman's legs. We lift her up like that, and tossed her into the well. [Voice diminishing]

And at that time, at that time, I . . . And that kid, because his mother had been thrown into the well, went round and round the well yelling, "Maa-maa, Maa-maa." But he was about four years old, you know? He couldn't quite reach. And there was a tapping sound—whether it was from inside of me or what I didn't know—and then he had a chair like a stand or a table that he dragged out. He used that as a stand, said "Maa-maa," then [pause] . . . he threw himself into the well. And we all had shiver right about then, you know? "Ohh, this is just too much," we thought. But this thing, you know, it's *alllways* been stuck in my head. And at the end, the old soldier said, "Kaneko. Throw a grenade in there." [Inaudible] We had these hand, hand-grenades—I primed the grenade and threw it into the well, and blew it up. Killed them both. And that's what happened. [Coughs]

That has stayed inside of me to this day. That stays with me no matter what.

[Later]

I didn't want to kill any kids. [Silence] When I shot kids, I would shoot them blindly. I would close my eyes and do it. I thought it would be bad luck if I stabbed them . . . I intended not to kill children. However, of course, I was using a machine gun, so it was just rata-tat-tat-tat—a machine gun. There were children there, and I had my eyes closed. I thought, "Forgive me if I hit you!" That's how it was.

———

My daughter does not blink. She watches me with eyes that have not found their true color, changing from blue to gray, brown to green, with the light. I hold my finger in front of her nose; still she does not blink. My finger floats toward her open eyes, reaching until it touches the fringe of her lashes. Her eyes remain open with stubborn trust, and I think: How many betrayals will she endure before she loses that trust, before she wants to close her eyes and never open them again?

— NORA OKJA KELLER, *COMFORT WOMAN*

Historian Will Durant estimates that humans have been at war for all but 268 years of the last three and a half millennia.[194] Jonathan Glover notes that from 1900 to 1989, eighty-six million people were killed in wars: "That is over 100 people an hour, round the clock, for 90 years."[195] Even more troubling, the wars seem to have gotten worse. At the beginning of the twentieth century, approximately 95 percent of all casualties in war were combatants. By the end of the century, some assert, the ratio had nearly reversed, with 90 percent civilian casualties. According to P. W. Singer, in the ten years straddling the turn of the twenty-first century, six million children were seriously injured in war, one million were orphaned, twenty-five million were driven from their homes, and approximately 300,000 had become soldiers. He claims this last number is up from "near zero" a few decades earlier.[196]

In his memoir, A Long Way Gone, Ishmael Beah explains that he was twelve years old in 1993 when his village was destroyed by rebel troops in Sierra Leone. By thirteen, he was a soldier addicted to speed, brown brown (cocaine mixed with gunpowder), and Rambo movies. He fought for two years, firing on combatants and non-combatants indiscriminately. He has no idea how many people he killed. He was, like the other boys, an effective and disposable perpetrator. As a friend of mine from the International Committee of the Red Cross once commented, "Children are the most dangerous because they do not know that they can die, so they fear nothing." One effective way of using them is this: if you want to draw the fire of your enemy so you can know where to aim, get a boy high and send him into the kill zone to wave his gun around and taunt the enemy. When they shoot the boy, you will know where they are.

It is hard to contemplate the murder of children, especially for those who have raised them. The difficulty is, in part, emotional. Children are so vulnerable, everything animal in us rises up to protect them. Moreover, children represent a category of person-hood that is, uniquely, both conceptually clear and universal. Not everyone understands what it means to be "a soldier," "Japanese," or "a woman," for instance, but everyone has experienced—from the inside—what it means to be "a child." The difficulty of contemplating the killing of children is more than emotional in these ways, however. It is also existential. It is because when killing boys and girls it is as if we are saying: *I do not wish to destroy only those who are; I wish to destroy the possibility of all who will be.* The death of a child is always a kind of apocalypse.

Fyodor Dostoyevsky, in what remains one of the most searching examinations of atrocity in literary history, insists upon thinking about children. And he insists that to think about children is to think not only about present sorrow but also about final meanings; to think, at least for people of faith, about the divine. Presenting the basic puzzle of theodicy, Dostoyevsky's embittered Ivan Karamazov tells his brother, the monk, the story of a small girl who is brutally tortured by her own mother and father. They trap her overnight in a frozen privy and force her to eat excrement. "Can you understand that a little being, who still can't even comprehend what is being done to her, in a vile place, in the dark and cold, beats herself with her tiny little fist on her strained little chest and cries her bloody, unresentful, meek little tears to 'dear God' to protect her—can you understand that nonsense, my friend and my brother, my pious and humble novice, do you understand why this nonsense is necessary and created?"[197] What kind of God would allow this?, Ivan asks. Would you? How could you bear it? What kind of God could bear it?

For many, the idea that God arises in wrath afterward to punish those who perpetrate such evils is emotionally satisfying. It restores our injured sense of justice, our sense that the universe must have balance. But Ivan is not satisfied by this. Eternal hell for evildoers doesn't provide relief to the tortured little girl, he argues. It only increases the amount of suffering among the created. What kind of God would consent to be the architect of a world organized around pointless pain and disproportionate retribution? Why, Ivan asks, should such a world exist at all?

"Has some Vast Imbecility," Thomas Hardy asks, "Mighty to build and blend, / But impotent to tend, / Framed us in jest, and left us now to hazardry?"[198] Or are we the playthings of a "vengeful god" who calls to us: "Thou suffering thing, / Know that thy sorrow is my ecstasy, / That thy love's loss is my hate's profiting!" The latter, at least, would be a kind of comfort for Hardy:

> Then would I bear it, clench myself, and die,
> Steeled by the sense of ire unmerited;
> Half-eased in that a Powerfuller than I
> Had willed and meted me the tears I shed.

But no, Hardy writes, our lot is much worse than that. Our suffering is only a matter of "hap," or chance, the arbitrary "dicing" of "purblind Doomsters."[199] Why should such a world exist at all? There is no reason. We are, absurdly, meaning-seeking creatures in a meaningless world.

Wars start, often, over the need to believe in transcendent things—sometimes the idea of God, sometimes the idea of a sacred people. The men I spoke to believed, as so many have before and will hence, that they were serving divine purpose when they sacrificed themselves to war; the emperor was a descendent of the gods. Sometimes campaigns of this sort vivify belief in the divine—particularly for the victors, or on homefronts that have remained safe from attack. But sometimes they make belief very hard, even for the most doggedly faithful. How can our concept of God survive a world where evil falls upon the heads of the innocent? "Lord, when will you hearken to our prayers?" cries the protagonist from Ha Jin's *Nanjing Requiem*. "When will you show your wrath?"[200]

In the Anglo-American tradition, recent religio-philosophical discussions of Ivan Karamazov's problem of evil often cite as a starting point J. L. Mackie's seminal essay, "Evil and Omnipotence." Mackie argued bluntly that we shouldn't believe in God—not because religious beliefs lack rational support (as had often been argued) but because the existence of evil shows us that religious beliefs are "positively irrational."[201] Crisply summarizing the argument, philosopher Susan Nieman writes:

> The problem of evil occurs when you try to maintain three propositions that don't fit together.
> 1. Evil exists.
> 2. God is benevolent.
> 3. God is omnipotent.
>   Bend, maul and move them as you will, they cannot be held in union. One of them has to go.[202]

As David Hume asks: "Is he willing to prevent evil, but not able? then he is impotent. Is he able, but not willing? then he is malevolent. Is he both able and willing? whence then is evil?"[203]

The problem of evil is often presented as if it is only a matter of logical contradiction—but the force of it is emotional. We can imagine a cruel God creating a world as appalling as this, the argument goes, and we can imagine an incompetent God doing so. But any reasonable all-powerful God, foreseeing what this particular version of creation would lead to, would've scrapped the whole thing before starting. Surely there was a better option. And if there wasn't, what need of Being at all?

Over the centuries, people of faith, people for whom God represents the final possibility of hope, meaning, or redemption, have struggled to find a response adequate to this grief-stricken charge. In the early eighteenth century, Gottfried Leibniz invented the word "theodicy" to describe these efforts to defend God, these attempts to "justify the ways of God to man," as John Milton audaciously wrote. Leibniz argued that creation proceeds according to divine plan; that which seems senseless, intolerable, or evil only seems so from the limited mortal perspective in time. We inhabit the best of all possible worlds. Things are as they must be. Hume imagined a handful of improvements, including the removal of pain as a source of human motivation, to be replaced by pleasure.[204] But Leibniz believed any repair we might imagine for the perceived damage of creation would only worsen matters in ways we are simply incapable of understanding, given our hopelessly narrow vision in a hopelessly vast universe. Or they would be impossible. Just as God couldn't, for instance, make a person who is taller than himself or make it the case that bachelors are also married, God also couldn't make a universe that is logically impossible. In other words, God couldn't make a universe of free souls who aren't free to harm each other.[205]

"All are but parts of one stupendous whole, / Whose body, Nature is, and God the soul," wrote Leibniz's near contemporary Alexander Pope, one of England's most celebrated poets. Pope made Leibniz's theodicy the centerpiece of his philosophical poem "An Essay on Man" (1733) in which he insisted even that history's perpetrators fit into God's plan: "If plagues or earthquakes break not Heav'n's design / Why then a Borgia, or a Catiline?"

> All Nature is but Art, unknown to thee;
> All Chance, Direction, which thou canst not see;
> All Discord, Harmony, not understood;
> All partial Evil, universal Good:
> And, spite of Pride, in erring Reason's spite,
> One truth is clear, "Whatever IS, is RIGHT."[206]

Pope has been reviled for his theodicy and characterized as a facile optimist (most famously by Voltaire). But Pope knew suffering. As a boy he was afflicted with tuberculosis of the spine—an incurable disease that made him shrink during adolescence rather than grow (to four and a half feet as an adult), and that gave him a limp, a curved spine, a visibly humped back, and lifelong pain.[207] Suffering was a mystery Pope knew he would never understand—but that failure to see was the fault of his blindness, not of God's design.

For many theologians and philosophers—from Augustine to John Milton to C. S. Lewis—the explanation for our pain is found in our freedom. Suffering is the price we pay for our free will, which is the gift God gives us to make our lives meaningful and which we have abused awfully. With our freedom we have fallen into evil and anguish. Made perfect, we have sinned ourselves into a "new species,"[208] becoming, as Lewis writes, "a horror to God."[209] But we mustn't believe that our fall surprised God (a version of the "incompetent God" argument). Rather, our fall, with all of its attendant sorrows, is a purposeful and productive tragedy. The freedom that would bring us to evil and pain would also deepen our being, bringing us out of the ignorant innocence of spiritual childhood, as William Blake expressed it, into the "organized innocence" of developed adult conscience. Augustine writes: "As a runaway horse is better than a stone which does not run away because it lacks self-movement and sense perception, so the creature is more excellent which sins by free will than that which does not sin only because it has no free will."[210] A world of free sinful souls is more perfect than a world of sinless slaves.

For such thinkers, therefore, it isn't puzzling to imagine a loving God creating a world of suffering and torment. The seemingly gratuitous pain of Being is, in fact, intelligible. Our suffering is the natural consequence of God's stern, uncompromising, and demanding love. Suffering is God's instrument of correction; suffering alerts us to His displeasure; the trial of suffering refines us spiritually; suffering is required for the existence of certain highly valuable goods (for instance, moral displays of grace and courage, or the experience of loving support and solidarity in grief); perhaps it is required even for the existence of the idea of "good" itself. Indeed, Mary McCord Adams argues that suffering is an aspect of God, that the capacity of each individual to realize the incommensurate good of beatific union with the Creator involves coming to understand the agony that is (in the Christian tradition that she represents) manifest in the crucifixion.[211]

As early as the second century, the early Christian church father St. Irenaeus argued that the sorrows and adversities of earthly life are the very things that forge us into the likeness of God.[212] The world, writes John Keats, is a "vale of Soul-making."[213] Indeed, hell itself, as Dante writes in the *Inferno,* is forged not only by justice but also by "primal love." In other words, even the final torture-house of the damned is an aspect of the infinitely loving gift of free will that alone allows for the soul's glory.

There are a host of ways to justify suffering, even ultimate suffering. But there are also a host of ways to negate such justifications. One might argue, for instance, that if the very meaning of creation hinges upon the idea of free will, then we free wills ought to be very free indeed—far more free than the genetically programmed, culturally conditioned, historically positioned, family fated, information deprived, resource craving, hormonally charged, chemically vulnerable, weak-willed beings that we are. Our freedom, indeed, seems a relatively feeble concept, rather like the freedom of the three-year-old child in Adams's stove analogy. A mother puts her three-year-old child into a gas-filled room, the analogy goes, and then before leaving warns the child not to fiddle with the attractive, brightly colored knobs that will, when turned, light the burners and ignite the gas, severely burning the child. Obviously, the mother cannot absolve herself of responsibility for the predictable explosion and consequent suffering simply by hanging it all upon the child's "free" choice. Nor can God.[214]

And there is, of course, the moral incoherence of what might be called "punishment theodicy." In Albert Camus's *The Plague,* Father Paneloux urges his congregants "to rejoice, yes, rejoice . . . This same pestilence which is slaying you works for your good"—"It is a red spear sternly pointing to the narrow path, the one of salvation."[215] Many religious justifications of suffering, including those I've just summarized, imply a link between pain and sin—and by extension, therefore, between happiness and virtue. Set aside the empirical implausibility of such thinking—the idea, for instance, that a virtuous people need not fear plague. The deeper problem is that imagining virtue can protect you from suffering *perverts* virtue, at least according to Immanuel Kant. The idea of virtue-as-holy-shield makes virtue into something we embody not for itself but for its instrumental value, as a matter of self-protection, even self-interested calculation. Is virtue really virtue when it is a good strategy? For Kant, Nieman writes, theodicy was awfully impious.[216]

Finally, there is the problem of logical impossibility for an omnipotent being. As Mackie asks: "Can an omnipotent being make beings which he cannot subsequently control? Or, what is practically equivalent to this, can an omnipotent being make rules which then bind himself?"[217] Both "yes" and "no" fail as answers to both questions. Mackie argues that we must therefore reject the concept of God's omnipotence—or the idea that we are free. Both can't be true at the same time.

I wish to believe. It is absurd, in the existential sense. But I cannot do anything else: I am the father of two small boys. I, like every parent, have known the terror of not being able to find my children, have imagined, with sick horror, that they might be frightened or lonely or hurt and that I *cannot get to them*. It is not to be borne. It is simply impossible to endure the thought that I will someday be kept from them forever. It is impossible to tolerate the idea that their small lives ultimately have no point. Sometimes late at night as I watch them sleep in the darkness, I let myself think this. It makes me lurch, hits me like a spasm of nausea.

Discussing God and the problem of evil, Hume notes that pleasure and pain are not, experientially, binaries. The heights of pleasure are difficult to achieve and degenerate rapidly; the depths of pain are swiftly entered and difficult to escape.[218] He writes:

> Were a stranger to drop, on a sudden, into this world, I would show him, as a specimen of its ills, a hospital full of diseases, a prison crowded with malefactors and debtors, a field of battle strowed with carcases, a fleet floundering in the ocean, a nation languishing under tyranny, famine, or pestilence. To turn the gay side of life to him, and give him a notion of its pleasures; whither should I conduct him? to a ball, to an opera, to court? He might justly think, that I was only showing him a diversity of distress and sorrow.[219]

In his grimly titled *Better Never to Have Been: The Harm of Coming into Existence*, contemporary philosopher David Benatar takes the asymmetry of pleasure and pain ("the absence of pain is good . . . the absence of pleasure is not bad") as an argument against having babies. "Although our potential offspring may not regret coming into existence," he argues, "they certainly would not regret not coming into existence."[220]

Humans, it seems, are designed to suffer. Psychologists today suggest that stress has a stronger physiological effect on people than relaxation, anticipated negative events have a stronger effect on mood than anticipated positive events, bad parenting has a stronger effect than good parenting, and our default experience of physiological arousal may be negative rather than positive.[221]

Most dismaying, there is no such thing as an opposite to trauma. That is, there is no concept of a positive event, in all the range of human experience, that can have as long-lasting, comprehensive, and severe an effect on human behavior as trauma.[222]

My boys, Mikey and Topher, are afraid to sleep alone in their bedroom. Each night after tucking, they creep into the same bed together for comfort, leaving one empty. They always ask me to stay, so I sit on the floor until their bodies go still and their breathing deepens, holding a book up against their nightlight and quietly turning pages. I watch them sleep and I yearn, with Ivan Karamazov, for the goodness of God.

———

My friend Barb read the previous section before publication and chided me for its despair. You are a teacher in a college, she reminded me. What are you teaching in your classes? I have often joked that I try to teach a touch of despair to the optimistic, idealistic, soon-to-change-the-world students in my human rights classes. I think of it as an inoculation against disappointment, an advance preparation for the harsh realities of human rights work that will prepare them to better adapt when they, inevitably, experience helplessness, disappointment, or failure while in the field. Idealists shatter, I argue—realists trudge on. But Barb is making me rethink this. Around the time of her remarks, I was reading Terry Eagleton's *On Evil*, which takes the argument that evil is the desire for nonbeing through destruction. Beneath his argument, it seemed to me, was the implication that despair, as a form of world renunciation, reproduces the structure of evil.[223]

Is there reason for despair now? According to *The Human Security Report 2005*, there might not be. The report claims that the most common statistics about how war and violence are getting worse over time—like the ones I cited earlier—are myths, evidence-light or evidence-free assertions that have acquired the solidity of political facts only because they have been repeated so frequently. On the contrary, the report argues, things are getting better—and not because of a random swing in world-historical patterns. It's because humanity has begun to create durable organizational structures for mitigating and preventing violence around the globe.

The report asserts a correlation between the post-1990s plummeting in the number of armed conflicts, politicides, genocides, and battle-deaths and the corresponding rise in the number of United Nations (UN) peacekeeping activities, preventive diplomatic missions, and economic sanctions in place around the world.[224] In *The Better Angels of Our Nature,* Steven Pinker argues more ambitiously that violence has declined dramatically over the broad sweep of human history. He attributes this to, among other things, the advances of "Enlightenment humanism." Another recent study provides striking evidence for the aptness of nonviolence as a tactic for human political organization. Analyzing 323 violent and nonviolent resistance campaigns from 1900 to 2006, Maria Stephan and Erica Chenoweth discovered that nonviolent campaigns were twice as likely to achieve strategic objectives as violent campaigns. We may have reason to be more optimistic about our collective future than our most commonly traded statistics suggest.[225]

We may also have reason to be more optimistic about the experience of human interiority than the psychological studies above suggest. Perhaps we are *not* designed to suffer. We may experience our negative memories more intensely, but we remember a higher proportion of positive events and are able to access them more quickly. People's self-conceptions are more often than not positive—often unrealistically so—and in certain circumstances their positive emotions seem to have greater capacity for contagiously spreading than negative ones. And while we certainly do suffer, many studies suggest that our suffering promotes increased social activity, affiliation, and even altruism. Experimental psychologists also note that it is more difficult to induce bad moods in subjects than good ones, and that it is even harder to sustain them. For this reason, according to Shelley Taylor, experiments are often set up to compare positive and neutral rather than positive and negative moods. Humans, naturally resilient, are equipped with a number of highly effective, sometimes automatic strategies for minimizing the experience of bad events. Thank God, a strong parallel doesn't appear to exist for our experience of positive events.[226]

Writing at the close of the nineteenth century, the American philosopher William James argued that certain facts in the world can only come into being if "a preliminary faith" in them exists. To paraphrase James, a declaration of faith in an athlete's ability can help to make real that athlete's power. We are therefore justified in adopting beliefs without sufficient evidence (a belief in God, for instance, or in ourselves) because of what adopting the belief can cause. He uses a striking analogy to explain the possibilities of belief: "A whole train of passengers (individually brave enough) will be looted by a few highwaymen, simply because the latter can count on one another, while each passenger fears that if he makes a movement of resistance, he will be shot before any one else backs him up. If we believed that the whole car-full would rise at once with us, we should each severally rise, and train-robbing would never even be attempted."[227]

In other words, to despair is to make a decision, with consequences.

Ebato-san

During the time when I was in the internment camp in Siberia, when we were doing outdoor manual labor, an old man came up to me, and he asked me a question. "Is the gulag [unclear]? Do you get enough to eat in the gulag?" he asked me. And when I said, "No, I don't . . ." This was in Siberia. He took an apple out of a bag. That apple, I believe, was a very precious apple from somewhere near the Ukraine. He held that one apple out to me. That was, in, well, in the midst of that cruel, harsh Siberian life, the most, ah, moved—happy I'd felt. There was such genuine affection for his fellow man there that I . . . Well, it left an impression on me that I'm not sure will ever go away. That's the feeling I got. This is, you know—whatever race you may be, you take the hand of your fellow man, where there is no war.

———

How selfish soever man may be supposed, there are evidently some principles in his nature, which interest him in the fortune of others, and render their happiness necessary to him, though he derives nothing from it, except the pleasure of seeing. Of this kind is pity or compassion, the emotion which we feel for the misery of others, when we either see it, or are made to conceive it in a very lively manner.

— ADAM SMITH, *THE THEORY OF MORAL SENTIMENTS*

We know something about what makes people perform evil acts. But what makes people resist performing evil acts, or perform altruistic ones? One way of defining altruism is this: it is voluntary, intentional behavior that helps others; the helping is itself the goal of the behavior; and it is done without expectation of external reward.[228] This kind of self-sacrifice and generosity is a less salient but more common human behavior than cruelty. It sutures the moments of each day. The most basic social units—families and neighborhoods—are impossible without it. But does that mean altruism exists, in a meaningful sense? Does self-sacrificing behavior (for instance, surrendering your well-being to care for a child or an aging parent, or, for that matter, resisting orders to harm others despite the threat of ostracism or punishment) reveal a principle of human motivation that transcends self-interest?

There are reasons to think not. Rational actor theory and sociobiology offer a range of ways to reframe ostensibly self-sacrificing behavior as selfishness. We choose to help because it gives us the pleasure of maintaining a (pleasing) benevolent self-conception. We choose to help because we want, as a matter of self-care, to unburden ourselves of the unpleasant sensation of watching others suffer. We choose to help because we've been trained to fear disapproval or punishment for not helping. We choose to help because we've been trained to expect approval or reward for helping. We choose to help because it is the only way we can rationally sustain our soothing belief that others would help us, too, if we were in grave need. We choose to help because it expresses and solidifies our social status (that is, we believe that when others accept our help they "tacitly acknowledge their dependency and inferiority" to us).[229] We choose to help because we have a taste for it—a taste, writes Howard Margolis, "not necessarily different in character from a taste for fancy motorcars or dollar cigars."[230] At the most basic level, altruists and egoists are the same: they are both just utility maximizers.

Or perhaps we don't choose to help at all. We can't help but help, and when we help what we're really doing is helping ourselves. This explanation is what evolutionary biologists call "inclusive fitness theory." Because life is a brutal, Darwinian struggle for individual survival, altruists would simply self-eradicate over time as they sacrificed their survival advantages to benefit others. But altruism persists, indeed thrives, because "fitness" (success at reproducing ourselves through breeding) is gene-based, not body-based. That is, when a human or nonhuman animal sacrifices its interests to support its kin, it is jeopardizing genetic reproduction in one body but enhancing the likelihood of that same genetic reproduction in other bodies. The calculus of advantage all depends on the math: how closely related, how many kin, how great the risk. As the pioneering evolutionary biologist J. B. S. Haldane is reported to have quipped when asked if he would risk his life to save a drowning brother: "No, but I would to save two brothers, or eight cousins."[231] Among the more repugnant implications of such a worldview is this claim: a parent will experience the most intense grief over a child's death when that death occurs during adolescence, because this is the child's reproductive potential peak. "Just as a horse breeder is more disappointed by the death of a thoroughbred the day before its first race than the day after its birth," explains Robert Wright of inclusive fitness theory, "a parent should be more heartbroken by the death of an adolescent than by the death of an infant."[232]

In other words, when we see love, or altruism, or any kind of rescue behavior, we may think we are seeing something nobly unselfish, but what's really happening is nothing more than the dumb work of, in Richard Dawkins's blunt words, "survival machines—robot vehicles blindly programmed to preserve the selfish molecules known as genes."[233] So we are not altruists, in any meaningful sense of the word. We are either rational actors driven by self-interest or we are herd animals. The pioneering evolutionary biologist George Williams writes: "As a general rule, a modern biologist seeing an animal doing something to benefit another assumes either that it is being manipulated by the other individual or that it is being subtly selfish."[234]

Most recently, however, the renowned biologist E. O. Wilson has argued that the foundations of inclusive fitness theory are crumbling. His research is about eusocial behavior, a special case of what evolutionary biologists consider "extreme" altruism. Wilson's argument is complex, controversial, and certain to be tested in the ensuing years, but the basic claim is that self-sacrifice for the common good simply cannot be redescribed as genetic selfishness. "Close genetic relatedness," he writes, "is the consequence, not the cause, of eusocial behavior." In loose translation: individuals did not cooperate because they were families; individuals that cooperated *became* families. "Human beings are prone to be moral—do the right thing, hold back, give aid to others, sometimes even at personal risk—because natural selection has favored those interactions of group members benefiting the group as a whole." Wilson concludes: "Authentic altruism exists."[235]

A great deal of energy has gone into disproving the disproving of altruism on other intellectual fronts. Multiple studies have been designed, for instance, to test the "aversive-arousal reduction" theory of altruism (that is, we only help to relieve ourselves of the distress associated with exposure to another's suffering). It seems the explanatory power of this theory is weak, successfully accounting for behavior only when personal distress is high and empathy is low.[236] In another study focusing on Central European rescuers of Jews during the Holocaust, researchers concluded that "rational actor theory is of little or no use in explaining rescue activity." Rescuers' motivations did not include cost-benefit analysis, cluster pressures, expectation of reward, or the desire to feel good about themselves.[237] Many seemed reluctant to talk about their experiences afterward and did not maintain contact with those they had rescued. Hoffman speculates that in some way shame must have adhered to the act of helping, "shame about what was required of them both, the degree of dehumanization that had to be reached in order for the need for such hiding to arise."[238] It's hard to account for such behaviors through models of self-interest.

Many have argued, more generally, that the explanatory power of the classic "self-interested man" model of economic theory has deficiencies so significant that it must be radically reconsidered. In the late 1970s, Nobel Prize–winning economist Amartya Sen attacked the narrow assumption that "every agent is actuated only by self-interest," insisting on the importance of ethical commitments that cannot be redefined as self-interest (unless self-interest is only the empty tautology: "what one chooses to do"). "The *purely* economic man," he wrote, "is indeed close to being a social moron."[239]

More recently, and further left on the political spectrum, economist Robert Rowthorn has attacked "the postulate of selfishness which still underlies most economic theorising, and the absence of any significant role for ethical or moral considerations in most analyses of economic activity."[240] The self-interest model predicts, for instance, that rational actors will contribute less to and consume more than their fair share of public goods when given the chance—the free-rider hypothesis—and that this will lead to a minimal production and maintenance of public goods. If I can get out of paying my fair share of taxes, I should and will; but when we all think this way, everybody loses. Global fisheries and carbon emissions are apocalyptic examples of this problem. But research on free riding has produced mixed results. Funnily enough, some studies suggest that if you want to get evidence showing that people are inherently self-interested and will therefore free ride, the best way to do so is to use economists and economics students as experimental subjects. Are economists just good at seeing when they're supposed to be playing a free-riding game in experiments? Or does continual exposure to the "self-interested man" model train economists to think in a way that promotes free riding?

In her work on "the tragedy of the commons," political scientist Elinor Ostrom (another Nobel Prize winner) finds multiple cases in which self-organizing groups effectively manage common pool resources despite the temptation to free ride.[241] While not evidence against the idea that we are egoists governed by selfishness (long-term cooperation involving internal sanctions is rather easily explained as self-interest), it nonetheless provides grounds for optimism about our capacity for prosocial collaborative action.

But rather than getting into a long discussion of fundamental questions such as "Are we governed by self-interest"? or "Does altruism exist?" let me return to the question I posed earlier, now rephrased. We know something about what makes people perform evil acts—but what makes people perform behaviors we call altruistic? There is an astonishing symmetry to these two very different processes.

1. Bystanders are more likely to be passive and perpetrators to be cruel when a victim is anonymous. When a victim's identity is recognizable, by contrast, it inhibits aggression and promotes altruism. The same logic applies to those observing the potential victim. An observer who feels personally anonymous is more likely to be impulsively antisocial or passive in the face of others' needs, while an observer who feels recognizable is more likely to engage in prosocial behavior and feel a heightened sense of responsibility to others. In one variation of the Milgram study, for instance, subjects delivered more shocks to victims when they played a subsidiary role

in the process, as compared to subjects who delivered the shocks directly. Indeed, when subjects were forced to deliver shocks by physically touching the victim, compliance dropped dramatically.

Relatedly, Oliner and Oliner found in their study of Holocaust rescuers that previous close contact with the victims played a significant part in helping behavior. Bystander-passivity experiments confirm this pattern. Subjects are much more likely to respond with helping behavior for victims whom they have previously met, even if only briefly.

2. If perceiving victims as out-group decreases the likelihood that we will help them, perceiving victims as in-group increases the likelihood that we will. Indeed, the in-group effect seems to determine not only what hold victims have upon us but also what hold other helpers have upon us. That is, we are more likely to help if we believe that the other helpers are in-group than if we believe they are out-group.[242]

Muzafer Sherif's Robbers Cave experiment is one of the most famous psychological studies on intergroup conflict. Posing as a janitor at a summer camp for twelve-year-old boys, Sherif observed the rapid formation of bitterly opposed in-groups. Here's a sample of his observations: "The Eagles, especially, were dead set against participating in any activity which had anything whatsoever to do with the Rattlers. In an early morning swim that day, the Eagles had discovered their flag in the water, burned the previous evening by the Rattlers. Upon making this discovery, they denounced the Rattlers as 'dirty bums,' and accused them of having put ice in the water (because it appeared to one of them as colder than usual), and of throwing rocks in their creek (because one of them stubbed his toes a number of times during the swim)."

Sherif determined that the most effective way to reduce intergroup hostility was to introduce "superordinate goals" for the Eagles and Rattlers—that is, to impose challenges that could only be resolved through cooperation. For instance, he caused a drinking water shortage that required everybody to work together, and later made the cost of screening a desired movie prohibitive for campers unless they collectively pooled their resources. Sufficiently motivating superordinate goals, in effect, made everybody in-group.[243]

3. Where information scarcity (for instance, in the form of censorship or euphemism) makes it easier for bystanders to ignore or support atrocities, information plenitude makes it more difficult. Information is coercive—hence the phenomenon of empathy avoidance. Because we know that we will be distressed by the suffering of others, and that this distress might then cause us to make personal sacrifices to help, we seek to avoid information that could elicit our empathy, especially personalizing information about people we expect to have to hurt.[244]

Relatedly, economists find in studies of the free-rider hypothesis that selfishness and exploitation of others is maximized under conditions of anonymity and disconnection from others, and is reduced when individuals have the capacity to personally communicate.[245] As Ostrom said in her Nobel Prize interview on the problem of free riding: "Humans are neither all angels or all devils. It is the context and institutional context in which they find themselves that enable them to have more willingness to use reciprocity [and] to trust each other."[246]

4. Where lack of visible dissent promotes conformity to antisocial behavior, visible dissent promotes defections. In varia-

tions of the Asch and Milgram experiments, for instance, subjects were much more capable of resisting pressure from groups or authority figures when they saw even one other confederate resisting.

Arendt, discussing the trial of Eichmann, argues in this spirit that public defection is a moral responsibility—private defection, however courageous, is a kind of failure. Propst Grüber was a German clergyman who ended up in a concentration camp because of his efforts to resist the Nazis. In his encounters with Eichmann, however, Grüber refrained from moral critique. Arendt notes approvingly that on this point, Eichmann's otherwise passive defense lawyer began to press: " 'Did you try to influence him? Did you, as a clergyman, try to appeal to his feelings, preach to him, and tell him that his conduct was contrary to morality?' Of course, the very courageous Propst had done nothing of the sort, and his answers now were highly embarrassing. He said that 'deeds are more effective than words,' and that 'words would have been useless'; he spoke in clichés that had nothing to do with the reality of the situation, where 'mere words' would have been deeds, and where it had perhaps been the duty of a clergyman to test the 'uselessness of words.' "[247] There is, in other words, no such thing as "merely symbolic" protest.

5. If we are less likely to help when victims are distant, intervention seems costly, and the situation is unclear or confusing, we are more likely to help when we are approached in person for help, and when the helping situation is "less costly, unambiguous, and highly urgent."[248] UN Undersecretary-General for Humanitarian Affairs Jan Egeland explains the way different narrative frames can affect willingness to intervene. Comparing the massive global interest in the 2003 tsunami to

the near total indifference to the conflict in Uganda and the DRC, he says: "Number one, they're in an endless cycle of misery and people *do not like* endless cycles. Number two, it's not so clear who's the good and the bad as it may be with the tsunami. Nature is bad, people are good, and aid workers succeed. It's a good story to tell. In Uganda it's incomprehensible terror carried out by an elusive rebel force that nobody knows. In eastern Congo, it's even murkier. It's not just one rebel movement, it's twenty different armed groups."[249]

6. If atrocity is a matter of "escalating commitments," as Waller puts it, so is helping behavior. According to Oliner and Oliner, rescuers frequently started down the path of risky self-sacrifice with limited attempts to help specific individuals for whom they had empathy. Over time they found themselves committed to more extensive and generalized rescue.[250] This kind of transformation is a strong version of the foot-in-the-door effect. In one representative study of foot-in-the-door, students who had been asked to sign a letter to the president emphasizing the need for assistance to the homeless were significantly more likely than those not previously contacted to agree to a larger request later on to take part in a food drive for the homeless. Such studies explain the amplification of altruism as the result of our need to maintain consistent self-perception. ("My previous actions show that I am an altruistic person who cares about this issue. Such a person would comply with this new, larger request.")[251] However, if we feel that we have helped because we have been pressured or given strong financial incentive to do so, we are less likely to perceive ourselves as altruistic and, therefore, less likely to behave in a manner that is consistent with such a self-perception in the future.[252]

7. Rescuers and perpetrators alike often characterize their behavior in the language of duress: *I had no choice*. The difference between them lies in where the "orders" are coming from. Speculatively: while many perpetrators feel coerced by external pressures or external models of personhood (I need to show others that I am a real man, a real German, etc.), many rescuers by contrast feel coerced by internal pressures and internal models of personhood. Eva Fogelman writes that Holocaust rescuers "had a strong sense of who they were and what they were about. Their values were self-sustaining, not dependent on the approval of others. To them, what mattered most was behaving in a way that maintained their integrity."[253]

   This kind of personhood, parents like me believe, can be cultivated. Philip Zimbardo, while best known for his studies showing how easily we slip into evil, in fact shares this optimistic view. He has a useful website, *The Lucifer Effect* (www.lucifer effect.com) that details a range of practices we can adopt and features we can cultivate in each other to help us resist negative social influences and build capacities for moral heroism.

8. If the pressure of cognitive dissonance makes us more likely to hold in contempt those we have hurt ("I have injured them, therefore they must be the sorts who deserve to be injured"), it also makes us more likely to have positive feelings for those we have helped.[254] If we are less likely to have empathy for those we have been trained to perceive as ugly or guilty, we are more likely to have empathy for those we have been trained to perceive as beautiful or innocent (and more likely to have empathy for children for both reasons).[255] Studies show, moreover, that once we have experienced empathy for others, we will respond with less aggression to provocation from those same others.[256]

9. If deindividuation can promote aggression, it can also promote
    benevolence. Ed Diener writes: "Deindividuation may release
    behaviors that many consider to be prosocial if these behaviors
    are inhibited by norms, by fear, or by long-term planning con-
    siderations. For example, the deindividuated person in a cer-
    tain situation might be more likely to donate a large sum of
    money to charity, might be more likely to risk his or her life to
    help another, and might be more likely to kiss friends—all be-
    haviors that many consider mandatory." Steven Prentice-Dunn
    and Ronald Rogers add that deindividuated persons "have been
    shown to follow the lead of models," and that "nonaggressive
    models can reduce the transgressions displayed by deindividu-
    ated individuals."[257]

10. If atrocity is a matter of training, with an emphasis on early
    education, so is altruism. Study after study emphasizes pa-
    rental influence as a key component for promoting altruistic
    behavior and inhibiting aggression in adults.[258] Oliner and
    Oliner identify several commonalities among rescuers, includ-
    ing "strong and cohesive family bonds," "broad social commit-
    ments, an intense sense of personal responsibility for the wel-
    fare of society as a whole," and an egalitarian upbringing.
    Non-helpers, by contrast, were more likely to have had au-
    thoritarian upbringings.[259] Other studies of personality traits
    associated with prosocial behavior see these regularities: al-
    truists are people "high in self-esteem, high in competence,
    high in internal locus of control, low in need for approval,
    and high in moral development."[260] They have "higher trust
    and faith in people" than non-altruists, "a spirit of adventur-
    ousness," a capacity for risk-taking, and an understanding of
    what it means to feel "socially marginal."[261]

For most of the processes above, storytelling is crucial. That is, exercises in narration and perspective taking can affect who we consider in-group, how thin or thick a person's identity is to us, how we interpret the reactive behaviors of those around us, how we frame complex or confusing events, how we see ourselves, what we identify as central to the particular meanings of our lives. I said previously that "information" is coercive, but what I really meant was "storytelling." As Sherif warns in discussing the Robbers Cave experiment, the "dissemination of specific information designed to correct prevailing group stereotypes . . . is relatively ineffective in changing attitudes. Stereotypes crystallized during the eventful course of competition and conflict with the out-group are usually more real in the experience of the group members than bits of information handed down to them." Information can pressure us, but it is relatively easy to adapt our interpretive frameworks so as to accommodate new information without changing our basic beliefs or behaviors. Stories, by contrast, can short-circuit the mechanisms of cognitive consistency and make us have *experiences,* make us interiorize rather than simply consider the identities of others.

But more on stories later. The primary point I want to emphasize here is this: for every powerful and structural force driving us toward inhuman treatment of others, there are equally powerful and structural forces available to us to promote prosocial behavior. Mark Osiel offers a detailed institutional model of this principle in his study *Obeying Orders.* If war crimes are the result of disorganization among the forces (atrocity comes from below), then create a better bureaucracy with "bright-line rules" rather than "general, discretionary standards" to control the behavior of soldiers.[262] If atrocity is instead the result of strict, depersonalizing, top-down bureaucracy (atrocity comes from above), then the bureaucracy must be restructured to incorporate a democratic ethos in discipline, codifying "generous qualifications and exceptions to the duty of obedience to superior orders" so that soldiers can reinterpret and resist illegal orders.[263]

If atrocities are then committed because of this discretion and ambiguity in orders, it will be for one of two reasons. First, soldiers might exploit ambiguity and latitude for discretion in order to create possibilities for unleashing frustration upon others (atrocity from below). Second, superiors might deliberately foster an atmosphere of discretion as a way of implicitly promising soldiers that extreme acts will not be punished and will possibly be rewarded (atrocity from above), rather than as a way of enabling soldiers to exercise restraint as conditions develop and complicate in the field. There are effective solutions for both possibilities. In the former case, emphasize the rule of manifest illegality, which holds troops responsible for criminal behavior independently of what they believe their orders require of them. In the latter, emphasize the rule of command responsibility, which holds superiors criminally responsible for the actions of subordinates.[264]

Finally, Osiel argues, training practices that brutalize troops, nurturing generalized hostility so that it might be turned upon the enemy, can be tempered by a "civilizing" of military law—for instance, by strengthening "the due process protections owed to troops by officers."[265] And the same sort of disciplinary rituals of "reintegrate shaming" that promote reckless aggression can also be used to promote virtue.[266] Just as martial cultures can produce bloody-minded behavior, they can produce restraint. "The best prospects for minimizing war crimes," he concludes, "derive from creating a personal identity based upon the virtues of chivalry and martial honor, virtues seen by officers as constitutive of good soldiering."[267]

It is a good thing to think strategically about ways to morally optimize human behavior. But it seems to me that it also requires maintaining internal vigilance about how one conceptualizes the human. Here's the problem: while all the above are sincere attempts to think our way out of the processes of depersonalization that release antisocial impulses, they also push us toward a model of self that is depersonalizing. The argument goes like this. Viewed in the aggregate and given certain conditions, our behaviors have a degree of predictability. This is a good thing—how else could we begin to regulate collaborative social life? It is because we have the capacity to step outside ourselves and view our behaviors in the aggregate—that is, view them objectively rather than subjectively—that we can design organizations that will promote behaviors we desire and inhibit those we disdain.

However, when we model personhood from the aggregate standpoint, the infinite nuance of individuality seems less important than location in organization or social group. And this not only flies in the face of our moment-by-moment sense of self, but also seriously undermines ideas that we organize our lives around, like integrity and authenticity. We experience ourselves from the inside, and our interior deliberations and personal freedom seem to matter a great deal from this angle. As philosopher Thomas Nagel argues, it is not that subjectivity appears limited and small when the world is viewed from the objective standpoint. Subjectivity does not appear at all when the world is viewed from the objective standpoint. The two perspectives are mutually exclusive.

Being careful about this split means, in this case, being careful not to suggest that extreme cruelty and extreme altruism reveal a universal truth about humans—that when certain psychological circuits trip, we become abstracted persons, depersonalized expressions of a behavioral principle. Indeed, even the most apparently senseless violence can be a marker of cultural and individual specificity. Alexander Hinton suggests that perpetrators, however constrained and even warped by circumstance, "remain active subjects who construct meaning and assert their self-identity through their violent practices."[268] Blame and resentment for injury are appropriate emotions because they are acknowledgments of another's agency. You can be angry that you hurt your foot on a rock, but you can't *blame* the rock. Blame is for those you respect as human.[269]

———

Yuasa-san

[Sighs] That was a long educational process, you know! Yeah. [In prison camp] I listened to Chinese people's stories, how they fought with the country of Japan and suffered a great deal, and they died. Through my daily education and, you know, watching developing conditions in China, I reflected on the unforgivable things I had done, and then finally, afterward, I realized what you say I realized. And so—but until then, I thought nothing but how to avoid my crimes—when I could return home.

But especially—the time I realized it the most was just before I was released, when I received a letter from a Chinese mother. And that was—ah [begins to recall the letter]—"Yuasa, I am the mother of [unclear] you performed a vivisection on. That day, my son was taken in by the military police, and I was standing in front of him. I remember watching this, waiting in the dirty road, and afterward, you—a car came along and you took him off somewhere." [*Not me,* Yuasa-san gestures with his hands, *my subordinate.*] "I panicked and ran down the hill . . . I lost sight of you, and a worried friend came by—'Ma'am, a notice came that your boy was killed alive at [unclear] Hospital.'" [Clicks tongue and sighs deeply] "Ohh, I cried and cried; I couldn't eat; I couldn't even plow a field. I just heard that you're in there, and I told the investigators that I wanted you to receive a harsh punishment."

But I—my mental state was such that I didn't even fear "harsh punishment," you know. Rather, I said, "Ma'am, you have found the culprit . . ." And I just bowed. Of the things I did, even if I thought at all about the people I killed, never before had my heart gone out to a *family* like this. I didn't think at all about that.

———

To begin thinking about blame and repentance for crimes like these, one must first give further consideration to the concept of evil. To judge something evil is to put the possibility of forgiveness into question in a way other judgments do not. What is evil? When can it be forgiven? Loosely conflating Kant's notion of "radical evil" with the Holocaust, Arendt writes: "All we know is that we can neither punish nor forgive such offenses and that they therefore transcend the realm of human affairs and the potentialities of human power, both of which they radically destroy wherever they make their appearance. Here, where the deed itself dispossesses us of all power, we can indeed only repeat with Jesus: 'It were better for him that a millstone were hanged about his neck, and he cast into the sea.'"[270]

Is Arendt's characterization useful? Is the concept of evil itself useful? Once out from under the immediate shadow of the Holocaust, many scholars began to think not. The concept of evil, as various scholars have characterized the position, "is simply a residue of an outdated theological perspective on the world." Evil is just "bad + God." Evil is "a useless or unwanted word." Evil is "a chimera, like Santa Claus or the tooth fairy."[271]

Western philosophy, in fact, has comparatively little to offer on evil. While wrongdoing has been a central topic of analysis, evil has not. Indeed, philosopher Claudia Card argues that a major strand of modern secular philosophy involves a "denial of evil." Card tracks this back to the influence of Friedrich Nietzsche, who argued that the concept of evil (as opposed to the concept of bad) was a trick foisted upon the world by resentful slaves who wished to constrain the power of their natural masters. Explaining this slave revolt in morality, Nietzsche writes: "Lofty spiritual independence, the will to stand alone, great intelligence even, are felt to be dangerous; everything that raises the individual above the herd and makes his neighbor quail is henceforth called *evil;* the fair, modest, obedient, self-effacing disposition, the *mean and average* in desires, acquires moral names and honours."[272]

Card explains that contemporary philosophical thought has been shaped less by Nietzsche's claims about morality—that we should admire the proud strength of the world's relentless Napoleons—than by his particular method of formulating such claims. Nietzsche's genealogy of morality, Card writes, helped to engineer "a shift from questions of what to do to prevent, reduce, or redress evils to skeptical psychological questions about what inclines people to make judgments of evil in the first place, what functions such judgments have served."[273] In other words, "What is evil?" is a question for pastors and theologians, not philosophers, political scientists, or other humanists; or, it is not a particularly interesting question; or, it is an interesting question only because it reveals something about the person asking it, because defining "evil" is an attempt to disguise subjective desires as objective imperatives.

Since 9/11, however, the concept of evil has resurged in Anglo-American scholarly research. Much of it has involved the philosophical spadework of attempting to devise a comprehensively satisfying definition of evil. Philosophers ask questions such as, How hurtful does something have to be to be evil rather than "extremely bad"? And once we've determined that, what should be the difference in our responses to each? Can accidents be evil? Or is malicious intent necessary? If malicious intent is necessary, could it also be sufficient? For instance, what if malicious intent never translates into actual harm?[274] This is persistently secular work. "You can believe in evil without supposing that it is supernatural in origin," explains Terry Eagleton. "Ideas of evil do not have to posit a cloven-hoofed Satan."[275]

In his own attempt to characterize evil, notably, Eagleton draws heavily from a view once dominant in Christian theology: that evil is fundamentally a privation of the good of being, that the desire for evil is a desire for the negation of being. The power of evil, he writes, "is essentially that of the death drive, turned outward so as to wreak its insatiable spitefulness on a fellow human being. Yet this furious violence involves a kind of lack—an unbearable sense of non-being, which must, so to speak, be taken out on the other. It is also oriented to another kind of absence: the nullity of death itself. Here, then, terrifying force and utter vacuousness come together."[276]

Eagleton's is a modernized, psychoanalytically inflected version of the privative theory of evil that dates back to St. Augustine. Augustine was unflinching on evil, believing even in infant damnation. In his *Confessions*, Augustine recalls an incident from when he was sixteen that dramatically illuminates his philosophy.

> There was a pear-tree near our vineyard, loaded with fruit that was attractive neither to look at nor to taste. Late one night a band of ruffians, myself included, went off to shake down the fruit and carry it away, for we had continued our games out of doors until well after dark, as was our pernicious habit. We took away an enormous quantity of pears, not

to eat them ourselves, but simply to throw them to the pigs. Perhaps we ate some of them, but our real pleasure consisted in doing something that was forbidden.

Look into my heart, O God, the same heart on which you took pity when it was in the depths of the abyss. Let my heart now tell you what prompted me to do wrong for no purpose, and why it was only my own love of mischief that made me do it. The evil in me was foul, but I loved it. I loved my own perdition and my own faults, not the things for which I committed wrong, but the wrong itself. My soul was vicious and broke away from your safe keeping to seek its own destruction, looking for no profit in disgrace but only for disgrace itself.[277]

Augustine's self-loathing is even more striking later, when he compares his pear-snatching to the atrocities of the Roman politician Catiline (villainized in the histories Augustine read) and judges his own crime the baser. Augustine here is radically interiorizing evil, focusing more on perversion of the soul than suffering in the world, more on motivations for an action than hurtful consequences. What is evil? Augustine insisted that it is a lack, an absence. We therefore know the nature of evil by not knowing it, just as we perceive darkness by not seeing it and perceive silence by not hearing it.[278] Augustine's theft is horrible because it is, essentially, motiveless. We may have a malicious desire to harm somebody, but it could be purposeful (we are acting from anger, jealousy, revenge, or ambition) or, more disturbing, it could be purposeless (we do it for no reason at all, or for the reason of evil itself, which is, in Augustine's thinking, nonbeing). Augustine's crime is the epitome of evil because he desires, quite literally, nothing.

Here's Eagleton once more, espousing an Augustinian view of evil. "Evil would actually prefer that there was nothing at all, since it does not see the point of created things. It loathes them because . . . being is itself a kind of good. The more richly abundant existence is, the more value there is in the world."[279] When one seeks evil, one seeks annihilation. Not only annihilation of other people and things, but also, and perhaps more centrally, annihilation of oneself.

———

DAWES. When he, when he looks back now at the man he was then, what does he see? During the war, the man he was in the war, what does he see?

INTERPRETER. With the person you are now, in the present day, how do you see—view the person you were during the war?

KANEKO-SAN. I think I was evil. What I did. However! [Very sudden, strong tone] However, okay? But we felt very strongly that war to the end was something that if from now on we get rid of—that it shouldn't happen. I think the things we did were really evil. We killed, we raped—because we didn't do anything really good, you know? We robbed. We took cotton, right? We took wheat, right? This kind of thing, we took mountains of it, okay? That wheat. Where do you think it went? I haven't got a damn clue . . .

DAWES. Can he make up for what he did?

INTERPRETER. Make up meaning that the, do that again?

DAWES. No, can he make up in the, uh . . . Is there redemption for him?

INTERPRETER. Redemption . . . in the sense . . .

DAWES. Is there a way to pay back what he did?

INTERPRETER. Ehh, so, Mr. Kaneko, supposing you were able to atone for that . . .

KANEKO-SAN. Eh?

INTERPRETER. If you were to atone, what sorts of things . . .

KANEKO-SAN. What's that?

INTERPRETER. If you were to atone . . .

KANEKO-SAN. That, of course, is opposing the war.

INTERPRETER. Ahh, of course . . .

KANEKO-SAN. That I will not fight such a war twice. No, not "that sort" of war—war itself I won't fight. Yeah. At this kind of time, [unclear phrase]. This isn't our, you know, theory. This isn't a theory we came up with. This is out of what we really experienced—when we lived through it, this is what we felt.

DAWES. Does he feel free of what he did, now? Does he, is he, is he redeemed?

INTERPRETER. Do you think that you've been forgiven now for the things you did?

KANEKO-SAN. You know, when it comes right down to it, I think I've really been forgiven. And it's because of that that we stress that we won't allow that sort of thing to happen twice—that we can't do that. This is our atonement. If I were to put it simply, that is what we're doing.

———

Japan has repeatedly acknowledged Imperial war crimes, and apologized for them—construing apology in a particular way. In 1995, the Japanese parliament passed the "Resolution to Renew the Determination for Peace on the Basis of Lessons Learned from History." Originally intended to be an official apology, it became instead an expression of "remorse" over Japan's "aggression-like acts" that lumped together Japanese war crimes with the "many instances of colonial rule and acts of aggression in the modern history of the world.[280] The prime minister later added his "apology," but as Norma Field points out, did so only at the same time that he insisted the Showa emperor bore no responsibility for the "mistaken state policy."[281] Over the years, in its relations with Taiwan,

Korea, and China, Field explains, Japan has expressed "regret" for "unfortunate events," made declarations of being "truly regretful for" and "deeply reflecting upon" the "unfortunate period" of colonialism, and asserted "keenly feeling responsibility for" and "deeply reflecting upon" the "great losses inflicted upon the people of China."[282] N. Muira finds in a series of resolutions passed by prefectural assemblies around the same time a similar pattern of evasive acknowledgment. Condolences for the hardships suffered by other Asian nations are coupled with explanations that Japanese soldiers died to guarantee the safety of their country and to ensure its future prosperity.[283]

Meanwhile, Field writes, reconciliation and reparations have taken "the form of loans and credit that paved the way for the penetration of Japanese capital into its neighboring countries,"[284] along with a fund to collect private donations for "sympathy money" for comfort women.[285] Because it is private sympathy money, Field notes, it is divorced from any notion of state responsibility for wrongdoing. Moreover, it reproduces "a patron-client relationship" that troubles many. "Sympathy money," says Song Shin Do, a former comfort woman who filed civil suit for an official apology and compensation. "It's just going to make people look askance at us."[286]

In a study of Japanese history textbooks, Christopher Barnard sees a series of subtle rhetorical maneuvers designed to minimize responsibility and agency. For instance, he notes, the Rape of Nanking is widely acknowledged in textbooks, but frequently with the qualifier that the Japanese people did not know about the atrocities at the time, and always in grammatical structures that present it as an anonymous, organizational crime—"in not one single textbook is it stated that Japanese *soldiers* killed Chinese people."[287] Many of these acknowledgments, moreover, suffer from "overwording" (a layering of synonymous identifiers that reveals an effort to avoid making a *particular* identification)[288] and from passive constructions (if "the Nanking Incident . . . occurs," to take one example, it's as if nobody did it—it just happened).[289]

Perhaps unsurprisingly, over the years that I have worked on this project, several people have asked me: You keep talking about "confessions" and "apologies" and even "redemption"—do you think these words mean the same thing to them as to you? Isn't what "confession" means for them (with its ties both to Communist political practice and to sincerity in Confucian thought) very different from what "confession" means for you (with its ties both to Augustine and Rousseau and to psychoanalysis)?[290]

In the very early stages of this project, I sometimes explained to fellow academics in conversation that I was spending time in Japan to "take confessions" from war criminals. I quickly learned not to do that. In using that language (of both the church and the police station), wasn't I implicating myself in confession as a cultural form explained by Michel Foucault? That is, a system of "power/knowledge" that produces truth as a form of social control? In the West we treat confession as the revelation, even creation, of an unfettered, authentic self. But, Foucault writes, the confession

> is also a ritual that unfolds within a power relationship, for one does not confess without the presence (or virtual presence) of a partner who is not simply the interlocutor but the authority who requires the confession, prescribes and appreciates it, and intervenes in order to judge, punish, forgive, console, and reconcile; a ritual in which the truth is corroborated by the obstacles and resistances it has had to surmount in order to be formulated; and finally, a ritual in which the expression alone, independently of its external consequences, produces intrinsic modifications in the person who articulates it: it exonerates, redeems, and purifies him; it unburdens him of his wrongs, liberates him, and promises him salvation.[291]

When I look at this quotation, I think about something that happened in a moment of organizational confusion during my time in
Japan. One of the local activists involved became frustrated; he had
an agitated exchange with our interpreter. Later, we pressed her
for details, but she demurred. While she never revealed what he
said in full, it finally became clear that the activist—an anti-
nationalist Communist devoted to the cause of forcing Japan to
confess its Imperial war crimes—had expressed in that moment
deep bitterness about how the very same white Westerners who
had bombed their cities had come once again to make their men
kneel before them.

I know the reasons I went to do what I did; I am at peace with
the reasons. But then, how different do I think I am? The theory
and practice of human rights has changed dramatically in recent
years, but we cannot shrug aside a long history of ignoring torture
and structural violence in our own backyards in favor of discovering it in the lands of racial others.

Sometimes colleagues expressed flipside concerns to me, concerns not about what I was up to, but about what the soldiers were
up to. Why do you think these men told you these stories at all,
and why in the way they did? What effect were they hoping to
achieve? As a literary critic, I can't help but think of these as "genre
questions." In her remarkable study of perpetrators in Argentina,
Chile, Brazil, and South Africa, Leigh Payne explains that confessions are not windows to the soul; indeed, they do not even necessarily represent "a claim to truth."[292] They are instead *performances,*
complete with actors, scripts, stages, and audiences. And there are
subgenres to confession; they can range from expressions of deep
remorse to heroic justifications, denial, and sadism. Payne identifies
the remorseful confession—the kind I am working with and the
kind most commonly seen as compatible with reconciliation—as a

"born again" narrative device that allows individuals "to trade their sinful pasts for saintly presents."[293] Like all confessions, she explains, they allow perpetrators "to reinvent their past through narrative."[294]

When injured, we crave remorse. But the remorseful confession is not necessarily less socially contentious than the heroic, self-justifying confession. Audiences rarely accept the sincerity of perpetrator remorse, so exceptional performances are required for success.[295] And even if sincerity is well performed, remorse may not work. "Remorse is irrelevant," declares Ana Maria Careaga, a torture survivor from Argentina's Dirty War.[296] As Payne writes, for many remorse is a "bait" to be rejected, because it sets in motion a process that pressures victims and survivors to grant perpetrators the profit of moral self-restoration. "Held to a standard of mental health and magnanimous spirit not expected of perpetrators," victims and survivors must forgive. They "are expected to be grateful" and "to regard the confessions as unexpected and generous gifts." Remorseful confessions, Payne concludes, "are felt to place undue burden on those who have already suffered—victims and survivors—in the name of individual and national healing."[297]

In whatever form they come, confessions can function as renewal of trauma. "Witnesses, particularly victims and survivors of authoritarian state violence, do not experience confessions at a safe and critical distance, but as part of their present lives. Perpetrators' confessions invade their safe spaces."[298] On top of that, confessions can also "traumatize bystanders and post-authoritarian-era generations, particularly victims of physical or psychological abuse."[299]

I have been haunted by such thoughts since starting this project. I hear them in my head like quiet voices. *These men had the power of gods during the war. They could grant life or take it away with a word. And their victims had nothing. Now, all these years later, you are giving them all the power once again.* For a long time I couldn't write anything, listening to these voices.

And yet.

And yet individuals, institutions, and cultures require confessions. They continually seek them out because confessions fill a basic need. They are antidotes to the psychically poisonous social silence of authoritarian violence, a silence that "perpetuates victims' self-blame, confusion, and rage,"[300] a silence that functions almost like a massive and cruel Asch conformity experiment. *We don't see what you see.* "It made you *psychotic,*" Renée Epelbaum, a member of the Mothers of the Plaza de Mayo, says of the lies and distortions of the Dirty War. "We could barely 'read,' let alone 'translate' the world around us. And that was exactly what they wanted."[301] Forgiveness aside, confessions can play a vital role in healing individuals and societies because they fight contaminated state fictions, because they make it more difficult for public discourse to violently deny the personal realities of survivors. Confessions rebuild social reality.

But what of forgiveness? In *The Sunflower,* Simon Wiesenthal tells the story of his encounter with a dying SS man, who had asked a nurse to "fetch a Jewish prisoner" to his bedside so that he might ask for forgiveness for his war crimes.[302] The man, a boy really, is in grievous pain, pitiable and truly remorseful. He confesses to awful crimes, in obvious moral agony. "I know that what I am asking is almost too much for you," he says, "but without your answer I cannot die in peace." Wiesenthal listens quietly, hears that there is "true repentance" in the confession, and then leaves the room of the blinded, dying boy with no response.[303]

Wiesenthal's friends tell him he was right to leave, tell him, indeed, that it would've been appalling for Wiesenthal to presume to forgive him. What right had Wiesenthal to forgive crimes committed against others? Wiesenthal, however, finds he is never after in his life able to make peace with his decision. What would you have done? he asks his readers.

Cynthia Ozick, answering Wiesenthal directly, has no doubt. "It is forgiveness that is relentless," she says. "The face of forgiveness is mild, but how stony to the slaughtered." She continues: "Often we are asked to think this way: vengeance brutalizes, forgiveness refines. But the opposite can be true. The rabbis said, 'Whoever is merciful to the cruel will end by being indifferent to the innocent.' Forgiveness can brutalize." Ozick concludes by recalling the moment in the memoir when Wiesenthal waves a fly away from one of the man's wounds—an unthinking act of natural animal pity. "Let the SS man die unshriven," she declares. "Let him go to hell. Sooner the fly to God than he."[304]

Patricia Hampl describes how her writing student Mr. Henle, a refugee from the Holocaust, came to a different decision. "There must be forgiveness," he said, explaining his decision to return to his hometown in Germany for a kind of reconciliation. He deliberately did not say "I must forgive," Hampl explained to me; he instead used the language of impersonal imperative. Some things are beyond the individual human heart. "The strict economy of history required pardon—not because there was no guilt to be assigned or no abiding outrage in the human heart, but because the force of time pushed green shoots out of the bloodied earth, and Mr. Henle bowed his gaunt head respectfully to the new growth. The future, uncaring though it was, had its rights."[305]

"Forgiveness," writes Wole Soyinka, "is a value that is far more humanly exacting than vengeance."[306] However, *being* forgiven is also exacting. South African Truth and Reconciliation Commission member Pumla Gobodo-Madikizela explains that forgiveness is the "victim's triumph" over the perpetrator. She describes the "sense of power" she felt over the murderous Eugene de Kock when she saw his needful remorse, "the distinct moral satisfaction" she derived from accepting it, knowing that it made her better than the man he had been. "Forgiveness," she writes, "is a kind of revenge."[307]

Discussing the East German truth commission, Molly Andrews describes an interview she conducted with B., a leader in the underground women's movement in East Germany. "We were naive in extending too quickly our forgiveness," B. said. "We had hoped that they [the Stasi] would readily say 'we were really wrong about this one'... We imagined that they would also feel relieved when they finally were able to come out of this role." Donald Shriver characterizes the problem B. faced this way: "alleged wrong-doers are [often] wary of being told that someone 'forgives them.' Immediately they sense that they are being subjected to some moral assessment, and they may not consent to it."

In a startling formulation, B. explained: "They still can't forgive us [for] what they did to us."[308]

———

Simon Wiesenthal's question about the place of forgiveness in the relationship between confessor and listener reemerged in 2010 in one of the most astonishing filmic collaborations of the new century, *Enemies of the People*. In the internationally acclaimed documentary, director Rob Lemkin follows journalist Thet Sambath as he meets, befriends, and obtains unprecedented confessions from dozens of perpetrators from the Cambodian genocide, including Nuon Chea, who was second in command to Pol Pot. It is an emotionally powerful film on many levels, but among its most subtle agonies are Sambath's simple kindnesses to Nuon Chea (a man often grouped together with the likes of Stalin and Hitler), whom Sambath befriends with a decade of gentle deferences and carefully paced inquiry. Sambath does not reveal until their last, disorientingly poignant moments together that his own family had been murdered in Nuon Chea's Killing Fields.

It would be wrong to characterize the film as an expression of sympathy or forgiveness for Khmer Rouge perpetrators—but there is, certainly, a nonjudgmental patience to the film that shares its emotional borders with empathy. When I talked to Lemkin about this, he explained that he was uncomfortable with the labels "perpetrator" and "victim." The powerful finality of the concepts curtails creative thinking and understanding, he explained. Judgment of this kind—if only because it shuts down communication—simply wouldn't have been useful to the project.

In our conversation, Lemkin recalled hearing criticism from some that he and Sambath must have been experiencing a mental imprisonment akin to Stockholm syndrome, that their desire to hear the other had become an overidentification with the other's worldview. But Sambath rejected the idea, Lemkin said, that he shouldn't be able to develop a "human connection with Nuon Chea which is like any other human connection, which has affection and positive emotions." "They've shared a lot of time together, in order to get the kind of information that he got over ten years," Lemkin said. "He had to meet him on a bridge of humanity, I think. They both had to come from the other side."

Reports of the film's reception among survivors of the genocide have been remarkable. At one point, a portion of the film was shown in a community center in Salt Lake City. Survivors were afraid to confront film footage of the men who had been in their nightmares for thirty years, but their children—having lived with loud silences their whole lives—dragged their reluctant parents along. The reactions were intense. The older women in particular, Lemkin told me, were surprised by their own emotions. The next time we go back Cambodia, they said, can you bring us to meet Khoun and Soun [the film's two key genocidaires]? "We really want to hug them and thank them for telling us the truth."

Lemkin later arranged for a videoconference between a group of Cambodian émigrés and Khoun and Soun. A man orphaned by the genocide, Bo Uce, translated. Repeatedly asked why they did what they did, Khoun and Soun responded that they had no choice. Their crimes were terrible, they knew, but they would've been killed if they disobeyed. The *LA Times* describes what happened next:

> As Bo translated for several observers who did not speak Khmer, he worried that this exchange might ease their consciences. At one point, one man said he would love to host them in Long Beach. Their confessions were taking on strains of heroism.
>
> Bo picked up the microphone. He was cool now. He wanted to ask something that would unravel their defense a bit, reveal its absurdity.
>
> "Greetings from a distance, proud uncles," he said. "I'm an orphan. I want you to know that I already forgive you."
>
> The men thanked him and smiled.
>
> "Uncles, you used to eat human liver or gall bladder," he said. "Did you do that on your own or were you ordered?"
>
> The men glanced at each other, looking uncomfortable. There was a long pause. Soun kept his hands clasped in front of his mouth.
>
> Finally Khoun took the microphone.
>
> "I only saw... I saw it a bit and I tried it to test it, I tried it out. The gall-bladder was for medicine so I wanted to try it. Just a little bit. That's my honest answer. Just one bit."
>
> Bo handed his microphone off, frustrated at the flatness of the exchange.

"Why did these people not kill themselves?" Bo Uce asked. "If they feel so bad about what they did, why didn't they kill themselves right after they did it? How are they able to live after they killed my family, all these families?"[309]

———

Kaneko-san

There was not a single higher-up person who said, "I feel sorry for you guys. I gave the order." Not even the Emperor. They'd say, "I don't know anything, I don't know anything." They didn't do a thing for us. That was when we all started feeling like, "Who is this Emperor guy anyway? That bastard worked us hard, and when we wound up like that he pretended he didn't know a thing!" You'd feel like that, you know? Up to then we thought the Emperor was a god, right? He's the god of heaven, we thought. Some god! He didn't do a *damn* thing for us.

The soldiers—they're just like this. The same with tissue paper. They just blow their nose with it and trash it. That's the life of soldiers.

Takahashi-san

It's too—too—you know. Things happened a long time ago . . . I don't look on it fondly. I *always* say this to my wife—you see, I don't ever have fun dreams. This is the Siberia issue . . . I feel like the Siberia problem might still have quite an effect on me. Hell, I wanna have a fun dream, but the fact that I don't have fun dreams . . . you know . . . those sorts of feelings. The feelings are somehow still with me. Yeah . . .

This was a stereotypical Siberian death, you see. So, labor during the daytime was extremely harsh, you know? In the cold weather, if you rested your hand even for just a minute, you'd be hit with the rifle of a Soviet soldier. It was more slavelike, you know, manual labor. And moreover, when you come home, the food was—there was no satisfying food, you know. Because you got a 350-gram slice of bread. And soup that was like water. And so your stomach was completely—for the whole year, you felt hungry. So you would get malnourished, right? And so when you were malnourished, the flesh on your legs would completely disappear . . .

It's just, it's up to if you could somehow by force of will suffer through that. Yeah. And those who were emotionally weak—you know, those with weak wills—and of course those who were sickly—those with some kind of handicap would be the first to go. And so before they would go to sleep at night, everyone would try to go to sleep with an empty stomach, you know? And so the only thing we talked about was food. This was instinctual. Because of this, in life in Siberia . . . there is a book about all memories of the Siberian internment camp, and when I ask around, everyone was the same. They get really excited, and they begin to talk about eating—talk about food. And it was the same with soldiers my own age really . . . [Pause]

They fall asleep hungry, you know? Then the next day comes, and you say to the guy next to you, "Hey, it's time for work. Get up! Get up!" But they are already dead cold. Those were the sort of conditions. Soldiers my own age—so my friends—I lost many this way. Yeah. And so now, no matter where you go, there are no graves or anything. 'Cause there isn't anything in the camps in the interior of Siberia. Yeah. And so I don't know what they died for. Because they died after the war had ended. It fricking sucks. That 60,000 died after the war had ended—if you said this to the parents, they wouldn't be able to take it. Hell no!

I don't have any memories except for my friend—friend dying in the bed next to me. The bad memories . . .

The people who in Siberia—who treated you that way in Siberia—can you forgive them?

Hell no! No way I can forgive them! I want to ask who the hell is responsible. I mean, whose responsibility was it, you know? It was the responsibility of those who started the war, too, for sure. And as soon as the war ended, really with the Potsdam Declaration, it was demanded that 60,000 Kantô soldiers be returned immediately to the army. However, they were all taken to Siberia, you know, *against* the Potsdam Declaration. And the one who approved, you know, of sending them to Siberia was the Kantô army. So there were guys like [name removed], and [name removed], a staff officer who lived until just recently. And he was—you won't fricking believe it—he was a powerful key figure in Japanese politics. This, [name removed], you know the kind, at the [name removed] Corporation—commercial corporation—he worked his way up to vice president—vice chairman, and then all the way up to fricking chairman! He was a staff officer of the Kantô. Believe it or not, we were in Siberia together. Us! Together!

However, until the end when he died, he said about the detainment in Siberia that there was no secret agreement with the Soviet army. But we think there absolutely was. That's where the goddamn responsibility falls. It falls on the Emperor. I most . . . Well, at its root, it was the Emperor. The Emperor's, umm, opening the war, the responsibility to begin the war. That during the war—by this I mean, the "Fall of Nanking," you know—whenever things like that happened, there would absolutely be—uh, the Manchurian Incident was like this, too—the Emperor issued words of encouragement. Words of praise. Awards. This—after the war ended and around the time when the war ended—the

decision, to come to end the war was late. You know. The Potsdam Declaration, you know—his acceptance of that was *waaay*
too slow. And he doesn't fricking try to take responsibility. This
is the most—in Japan's—modern society—it's extremely
backward-looking . . .

———

When pressing me to think about the genre of perpetrator confessions ("Why do you think these men told you these stories at all,
and why in the way they did? What effect were they hoping to
achieve?"), people sometimes turned the questions to me. Why are
you telling their stories the way *you* are? Cutting the interviews up
into pieces? Moving unpredictably back and forth between setting
things in historical context and abstracting away from it? Why the
continually shifting narrative voice and disciplinary perspectives?
Those who knew that I had collected fuller life biographies of the
men were sometimes baffled. Why did you exclude those, choosing to reveal the men only through their most awful crimes? In a
reading I gave at the University of Minnesota when I was first ex-
perimenting with juxtaposition as structure, Gourevitch, who was
in the audience, asked during the Q&A session: Why would you
want to put these ghastly images in my head—and why, especially,
in this violently decontextualized way? It had been my secret fear
that somebody would ask this question. I told him, honestly, that I
didn't know why.

In my effort to answer questions like that, I reread a seminal
book of criticism on human rights representation, Kay Schaffer and
Sidonie Smith's *Human Rights and Narrated Lives*. Their book analyzes the subgenres of the U.S. prison memoir and the nongovernmental organization (NGO) prison report to show how mainstream organizations attempt both to give power to the voice of

others and to use the power of the voice of others, while retaining the objectivity that provides ethical insulation.

The classic model for understanding detention, they note, derives from Peter Berensen's "An Appeal for Amnesty 1961" in the *London Observer*, calling into being Amnesty International by organizing outrage over what he termed "prisoners of conscience." Given that audiences of human rights narratives are deeply conditioned by this ur-narrative of "innocent victims," how can subgenres of work by and about *criminals* be effective? Tracking the strategies Human Rights Watch uses in constructing a report on U.S. prisons, Schaffer and Smith identify a series of generic moves used to address this problem. Short pieces of testimony describing prison rape in "ungrammatical, fitful, brutally direct" detail are embedded in the authoritative, objective language of human rights. Powerful but controlled glimpses into prison life are attached to very selective biographies: inmates convicted for property crimes as juveniles are chosen over those convicted for violence against persons. And careful attention is paid to the way prisoners are framed as agents. Action as such is not avoided—since helpless victimization is as alienating as a threatening capacity to act—but is rather reframed, expressed through stories of successful advocacy on the part of the inmates. Schaffer and Smith explain how this combination of moves underscores "the importance to an activist agenda of turning the inmate/perpetrator into victim/activist." They offer their reading as a formula for better understanding other works in the genre of prison memoir.[310]

In obvious ways, I seem to have aped some of these strategies (the embedding of short, brutal testimony; the emphasis on postwar political activism). In other ways, I seem to have deliberately avoided them (establishing clear individual identities through coherent biographical sketches). All writing is a kind of manipulation, but sometimes it is a manipulation the author is not fully in control of, or does not intend, or does not know he intends. Perhaps I cut up the testimony of the men as a genre reflex, an unthinking habit developed from repetitive exposure to the very reports Schaffer and Smith describe. I think I deliberately cut the interviews up because they're unbearable to read at length, without some emotional break. And I think I insisted on including so many of the language fractures—repetition, subvocalizations, words or phrases broken halfway—because I *worried* about how I was cutting their stories up, about whether it was manipulative, and therefore wanted to avoid as much as possible other things that felt inauthentic (like extensive copyediting for grammatical felicity). I think I often shunned historical context because I simply couldn't dare, as a U.S. citizen at this time, to launch a detailed and righteous critique of the war crimes of others. And I think the shifting perspectives and limited biographical information helped me resolve—or rather, postpone—an inner tension about my stance toward the men. I just don't know how I should feel about them, and fracture is a kind of insulation.

But there's more to it than that. I think I cut up the interviews in this way—with the relationships to the accompanying text sometimes clear and sometimes only suggestive—for two deeper reasons. First, I believe that atrocity, from the inside, is itself a relentless cycle of disorientation and reorientation. It certainly was for the veterans, who lost themselves in fresh confusion at each new level of hell. And it was also for me, shuttling back and forth between their monstrous cruelties and the gentle intimacies we shared (eating together, exchanging gifts, meeting their wives and children). I think I wanted my readers to feel something of that confusion, that jolt of moments experienced as if without stable or sensible context. Second, I believe that in all this there is something *more*, something beyond, something that truly cannot be explained in words but that, perhaps, we can begin to feel our way toward through the un-logic of decontextualized association and juxtaposition. Writing with linear closure and fixity of structure on such matters, as I did at first, made me feel not like I was offering readers my perspective but like I was limiting them to it.

It's also possible, however, that I wrote this way because I was somehow under the sway of the photographer's work (his pictures are haunting and beautiful, and I wish I could share them with you). It's possible that I was seeking a literary equivalent to the photographic image. But I think there's something self-serving about me saying this. It's as if I'm seeking refuge, seeking to claim for myself a justification that might belong solely to photographers. Susie Linfield gives this answer to people who accuse photojournalists of turning pain into pornography by objectifying and decontextualizing it in snapshot images:

> These critics seek something that does not exist: an uncorrupted, unblemished photographic gaze that will result in images flawlessly poised between hope and despair, resistance and defeat, intimacy and distance. They demand photographs that embody an absolute reciprocity between photographer and subject, though absolute reciprocity is a hard thing to find even in the best of circumstances. They want the worst things on earth—the most agonizing, unjust things on earth—to be represented in ways that are not incomplete, imperfect, or discomfiting. Is there an unproblematic way to show the degradation of a person? Is there an untroubled way to portray the death of a nation? Is there an inoffensive way to document unforgivable violence? Is there a right way to look at any of this? Ultimately, pious denouncements of the "pornographic" photograph reveal something that is, I think, fairly simple: a desire to not look at the world's cruelest moments and to remain, therefore, unsullied.[311]

At lunch after my reading in Minnesota, Gourevitch continued to pressure me to think more clearly about what I was doing. You have to have a very good reason for telling people explicit stories of atrocity and horror, he said, a reason that you make clear *in the way that you tell them.* You have to tell me what they mean, and what you mean by demanding that I pay attention, why I should listen or look. To tell them without such a compelling sense of purpose and meaning, simply as graphic flashes of extreme brutality—it's not an intellectual activity, he said, it's an assault, and you almost guarantee that I will recoil, shut down, stop reading. What's the good in that?

I had to confess I didn't know if there was any good.

Afterward, a friend who was listening to the conversation came up to me. I think I understand why you did it, she said. It's the law of pain. Pain has to be passed on. It's the difference between knowing and *knowing.*

Maybe that is right. In academia, trauma studies is a long-enduring and lurid subfield. We professors circulate the traumatic stories of others for professional profit and pleasure, for easy access to the feeling that what we do has important stakes. Some say we play with painless pain. Fellow English professor Patricia Yeager explains elegantly: "The traumatic narratives we read and write so freely may have the effect of creating a safely pleasurable source of self-shattering."[312]

So maybe it's this: insofar as I'm able, I want this to be unsafe, to hurt.

Sakakura-san

When we got in to the [camp], everybody had "War Criminal" written on them, actually. "Were we really war criminals?" we thought. Why? . . . We all said we did them because we were ordered to by our superiors. We did it because our superiors ordered us to. And that's—we're talking war criminals, so everyone—every soldier—every single person in the army was a war criminal, then, weren't they? That's how we thought about it. And we got lectures, right? And life sort of went on. And gradually, gradually, you know—like snow hit by the morning sun, little by little, we melted. It sunk into us. If we played sports, for instance, a staff member would say, you know, "You play volleyball like this," and teach us the way. Basketball was like that too. And so, in all kinds of [unclear], they'd let us do all sorts of Japanese folk songs, and we did things like make cultural [unclear phrase]. Even watching movies; we watched a movie, like [unclear title] or something, there'd be something that fit right in my heart . . .

There was this teacher on staff, and every day there was a broadcast, you see. This broadcast—lecture. And we were listening to that lecture. And what lecture was that? It was on theories of imperialism! And while I was listening to that, I thought, Wow, this is really incredible learning, I thought. This is really the best thing I could study, I thought. As I listened, more and more I felt joy inside. This is amazing, I thought. Up until then, I was a person without any education, you know. I didn't even go to middle school! And so words, language like that were of course very rare and unusual to me. But, listen, as the lecture proceeded, when we got to the end, from then it was, from here on there will be cases of leaving the stage of capitalism and entering the stage of imperialism. That's what the teacher said. "You've all studied your hearts out so far, and now you should take those theories of imperialism and link them to yourself! This is the end of my lecture." And when he said that, you know, I was in trouble! What did he mean to "link" the theories of imperialism to myself? I had no idea. No matter who I asked, nobody answered me. Nobody told me, you know, "It's like this."

However, while I was doing that, one day, at a place that unit [inaudible] had gotten together, one of those—the commander of the 39th division—he was named M——. This person, everyone—in front of everyone, researched his own opinion, and in the end expressed his opinion to me: "I have up until now, as a company commander, have made fresh recruits, for the purpose of making them braver, as training, made them kill six or seven local farmers. And in this role, in order to test the cut of a blade, I've cut off some heads. And then I've set fire to villages. I've burnt villagers' homesteads completely to the ground for holding animosity toward the Japanese."

These sorts of [unclear—possibly "sins"] he shared with us piece by piece. "And though I have, of course, committed these on the orders of my superiors, I've committed them also of my own volition. And so, when I think about this, whether I like it or not, I wish to be put to death."

He said this—in front of everyone, with his head lowered, you see. When I heard this, I . . . "linking myself" with the theories of imperialism—that just means I'm an imperialist, doesn't it? . . . And then, ahh, "I must work hard to recognize my crimes." That's what I was learning, I thought. And then, for the first time, I felt that I needed to understand the hearts of the people I'd killed in China. And not superficially—I felt it from deep inside.

And then before long, we—well, August of that next year, I was released and went home. But going home, you know, [they said to us]: "Everyone, you know, up until now—may have had the relationship with us of war criminal, but from today on, all of you are our old friends." That's what they said. And so, "Go back to Japan, get a new house, and just live out a peaceful life." And of course, they didn't say one word at all about it being for Japan-China friendship or anything. Just, "Go on and get a peaceful home and live out your life"—that's what they said, you know? Mm. Ah, and when I heard that, I thought, Ohh, if I say this to [unclear name], what shock. But not just that time, but from the very start: "We will not do this again. We won't." And that sort of thing—"Well, confess to your own crimes—confess, testify to your own crimes, and come to really oppose the war—that's what we want," they said. And so, you know, uh—it was because I felt that way that I went on the Peace Boat missions that I did.[313]

———

There is one last question people have tended to ask me. Do you believe everything they told you?

That's complicated. I'm convinced by Payne that confessions can be manipulative and self-serving, and that memory is "partial and selective," "imperfect and unreliable," a "salvage operation" that retains "certain parts of the remembered past" and jettisons "others that do not fit 'present-day discourses and desires.'"[314] But in a context where confessions of war crimes have been nationalistically dismissed as Communist brainwashing, and where confessions fight against historical revisionism, an attitude of open, generous acceptance seems required. There is so much lying from the other side. One common position of contemporary Japanese historical revisionists, for instance, is what Barnard calls the "'accidental involvement theory of Asian suffering': Japan was fighting against the Western imperialists, but unfortunately some Asians were killed in this war."[315]

Sometimes the question of what it means for something to be true just isn't straightforward. The reception history of Rigoberta Menchú's life story *I, Rigoberta Menchú: An Indian Woman in Guatemala* (the result of a series of interviews with anthropologist and editor Elisabeth Burgos-Debray) is an instructive case study.

Not long after it was published, literary critic John Beverley presented *I, Rigoberta Menchú* as a model for understanding and organizing a wide range of Latin American Spanish writing. Beverley was working in the tradition of Marxist literary theory, which argues that literary genres emerge as ideological practices for producing subjects consistent with broad economic and cultural transitions—because the shift to capitalism, for instance, required people to understand themselves as autonomous and individualistic rather than, say, communally determined, various forms of cultural expression began to help model that new kind of personhood. Beverley argued that in our time watershed cultural, political, and economic changes were producing and being produced by a genre called "testimonio," a first-person novel-length narrative told by the witness of the events—often through an editor or "compiler"—that depicts a collective social problem through the individual's life narrative.[316] The testimonio, he wrote, embodies "the social forces contending for power in the world today," including movements of ethnic or national liberation and the women's liberation movement. Studying this genre could, therefore, help us see more clearly the possibilities for emancipation in our time.[317] Beverley offered *I, Rigoberta Menchú* as an important case study.

I, Rigoberta Menchú was at that point already a literary and political controversy. When Stanford in 1988 replaced its Western culture course requirement with the more intellectually inclusive Culture, Ideas and Values requirement, the *Wall Street Journal* editorialized in outrage:

Of the 15 great works previously required only six remain. The rest have been replaced by lesser known authors. Dante's "Inferno" is out, for example, but "I...Rigoberta Menchú" is in. This epic tracks Ms. Menchú's progress from poverty to Guatemalan revolutionary and "the effects of her feminist and socialist ideologies." ... The 18-year-old freshmen end their first term at Stanford with seven classes on Forging Revolutionary Selves. Much of this amounts to an intellectual fashion known as "deconstruction"—reading texts not as inherently worthy but to serve some professor's private agenda. We await the lecture that interprets Marx (still required) through the work of Groucho and Harpo.[318]

Three years later, Menchú received the Nobel Peace Prize, and the plight of Guatemalan Indians received worldwide attention. Soon after, the powerful conservative backlash was revived when anthropologist David Stoll charged Menchú with fabricating certain details of her story. In an early reply to this charge, Beverley wrote (in language doomed to infuriate nonacademics): "There is not, outside of discourse, a level of social facticity that can guarantee the truth of this or that representation, given that what we call 'society' itself is not an essence prior to representation but precisely the consequence of struggles to represent and over representation."[319] In response to these sorts of arguments, conservatives like David Horowitz harshly attacked the credibility of "human rights leftists" (his essay in *Salon* on the topic was called "I, Rigoberta Menchú, Liar").[320]

Did Rigoberta Menchú tell the truth? Did she lie? What counts as "the truth"? As discussion proceeded, *I, Rigoberta Menchú* became an opportunity for scholars and activists to examine the role of storytelling in human rights advocacy. It was not, Beverley insisted, a matter of unscrupulous "deconstruction" or postmodern recklessness, but rather a matter of negotiating the complicated relationships among truth telling, politics, trauma, and memory, of understanding the way narrative structures all political discourse.

What *I, Rigoberta Menchú* forces us to confront is not someone who is being represented for us *as subaltern*, but rather an active agent of a transformative cultural and political project that aspires to become hegemonic in its own right: someone, in other words, who assumes the right to tell the story in the way she feels will be most effective in molding both national and international public opinion in support of the ideas and values she favors, which include a new kind of autonomy and authority for indigenous peoples.[321]

As Doris Sommer emphasizes, Rigoberta Menchú's testimony came as a series of responses to "possibly impertinent questions" from Burgos-Debray. Menchú, Sommer writes, exercised an "uncooperative control" that turned "a potentially humiliating scene of interrogation into an opportunity for self-authorization."[322]

I, Rigoberta Menchú is an exceptional case, but as Shoshana Felman and Dori Laub reveal, truth and storytelling can be a complex problem for human rights work in a range of ways. They recall the testimony of a Holocaust survivor who, describing an uprising at Auschwitz, spoke in detail about the sight of four chimneys being blown up. Because, in fact, only three chimneys were blown up, some historians were insistent that her testimony as a whole could not be accepted. "It was utterly important to remain accurate, lest the revisionists in history discredit everything." One psychoanalyst disagreed, explaining:

> The woman was testifying not to the number of the chimneys blown up, but to something else, more radical, more crucial: the reality of an unimaginable occurrence. One chimney blown up in Auschwitz was as incredible as four. The number mattered less than the fact of the occurrence. The event itself is almost inconceivable. The woman testified to an event that broke the all compelling frame of Auschwitz, where Jewish armed revolts just did not happen, and had no place. She testified to the breakage of a framework. That was historical truth.[323]

EVIL MEN | 160

Takahashi-san

No, no, the first time that something like that came up was after about three years had already passed [in Chinese prison camp]. Three years. And after about three years had passed, everyone's studies had progressed to a certain point, and they had begun to be aware of their own wrongdoings. And their guilt was they took part in the Japanese army's crime of invasion, and they became aware of that. That was the self-awareness. They came to be self-aware of it, and for the first time, everyone announced to everyone else his own wrongdoings, and confessed to the realities of the sins committed. There was the process of confession. It's not like everyone was talking about it from the start. That's because the first two or three years, everybody thought that if you talked about stuff like what you did bad, you'd get punished for it.

They were *alllways* kind to us. They were really extremely kind. The ones I was in direct contact with were the three so-called instructors. There were three instructors, and then there were the "observers," guards who observed—people who watched us; they were there. But especially the three instructors were extremely impressive, you see. These were young officers with extremely good Japanese. These were very distinctive, unique people, but they were just so kind, you know? Above all, they were kind. They were also sincere. And then one of them was extremely strict. One of them was very quiet and gentle. One was very logical. Each was a very unique person, and each took responsibility such that if one of us had a question, they would answer it. You see? And if there was something we wanted, they'd supply us with the materials we wanted.

And so we, for the first time, came to read books on the doctrines of Marx and Lenin. We came to study things. Like Lenin's

Imperialism, and the history of the development of capitalism in Japan, and the true nature of the Emperor, and the, you know, reality of Japan's aggressive wars, all things like that . . . And then Mao Tse-tung's book—I read and was moved by it a lot. For the first time—the first time in my life . . . that sort of philosophical . . . Mao Tse-tung. You know Mao Tse-tung, right? Mao Tse-tung's *On Contradiction,* or his *On Practice,* or his [unclear title], these books representative of Mao Tse-tung were philosophy books and books on revolutionary theory, you know? I read things like this, and for the first time I ended up thinking about how I view things. "Ahh, the contradictory—the development of my brain has been a development of contradictions, a development of issues." You see, those kind of things were explained in a way that was extremely easy to understand, so this was a very good textbook.

And along with that was, uh, I started connecting the wrongdoings that everybody came to confess to the aggression of the Japanese army. And for the first time, I realized what a war of aggression is; why Japan's wars were aggressive wars in the first place—and why we all unquestioningly accepted the war, and the essence of the emperor system. We studied all of these things . . . So it was a question of recognition, for me. Recognition gradually, gradually sank in deep on a huge scale. And moreover, it was correct recognition that I came to be capable of, you know? I, too, knew what aggression was; what democracy was; what socialism was; what communism was; what development was; what the emperor system was; what the structure of Japanese society was. Little by little, for the first time, I was able to theoretically grasp these things. And then I came to understand the evilness in our experiences.

The Chukiren have often been accused of being brainwashed while in China. What is brainwashing?

Reports from U.S. Korean War veterans about their experiences in Communist Chinese prison camps after 1950 reveal a set of tactics, referred to as "the lenient policy," that appear similar in many ways to those employed at Fushun. U.S. analysts call it brainwashing; Chinese officials, and the Chukiren, call it enlightenment. Lifton characterizes the perspectival clash this way: "What we see as a set of coercive maneuvers, the Chinese Communists view as a morally uplifting, harmonizing, and scientifically therapeutic experience."[324]

In a famous speech in 1942, Mao Tse-tung described the basic principles of Communist thought reform as a matter of punishment and cure: "Past errors must be exposed with no thought of personal feelings or face. We must use a scientific attitude to analyze and criticize what has been undesirable in the past . . . This is the meaning of 'punish the past to warn the future.' But our object in exposing errors and criticizing shortcomings is like that of a doctor in curing a disease. The entire purpose is to save the person, not to cure him to death."[325]

The United States first encountered Chinese thought reform during the Korean War. Early in the war, North Korean forces reportedly shot captured U.S. prisoners often enough that it became an expected outcome among many U.S. soldiers.[326] But after the Chinese entered the war, tactics changed dramatically. One U.S. colonel describes the moment of capture: "The beginning would be like this. The Chinese to our great bewilderment would greet each captive with a smile, a cigarette, and a handshake . . . The American was completely unprepared. It put him off balance. Right then and there, the process of indoctrination began."[327] As another officer explained, captured U.S. soldiers were treated not as enemies but rather as uneducated pawns of the capitalist-imperialist war machine, men who could be taught the value of Communist peace efforts. They received greetings such as "Congratulations! You've been liberated!" and "You have now joined the Fighters for Peace."[328]

In prison, pre-existing formal and informal group structures were dismantled; visible leaders were removed; and information from the external world was restricted. Insofar as prisoners showed a willingness to study, to meaningfully self-criticize, and to repent, they were rewarded. "Reactionaries"—those who remained noncompliant—were segregated. One analyst characterized it as "a means of isolating every person emotionally from every other person, permitting each one to turn only to the system for guidance and friendship."[329]

Other compliance-inducing techniques included "prestige suggestion"—for instance, showing confessions from respected superiors (recall the effect commander M——'s confession had on Sakakura-san)—and "the principle of participation, the principle of repetition, and the creation of meaningful contexts for attitudes."[330] Men were invited to participate in their conversion rather than simply coerced into it. Over and over again they attended lectures, joined discussion groups, and wrote autobiographies—always with a view to achieving clarity about the flaws in their previous beliefs.

Notably, the pacing and incrementalism so important to making the Japanese soldiers into war criminals was also important to making them repent for their war crimes:

> The GI's, for instance, were puzzled when their captors bawled them out violently for some trivial offense such as not brushing their teeth. Of course, they rose meekly before everybody and publicly confessed they hadn't brushed their teeth. It seemed too foolish a thing to take a stand on. But once they had humbled themselves, even about

something as minor as this, the Communists found it easier to get them to criticize themselves and other prisoners on more important questions. The men did not realize that acceding in these matters was alienating them subtly from each other and making them emotionally dependent on the system, till it was finally the only source of either praise or blame.[331]

Lifton describes this process through what he calls the "psychology of the pawn." Unable to escape the people and forces dominating him, the prisoner eventually orients himself completely around adaptation. "He becomes sensitive to all kinds of cues, expert at anticipating environmental pressures, and skillful in riding them in such a way that his psychological energies merge with the tide rather than turn painfully against himself."[332] This testimony from an American priest imprisoned in China is a portrait of such adaptive helplessness: "After a while one wants to talk . . . they press you, so you feel you must say something. Once you start you are deceived: you are at the top of the tree and you go down . . . If you say the first word, there is always something more: 'Lao shih'—No, no, be a good boy! Say the truth!—, 't'an pai'—Confess!—are constantly repeated every two minutes. I felt myself wanting to say more to make him shut his mouth, he was so insisting . . . It made me weak; it made me want to give in."[333]

While this is an extreme case, it nonetheless illuminates what Peter Brooks argues is a core logic to confession generally: the more you confess, the more you want to confess. "As a speech act, 'I confess' implies and necessitates guilt, and if the guilt is not there in the referent, as an object of cognition, it is in the speech-act itself, which simultaneously exonerates and inculpates." In other words, the content of the confession produces guilt, but so does the *form* of the confession. Guilt generates confession and confession generates guilt, "in a dynamic that is potentially infinite."[334] Once you confess, you are a criminal.

I should be up front about this: I hesitated almost to the completion of the manuscript before including the foregoing. It isn't new or controversial information, but it is nonetheless personally disconcerting to detail "evidence" for the charges of brainwashing that war-crimes deniers and historical revisionists continue to level against the Chukiren. But it is of course possible for both things to be true at the same time. That is, the soldiers committed the crimes they describe, and they were also subjected to a powerful system of psychological coercion.

———

Kubotera-san

The Chinese government, in contrast with how horrible the things we did were, well, they treated us in a way that was on par with the Japanese lifestyle. And moreover, in prison, though I thought I'd probably starve, I ate 'til my stomach was full, and they gave me a new futon, and they allowed me to study. This is something the Japanese could not do. Mmm. Japanese couldn't do it. It had to be the Chinese—well, to tell the truth, the Communist Party, I guess, their policies revived us as human beings.

Interpreter: In the camp in Fushun, when you first summoned the courage to talk about the time that you killed the child, what was it like?

Well, I was always in this large room with fifteen, sixteen people. There was what was called an "indictment movement" that took place among the Japanese, in which we criticized each other—and I was criticized. But in the middle of all that, I was just thinking,

"Well, I don't care what happens to me." I'd made up my mind, and so I said it for the first time. And after that, well, if the Chinese government were to sentence me by trial, I didn't care. That's how I'd made up my mind. That was what happened.

So, the bunch of us who came back from Fushun, they think we have had our minds reconstructed . . . However, when I came back to Japan and dozens of years passed, however I think about it, there is no other way that human beings should be except what I've said. All the rest is a lie.

Inaba-san

I spent ten years in the prison . . . In there—in the prison—I had a chance to reflect, and by their lenient policies, I returned to Japan. By that itself my way of thinking about it really changed, you know? And of course, at the time we thought we might be shot—that we would be killed, and there was nothing, nothing we could do about it. That's what we thought at first. But we were released scot-free. And so, due to the fact that we were released—especially due to that, you know?—my way of thinking changed. So you could say that having that much opportunity for deep reflection will change a person. It will fundamentally change them . . . I came to understand all the way from why the war itself had occurred and then, well, what I myself did. And then in the midst of really reflecting on all this, as I understood more and more who had killed these people and for what purposes, I began to realize what I was—a real demon . . .

It was in steps, yes. At the beginning, when I was caught, I believed in the Japanese army, and though I understood that I had been caught, you know, there was still some resistance there. However, through the long span of ten years, I thought and reflected little by little, and due to all sorts of things that happened, things change one after another, you know? So the period of time here was really quite long.

Something my dad said once was that some Japanese police came, and said since I'd come home from China, I might be a complete and total Commie now. So they came to find out how Commie I had become, he said . . . He just said, "That's ridiculous," you know. Apparently they were investigating whether I might have joined the Communist Party and come over to Japan to work for them here, see.

Yuasa-san

Other prisoners—800 other prisoners—everyone was the same; everyone cand—candidly confessed . . . And then, one time, our Chinese instructor—our political instructor, talked to everyone about that. He was having everyone write down the crimes they had committed in the war. But he said: "Everyone's heart is uneasy, I bet. You feel anxious. But the people of China know that not a single one of you went ahead of your own volition and waged war on China. Everyone was, by the power of the state, forced out, and forced to commit crimes. The people of China know this well," he said. And when he said that, I felt—oh, I felt so grateful, so grateful. "The Chinese understand us that well!" I thought. But though you might think, well, they would just forgive us and let us go home like that, he said, "But the Chinese have suffered a great deal because of everyone. You were the hand; you all *did* these things. So now, at last, write all of these things out," he said. "Confess." And I believed him, and wrote it all out.

But it was, like I said earlier, an insincere, evasive confession. It was not a confession meant to apologize. However, as part of the thought-reform education given to us by the Chinese, we were to think about the nature of our offense—reflect on it, as a first layer of reform. Another part was manual labor—manual labor—a means to return to the people. And I was able to listen to talk about world affairs and the war; political education. And through those things, I gradually began to think that I had to reflect more on my crimes, and then again and again I confessed to the things I was hiding.

I was quite hounded by questions like, [disrespectful tone] "You engaged in germ warfare, right?" I had no memory of it, so I said, "No, no." I was questioned this way, and harshly condemned. "I had nothing to do with it, nothing," I said. [But I saw] a battalion commander, and this is what he said. "Ehh, in our invasion, when we entered, we received bacilli from [unclear], and those we cultivated and scattered into the population." I saw him make this confession. I was shocked. Well, where did those bacteria come from? I used to pass along fresh, new, strong bacteria I had just extracted from patients. When a [unclear] comes, everyone passed that stuff to an orderly—my subordinate orderly, and I never especially heard about it, nothing like germ activity. But by his confession, [I realized] "Ahh, these bacilli I passed along were used like that!" Just a little before my release, I finally realized and, to apologize, I said, "Forgive me. I learned that I too was used in germ warfare. Please forgive me." I wrote that down.

———

The Chukiren referenced President Bush and Iraq many times during my time in Japan. Some people back in the United States reacted angrily when I told them about this. Was this some kind of attempt to deflect blame from themselves? To put me in my place as an American? Was it possible they were claiming that the invasion of Iraq was no different from the Rape of Nanking? That President Bush was morally inferior to other world leaders or previous U.S. presidents?

I think the answer is "no," on all counts. I was prepared to be put in my place, and felt (indeed, still feel, as this section will show) the need to prove to them that I was able to subject my own history to the same moral scrutiny they gave to their own. But they weren't angry at President Bush, and didn't require me to display anger of my own to earn their trust. They weren't really interested in the "Americanness" of the Gulf Wars, if that makes any sense. They were interested, instead, in a feature of war that is truly transcendent—and at that time, President Bush happened to be the example at hand. I am convinced that if I had gone later, they would have asked about President Obama, the Nobel Peace Prize winner, and drones and civilian deaths in Afghanistan. Or, if I had gone earlier, about the number of military deaths around the world under President Clinton. The primary point of all their confessions was to reveal that they had lived in a world of lies, that war had made them blind. In asking about Iraq, the Chukiren were just interested in what I was able to *see*.

War makes it hard to discern what is true. It has always been thus. Wars are made possible, sustained, and won or lost through deceit and the confusion of reference. The lies of war extend even into its most basic physical operations. "Strategy," Elaine Scarry writes, "does not simply entail lies but is essentially and centrally a verbal act of lying." Codes, for instance, "are attempts to make meaning irrecoverable," and in camouflage "the principle of lying is carried forward into the materialized self-expression of clothing, shelter, and other structures." War, she writes, is defined by its "disappearing content."[335] It is, by its nature, a matter of cover-ups. In Iraq, the United States used a blanket of propaganda about smart bombs and high-tech "postmodern warfare" to cover up the reality of civilian-targeting cluster bomblets and radioactive dust from depleted uranium-tipped shells.[336] And it covered up the reality of failures on the ground with a campaign of essentially fictional letters-to-the-editor from soldiers extolling successes.[337] Just so, in a moment of wrenching symbolism, UN officials draped a shroud over their tapestry of Picasso's *Guernica* as Security Council members discussed the possibility of war in Iraq, lest the international media snap a picture of an official near the arresting antiwar image.[338]

In Gabe Hudson's comically macabre *Dear Mr. President,* a twitchily nervous George Bush Sr. will only visit soldiers behind a vision-obscuring gas mask. Hudson makes this refusal to see a primary metaphor not only for wartime culture, but also for what happens after combat ceases—especially with the bodies of injured soldiers. While Hudson's veterans sprout third ears and disintegrate into human blobs, the U.S. government steadfastly denies Gulf War syndrome and Veterans Affairs doctors diagnose stress and prescribe Prozac. (Ian Buruma recalls seeing, in the 1970s and 1980s, "the blind and maimed veterans of the Imperial Army standing on crude artificial limbs in the halls of railway stations," begging for spare change, quietly ignored.[339])

It is difficult to gaze upon injured bodies after war, to acknowledge both the depth and the durability of damage. It is also difficult, after war, to look carefully at the reasons for going in the first place. The original public explanations and exhortations, once so bright and clear, once so emotionally overwhelming, seem by the end so misguided, so misleading, so disproportionate to the reality of amputated limbs and burn scarring. And when alternative explanations for why we fought, inevitably, begin to emerge, it is especially painful.

Four years after President Bush declared "mission accomplished" in Iraq, Naomi Klein insisted that U.S. attempts to privatize the country, and to privatize warfare itself, were central rather than incidental goals. Just eight days after announcing the end of combat operations in Iraq, she notes, President Bush revealed his hand by calling for the "establishment of a United States–Middle East free-trade area within a decade." Two weeks after arriving in a Baghdad he himself described as "on fire," Paul Bremer declared the country "open for business." As Klein was told by a delegate at the second Rebuilding Iraq Conference: "The best time to invest is when there is still blood on the ground."[340]

"During the first Gulf War in 1991," Klein writes, "there was one contractor for every hundred soldiers." Four years into the Iraq War, "there was one contractor for every 1.4 U.S. soldiers." Halliburton alone received $20 billion in contracts, almost four times the entire UN peacekeeping budget for 2006–2007. Paul Bremer played his part in funneling money to such corporations by barring Iraq's central bank from providing financing for state-owned enterprises, effectively slashing away at its public-sector infrastructure. Free-market fervor, Klein argues, extended even to the postinvasion looting. Peter McPherson, senior economic advisor to Paul Bremer, "said that when he saw Iraqis taking state property—cars, buses, ministry equipment—it didn't bother him." Describing the pillaging as a form of public-sector "shrinkage," he commented: "I thought the privatization that occurs sort of naturally when somebody took over their state vehicle, or began to drive a truck that the state used to own, was just fine."[341] The rise of private mercenary armies, chillingly documented in Jeremy Scahill's *Blackwater,* was inevitable under such leadership.

Comparing U.S. nation building in Iraq to nation building in Japan after World War II, John Dower writes: "Just as in Iraq, creating a sound capitalist economy was always a goal in Japan. What was understood as 'capitalism' (and 'sound' as well) was another matter entirely." After World War II, it was taken for granted that the state—that is, the U.S. and Japanese governments—"had to play a major role in economic development."

By contrast, once the Americans found themselves plunged willy-nilly into reconstructing Iraq, they pursued this with a zealotry that reflected the reigning dogmas of market fundamentalism. "Privatization" became the catechism of these latecomers to nation building. At one critical early point, much of occupied Iraq's economy appeared to have been put up for sale. At every point, an immense portion of the tasks and functions involved in planning and directing civil affairs in a shattered nation were outsourced to private and largely American contractors—even "civil affairs," even intelligence gathering, even security, even reconstruction endeavors that in Japan had been left to the Japanese and could have been done by Iraqis with greater efficiency and far less expense. The result was a level of confusion, cronyism, non-transparency, and corruption that had no counterpart in Japan.[342]

In an article entitled "Let's All Go to the Yard Sale," the *Economist* described Iraq—with its new 15 percent flat tax for individuals and corporations and its tariffs eliminated or slashed to 5 percent—as a "capitalist's dream."[343]

While it will be impossible to ever fully track all of our spending on the war, Linda Bilmes and Nobel Prize–winning economist Joseph Stiglitz put it at $3 trillion. "Even in the best case scenario," they write:

These costs are projected to be almost ten times the cost of the first Gulf War, almost a third more than the cost of the Vietnam War, and twice that of the First World War. The only war in our history which cost more was the Second World War, when 16.3 million U.S. troops fought in a campaign lasting four years, at a total cost (in 2007 dollars, after adjusting for inflation) of about $5 trillion (that's $5 million million, or £2.5 million million). With virtually the entire armed forces committed to fighting the Germans and Japanese, the cost per troop (in today's dollars) was less than $100,000 in 2007 dollars. By contrast, the Iraq war is costing upward of $400,000 per troop.[344]

In the unflinching documentary *War Tapes,* a staff sergeant offers a telling detail: "Army truck drivers make seventeen grand a year, you know, E-5, so they outsource it, privatize, save the Army money, and now we pay KBR [Halliburton] one hundred twenty grand to do the same job." Another soldier complains about the KBR convoys: "Why the fuck am I sitting here guarding this truck full of cheesecake? Are these people crazy? I feel like the priority of KBR making money outweighs the priority of safety."

War profiteering and business-government collusion have always been sources of moral nausea in postwar discourse, from John Dos Passos's claim that World War I provided "good growing weather for the House of Morgan,"[345] to Anthony Swofford's grim joke about being transferred from the Marine Corps to the Oil Corps, his life "squandered" to secure the financial interests of Bush Sr. & Sons.[346] In the United States, when we evaluate the cost of our wars afterward—the appalling expense of blood and treasure paid by some, and the astonishing profit gained by others—we are always surprised.

———

After photographs were released in 2004 depicting prisoner abuse in Abu Ghraib, I began to receive invitations to speak at nonacademic public forums to discuss the war in Iraq. In the Q&As, conversation inevitably turned to torture: Is torture effective? What separates torture from coercion? Are we torturing? In particular people wanted to ask about waterboarding. What is it? What does it look like? They wanted to know what we were doing, and how they should feel about it. It was curiosity as civic duty.

Sometimes in these conversations, I was reminded of a book review by J. M. Coetzee called "Into the Dark Chamber," about torture novels. Coetzee wanted to explain why writers in South

Africa seemed to have a "dark fascination" with torture. "The torture room," he wrote, "is a site of extreme human experience, accessible to no one save the participants." Novelist and reader stand
outside the door, "wanting to enter the dark room but unable to."
"In creating an obscenity, in enveloping it in mystery, the state creates the preconditions for the novel to set about its work." The torture chamber, Coetzee concluded, is the "origin" of a particular
kind of fantasy.[347]

So what *does* waterboarding look like?

Sakakura-san

And so, I—with my buddies, the three of us, we got one man, a 35-,
36-year-old burly man, you know? We took him inside a house. And
then, we broke down a door and went to where the door was, and
that man—we made him lie on top of the door. "Lie here," we said.
He looked up at us dumbfounded, so dumbfounded . . . And then
we all pushed him down and tied him to [inaudible]. His hands and
legs. Here and here, both of his hands, we tied all of that to the
door. And then, here he got angry, you know. Why are you tying
me up?!—yelling at us like that a few times. But since we'd already
tied him up tight with a rope, you know, once bound like that you
can't move. And, it's just, where do we go from here?

Well, hm, the older soldier had experience, you know, so he said,
"Go draw me some water." Well, I went and got some water, and
after that, he said, "Go get me a rag." And I got a rag, um, any sort
of cloth—"Anything'll do; just get me a rag." And then he said,
"Now make him drink some water." And so he put the rag on his
head, and then I put the spout of the kettle up to his nose, and *glug
glug glug glug,* I poured water into him. And then, while I was

making him drink, I asked, "Are there any weapons here? Where is the Eighth Route Army?" And while we were asking these questions, he looked pained, writhing and blubbering. Well, at first the water didn't go in too well; however, as I did it, gradually water got into his air pipe. And then—even still [we continued], no matter how much it hurt, "Stop! Stop!" [Inaudible] And he was just completely exhausted. "Don't know *nothin'* . . . [about the Eighth Route]," he'd say.

And while we were doing that kind of thing—uh, when we'd been doing it about thirty minutes, then, that guy's stomach had grown out like this [gestures] . . . Because we'd been making him drink water, you know? With a cloth on your face like that, you'll just keep on drinking water, you know? Every time you breathe, no matter how much you don't want to, you'll drink. So you should take the cloth off—but your hands are tied up, right? Your legs are tied up too. So all you do is thrash. Squirm around. And shaking your head doesn't do much either. Because there's somebody holding your head. And then, because he'd been drinking his stomach had swollen out now, so the old soldier said, "Good." Then took his foot and placed it on the man's stomach. And BAM, he stomped on it. Water shot out of his mouth, and he shot out blood too. Yeah. Even then, "I don't know nothin'," he said.

And so we kept on doing it, all of it, for an hour, we just kept on doing it—making him vomit water, making him drink it again—about an hour passed that way. But, if he won't talk even with all this, maybe we should make him drink some *shochu* [Japanese liquor], make him drink some alcohol [unclear phrase]. And so now I went out to look for some alcohol. And since it was the Chinese New Year, every house had alcohol in it. So I searched out and brought back alcohol from who knows how many houses. And this time we put—we took away the rag that was up against his face and changed it for a new one, and now we slowly, from the nose—from the mouth, we made him drink the *shochu*. There's no way to make him drink it all at once. So to make him drink it, we'd pour little by little—and we thought he was drinking it pretty well! We'd brought twenty bottles or so. Or was it more? We made him drink most of that. And then in the end, when it was finally the end—*finally*, you know?—"I'll talk! I'll talk, I'll talk!" he said. And we thought, "We did it."

We untied his rope and made him stand—he couldn't stand. So we lent him a hand, and the place we went—*where are we going?* I thought. And we went into the house, where there's a heater, you know? And he said, "It's here!" and he shut his eyes. "Here, they're in here," he said. This ridiculous—it's just weird. There's no way there could be weapons in a place like this, I thought. And then that man just flopped right down. And that was the end. And my boss said it was hopeless, and we just left him like that . . .

(Sakakura-san's wife died long ago. He lives with his adopted daughter, her husband, and a grandchild. At the time of this writing, he was hospitalized but in stable condition for complications from dialysis.)

———

Douglas Johnson was until recently the executive director of the Center for Victims of Torture in the Twin Cities. When international controversy over U.S. torture in Abu Ghraib was at its height, he gave a public lecture that I attended. In it he discussed the intelligence value of torture and the famous "ticking time bomb" scenario.

The "ticking time bomb" is a thought experiment designed to torment people who are moral absolutists about torture, who condemn it without exception. What if there's a bomb somewhere in New York City, about to go off? Would you torture the person who knows where it is and how to defuse it? What if the bomb will kill 100 people? Is a terrorist worth more than a hundred innocent lives? Is your moral purity worth more than 100 lives? What if it will kill 1,000 people? Is a terrorist worth more than 1,000 innocent lives? Is your moral purity worth more than 1,000 lives?

And so on. There is a number where every sane absolutist breaks down and hypothetically authorizes torture.

But this is science fiction, Johnson explains. *This is not how torture works. Let me give you a more realistic case. There is a bomb at a nearby shopping mall. If it goes off, it will kill 100 or more people.* Johnson pauses and looks around the lecture hall, as if searching for something among the fifty or so spectators. Then he locks his gaze on the first row.

We know that somebody in the first row knows something about this bomb.

Looking back to the rest of the audience, he asks: *Would you be willing to torture them all to find out who that person is, and what he or she knows?*

I am not sitting in the first row.

He continues: *OK. Let's imagine this. We know somebody in the first two rows knows something about this bomb. Would you be willing to torture them all to find out who that person is, and what he or she knows?*

The first three rows?

This lecture hall?

And so on.

There is a number where every sane torture-defender breaks down.

In 1942, writes Yuki Tanaka, operatives of the Kempeitai, a special Japanese military force, raided a home in Banjarmasin and found a radio transmitter that they believed locals were using to communicate with Allied Forces. In the investigation that followed, 257 people were tortured and murdered. While this was happening, "a groundless rumor" of a radio being used in Pontianak popped up. Eventually more than 1,500 civilians were arrested, and most were tortured and killed. Tanaka explains:

> Kempeitai members were projecting their fears onto the local population and thus constantly "discovering" new conspiracies. They were usually convinced of the guilt of those arrested before any interrogation had taken place. The confessions extracted after days, weeks, or even months of torture were usually given by victims who would confess to anything, even crimes punishable by death, in order to end their ordeal. Those named in such confessions would also be arrested and tortured, so the circle of false confession and torture would widen and fuel the paranoia of Kempeitai operatives, who became increasingly convinced that they had uncovered a comprehensive network of resistance activity.[348]

This is a common pattern: torture produces bad information, and a lot of it. Torture one innocent and you will eventually get a list of names. The person you are torturing will say anything to make you stop, and she thinks you want names. So now you have a handful of names. These people are of course innocent, but you cannot know that, so you will torture them, too. Some will take longer than others, but eventually you will find that each of these people also has a list of names to give you. Now you have a conspiracy unraveling in front of you; you are onto something. Security resources are scarce, and occupied elsewhere—but this is important. Resources will simply have to be redirected.

But torture doesn't only produce bad information; it also shuts down good information. Executive Director of Human Rights Watch Kenneth Roth claims that, among intelligence personnel, it is widely agreed that the best source of information comes from cooperative communities providing information and tips. And in Iraq, he explains, Muslim communities stopped cooperating with the United States once it became clear we were using torture. Why would anybody provide information about peculiar or suspicious activity, if that might lead to cruel and inhumane treatment of Muslims or to the torture of innocents?[349] Who would want that on their conscience? Best to keep quiet.

But this is not to say that torture is never effective, exactly. Apologists for torture, for instance, will often cite as evidence in their favor the French victory over FLN (National Liberation Front) guerrillas in the Battle of Algiers. Here, too, torture was deemed generally ineffective for getting information—but that fact, as we will see, wasn't relevant.

The first commander to officially use torture in the Battle of Algiers insisted: "Infiltration and information obtained spontaneously from the population are the most useful methods. I repeat, the use of pushed interrogations [the euphemism for torture] is only valuable if one is dealing with someone who is certainly guilty and if the information can be immediately exploited."[350] But torturers from the Battle of Algiers, Darius Rejali recounts, rarely found "certainly guilty" people with information that could be "immediately exploited." "No one cites his role in preventing a ticking time bomb from going off," Rejali writes. "Such rumored successes always happen elsewhere and are things interrogators have only heard about."[351]

In fact, torturers regularly complained about the problem of false confessions, and later lamented how the torture deprofessionalized soldiers and fragmented their military institutions.[352] Nonetheless, torture was used aggressively throughout the Battle of Algiers and it did, temporarily, defeat the enemy. Why? Because torture *isn't* about getting information. It wasn't torture as a strategy for gathering information that defeated terrorism. It was torture *as* terrorism that worked. As Rejali recounts, approximately one-third of the city was arrested within nine months, and "at least fifteen innocents were tortured for every FLN operative."[353] This was a great way of winning a battle and closing down a city, even if it meant losing the war.

———

Sakakura-san

And on the way home . . . we came across them tying a woman to the roots of a big tree—another [unclear]. They tied her up, and then another soldier was holding her kid. And one guy—that woman—uh—my—there was a woman, you know? And they stuck out their bayonets. "Where is it? Where are they? Where is it?" you know. They did these two things and whatnot, and the mother—it was like she went crazy. Because the one we had under the bayonet wasn't the woman, it was her kid.

They held the bayonet to the kid like this—"Where are they? Where?" they asked. And to get her to talk, they'd, you know, do this to the kid, and the mother would go completely crazy—kick and scream, you know? But even still they didn't let the kid go. And they kept doing that sort of thing. And we thought, well, you see these things sometimes. And if you tell the company commander—well, the company commander went and rounded up twenty villagers. And one, you know, village leader—we took the village leader and hung him upside down by the branches of this gigantic willow tree. With his hands [unclear]. And we just hung him there. And [unclear], your bones slip out of the joints. And now to the villagers we shouted, "Where are the weapons?" you know. "Where is the Eighth Route Army?" We gathered that sort of information. Every time, the villagers said there were no weapons here, no Eighth Route Army here. "If you don't say—if you bastards don't say, we'll kill your village leader!" we'd say. And then, every time, the villagers got mad. And whenever they got mad, we twenty or so soldiers closed ranks. And while we were doing that sort of thing over and over, the company commander finally said, "This is useless." And he said to a subordinate officer, "Okay, cut him down." He ordered him. And the officer—he didn't have much choice, you know? And it was his first time, of course—and so . . .

Taking out your katana in front of everyone and chopping off a man's head—that's not in [unclear], is it? And, his legs were shaking a little, you know? Hm. And then he cleaned the sword in a bucket of water—in a bucket of water, you know? And then we lowered the village leader—we lowered the village leader from the tree, and in front of the well—this well was dug out—everywhere in China here are these wells dug out of the ground, you know? He made him sit by the well, and then the officer, he picked up the ka- tana, and *whish,* took off his head in a flash. His head thumped down in front, and blood shot up about two metres into the sky. And just when I thought it was over, then he took his leg and gave him a swift hard kick. That man, that village leader popped down into the well, and that was the end.

It was so easy, this sort of thing . . . Well, the way I really felt, you know, was something like—"Won't they just give up informa- tion?" "It'd be great if we had such-and-such information"—and you know, for us, it was the success, the merit we were after.

In torturing, in setting fires—if something really came of it, that would have an impact on our army record. And so if we didn't get what we wanted, we were disappointed. And so—it wasn't a very good feeling when some enemy [or civilian] died, but we felt like, if they do die, we don't care. At any rate, we were happy if we got information out of them. So that—success in the world, I suppose? Our record. We did that stuff thinking we were going to get a better record for it.

[Later]

When I went off to the army [my mother] said, "Give 'em hell." She also said, "When you go over there, don't get any weird diseases!" That's what she said. Don't get any weird diseases, she said. And I remembered this well, you know—don't get, you know, any of the army's weird diseases.

———

When I first got back home after meeting these men, I tried to tell people about it. But I didn't know how to explain things, how to turn any of it into coherent stories that could be shared. Something in me kept needing to try, though. I ended up saying inappropriate things at inappropriate times in inappropriate ways. I would start a story and then not know where to go with it, how to wrap it up, how to make it fit back into the flow of a reciprocal conversation. And so I found myself mouthing familiar bromides that allowed me to end my turn in the conversation and that changed each time I spoke: how it made me cynical about people and about our collective future; how it made me see opportunities for change and reasons for hope. One time I found myself talking about the things these men did on the sidelines during a community soccer game, another time in a holiday party chatter circle. The way people looked at me—after that I decided to be quiet.

Over the next year, I spent a lot of time thinking about how to share these stories and about whether to. At the same time, I was teaching courses at my college on the theoretical and ethical structures of storytelling and human rights. It all became knotted up together in my head, so that I couldn't separate the specific practical questions about my own writing from the broader philosophical questions about the nature of writing in general. I felt like there was an answer, even though I wasn't sure about the question. It was like that feeling you get, momentarily, when you can't remember a name that is intimate to you. But in this case, the feeling lasted many months.

Anyway, it is now years later, and I have built my own twisted little walkway to something that feels like resolution, or as close as I'll manage. It winds itself around the ideas of storytelling and human dignity, and advances through a series of interlocking pieces that culminate in a single sentence. Standing alone, it is an empty final sentence, but by the time you get to it I hope you will see what it means to me.

The path starts with a question I asked one of the soldiers who was, like me, a teacher. In advance of our meeting, this man was a *worry* for me. He specialized in ethics at his university under a prominent Japanese moral philosopher, loved Tolstoy, and immersed himself in Shirakabaha literature (a literary movement that promoted individualism and humanism). He worked for the Ministry of Education after graduation but, as a man of conscience, quit in protest when asked to perform an "ideology inspection" on a scholar he admired. After that, he worked as a teacher at a teachers' college. He was then drafted and became a war criminal.

You were the kind of man who disobeyed and sacrificed so many things before the war, I said to him. *You spent all this time in China and engaged in acts that strongly contradicted your philosophical position. How, besides rationalizing it as orders, did you make sense of your actions?*

Ebato-san

Well, at Tokyo University, I learned logic; and I primarily learned the logic of Kant. Particularly Kant's ideas on human dignity had a definite influence on my life, I think. And, to go into specifics, I entered the army and particularly when people would, day in and day out, be punished with beatings as part of what was called recruitment training in the Japanese emperor's army . . . Though I was slapped in the face, I did not yield; and I was able to live the army life. Even if I went to the front and did terrible things—and you know, they did a lot of them—for me myself, doing even one of those things is too many. But, as I just mentioned, there is the fact that a superior's order is the emperor's order; and so, if you execute such a thing—if you execute such a thing, you yourself cannot live on . . . But, we lost, and if I were to rephrase it, I also didn't act on my conscience . . . The fact that I committed those crimes is, well, the biggest regret of my life.

Well, we intellectuals, you see. There's something common to the intellectuals in the Japanese army . . . All of these war crimes—we simply can't approve of them. Therefore, the intelligent or intellectual soldiers—I don't think they committed any war crimes but what was ordered by their superiors. You know? They didn't do anything else. But, well, since I'm speaking from the present, if you really thought seriously about the contradictions of daily life, you would have a nervous breakdown.

So, in the context of the war, in order to keep that at bay . . . Well, uh, you place yourself outside of the war—put yourself out-of-bounds. So. Although in reality you're participating in a war of aggression, you yourself are separate—you've, you know, left yourself in a make-believe world. In other words, you have an aggressive war, and even while you participate in that, the intellectuals—how do I put it—mmm, they say that they are something apart from this aggressive war. And I—to talk about myself now—I took the position that I was doing a sort of rehearsal . . . So, in order to escape from the world that has this painful war—for instance, I didn't come for the purpose of killing people—I came for the beautiful scenery, or to connect with the natural side of the country, and to find my *raison d'etre,* or something like that—I escaped into thoughts like that. That's what I think. But I—so I wrote it in my own record of the war . . . I think that I myself was like that, you know? But in the end, well, I committed great crimes. Do you understand?

One time [in prison camp in Siberia], I was called in by a Soviet political staff member, and my very best friend, [unclear several words]—in other words, he compelled me to betray him. He had, long ago, been a police officer in Manchukuo. And if this leaked out—if they learned this—he wouldn't be able to go home—and he'd revealed all of this to me. That political staff member was telling me to look into personal history, his career history, and report back with it all. He told me it was an order, and threatened me. But my conscience rejected this. "Even if it is an order, I can't do it," I said. He was furious. "Leave!" he said. "But I won't let you go home!" And then . . . And, at that time, I fell into a depression for a bit, but then I remembered in my heart something I'd studied in the past, Kant's epitaph, on his tombstone—his epitaph. [*Ebato-san quotes: "Two things fill the mind with ever new and increasing admiration and awe, the more often and perseveringly my thinking engages itself with them: the starry heavens above me and the moral law within me."*]

When I refused that order in the Soviet Union—well, I didn't mean to do anything that would end up in my not being able to go home. No way. However, when you put it like that, it seems so hopeless. But at the time, I was okay with that, I thought. To have obeyed my conscience is to have done the right thing—that's the experience I had. Yeah. So that was the very, uh, best experience to have occurred in my life, I suppose; the time for which I most want to praise myself. That's what it is.

———

In *The Defense of Poesy,* Sir Philip Sidney describes the tyrant Alexander Pheraeus, "from whose eyes a tragedy well-made and represented drew abundance of tears; who without all pity had murdered infinite numbers, and some of his own blood, so as he that was not ashamed to make matters for tragedies, yet could not resist the sweet violence of a tragedy."

In the West for some time, it seemed a contradiction that in the Holocaust, highly cultured people could do barbaric things. "How was such a horror possible?" Bauman ventriloquizes the voices. "How could it happen in the heart of the most civilized part of the world?"[354] The city of Weimar was home to Johann Wolfgang von Goethe and Friedrich Schiller; it was also only a handful of miles away from Buchenwald concentration camp. Jorge Semprun, a survivor of Buchenwald, depicts an American soldier's astonished confrontation with Weimar's inhabitants during the camp's liberation: "Your pretty town, so clean, so neat, brimming with cultural memories, the heart of classical and enlightened Germany, seems not to have had the slightest qualm about living in the smoke of Nazi crematoria!"[355]

In our imperial arrogance, we have always believed that there is something fine and unique in our cultural achievements, that these have a transcendent value and therefore reveal something transcendent about us. Indeed, there are still today those who find their moral foundations shaken by the Holocaust, but not, say, by the Rwandan genocide. Again, François Mitterrand: "In countries like that, a genocide is not very important."[356] Mitterrand's racism is glaring and has been appropriately condemned. But according to Wole Soyinka, subtler versions of this racism regularly escape notice. He rails in particular against the argument that the Holocaust "placed the first question mark" on European humanism. This idea, he insists,

> merely provides further proof that the European mind has yet to come into full cognition of the African world as an equal sector of a universal humanity, for, if it had, its historic recollection would have placed the failure of European humanism centuries earlier—and that would be at the very inception of the Atlantic slave trade. This, we remind ourselves, was an enterprise that voided a continent, it is estimated, of some twenty million souls and transported them across the Atlantic under conditions of brutality that have yet to be beggared by any other encounter between races.[357]

Is there a version of Sir Philip Sidney's wonder at the coexistence of aesthetic sensitivity and cruelty that isn't bound up in ethnocentrism and racism?

Let me start to approach this question with what might be called the deep history of human rights and the arts. In *Inventing Human Rights*, Lynn Hunt makes the argument that the human rights movement was made possible by evolutions in narrative practice. She claims that modern conceptions of human rights are derived from the principles of the eighteenth-century Western Enlightenment, which in turn were made possible by (or developed the way they did because of) changing practices of storytelling: namely, the rise of the epistolary novel.

You may recall reading as an undergraduate Samuel Richardson's *Pamela: Or, Virtue Rewarded* (1740). It's the story of a young maidservant—told through her letters—who successfully resists the sexual assaults of her master, Mr. B., and in so doing earns the "reward" of marriage to him. It's as hard to overstate the revolutionary popularity of this novel as it is for some readers today to understand it. In one village, Hunt writes, "the inhabitants rang the church bells upon hearing the rumor that Mr. B. had finally married Pamela."³⁵⁸ Arguing for something like an eighteenth-century version of the CNN effect, Hunt claims that widespread reading of newly available dramatic novels like this, centering on the emotions of common individuals, played an important role in developing a new sense of empathy for physically or socially distant persons.

> Novels made the point that all people are fundamentally similar because of their inner feelings, and many novels showcased in particular the desire for autonomy. In this way, reading novels created a sense of equality and empathy through passionate involvement in the narrative. Can it be coincidental that the three greatest novels of psychological identification of the eighteenth century—Richardson's *Pamela* (1740) and *Clarissa* (1747–48) and Rousseau's *Julie* (1761)—were all published in the period immediately preceding the appearance of the concept of "rights of Man"?³⁵⁹

Margaret Cohen argues similarly that the sentimental social novel turns pity into "a political or social idea"; moreover, that such novels self-consciously position themselves "as participating in the march, if not battle, for progress."³⁶⁰ As Lynn Festa explains, the sentimental novel's "repetition and rehearsal of emotions" for the disenfranchised contributed to the broad reimagination of a more inclusive human community. Novels like *Pamela* helped to carve out a space "of abstract humanity that anticipated the ideal of universality upon which Revolutionary doctrine was ideally or theoretically based."³⁶¹

It is an intuitively persuasive idea—that new technologies of representation (the novel, the camera, the television, the 24-hour news network, the Internet) can produce new kinds of social relations and even new kinds of empathy. Many have criticized such arguments, however, for relying upon, without fully developing, a theory about how representations can perform cultural labors that bring about broad perceptual shifts. But whether or not it is true that the rise of the novel, for instance, played a role in *causing* the changes that made modern human rights possible, the novel as a form certainly *reflects* those changes. The novel, in other words, is an artistic development that is dependent upon a certain conception of the human (individualistic, autonomous, defined less by status than by valuable interior feelings that, implicitly, all can share)—a conception that is likely also a prerequisite for the modern, liberal conception of (natural, equal, and universal) human rights.

The current interest in the connection between narrative and human rights is perhaps best understood within the larger context of aesthetics and ethics in intellectual history, in the broad study of the way art provides a foundation for human dignity. The defense of poetry by what amounts to ethical consequence has a long history. "Taste alone brings harmony into society," Schiller writes, "because it fosters harmony in the individual."[362] And Ludwig Wittgenstein declares: "Ethics and aesthetics are one and the same."[363] Writing after the French Revolution, William Wordsworth finds in the pleasure of poetry "an acknowledgment of the beauty of the universe . . . homage paid to the native and naked dignity of man, to the grand elementary principle of pleasure, by which he knows, and feels, and lives, and moves." This pleasure, he writes, is itself the foundation of universal human sympathy. "In spite of differences of soil and climate, of language and manners, of laws and customs, the poet binds together by passion and knowledge the vast empire of human society, as it is spread over the whole earth, and over all time."[364]

This Romantic view of art, long dormant, has resurged of late in a series of scholarly works arguing that the aesthetic as a category helps us develop richer lives and better social arrangements. Helen Vendler, drawing upon the poet Wallace Stevens, explains that art brings us into "a pervasive being": "To lack a pervasive being is to fail to live fully. A pervasive being is one that extends through the brain, the body, the senses, and the will, a being that spreads to every moment, so that one not only feels what Keats called 'the poetry of earth' but responds to it with creative motions of one's own."[365]

Scarry argues that the transcendent experience of beauty not only deepens our personal being, it also prepares us for social justice. When we submit, in rapture, to the beautiful object, we are doing more than making it the center of our attention—we are temporarily making it the center of our universe. Beauty in this way short-circuits our default self-centeredness. It makes us forget ourselves; it trains us not only to be other-regarding but to take pleasure in this stance. Moreover, because beauty inspires us to share (we photograph it, draw it, describe it, invite others to witness it), it trains us in fair distribution and symmetry. For Scarry, fundamentally, the double meaning of "fair" is material rather than accidental; and fairness as justice, she argues, is the opposite of injuring. "Beauty is pacific," she writes. "Its reciprocal salute to continued existence, its pact, is indistinguishable from the word for peace."[366]

Beauty has enjoyed a resurgence in recent years not only among literary and cultural critics but also among philosophers. Marcia Muelder Eaton argues that "aesthetic response, like emotion, is tied

to a culture's moral order and, like emotions, will be used to prescribe and proscribe the sort of life one has and leads."[367] And Martha Nussbaum highlights the links between philosophical ethics
and literary aesthetics. The practices of the Greeks of the fifth and
early fourth centuries BC, she argues, reveal that "dramatic poetry
and what we now call philosophical inquiry in ethics were both
typically framed by, seen as ways of pursuing, a single and general
question: namely, how human beings should live."[368] Narrative art,
she writes elsewhere, is a valuable resource "for the formation of
decent citizenship."[369] Moreover, in developing with Sen the highly
influential "capabilities approach" (the idea that we should evaluate
principles of social organization based on how well they promote
human flourishing by allowing for the functioning of universal,
basic capabilities), Nussbaum has emphasized the capacity for aesthetic expression as an important element in deriving a universal
ethics.[370]

We value art because it is essential to the free and full development of personality and because it promotes human flourishing.
Indeed, art is a basic human right, protected in Article 27 of the
Universal Declaration of Human Rights (UDHR). Even the foun-
dational texts of human rights, it might be argued, are designed
according to aesthetic principles. René Cassin, the primary drafter
of the UDHR, compared the document to the portico of a temple.
In so doing he invited us to consider how the document's form reinforces its values: the textual architecture persuades us with its
stately solidity and implications of the sacred; and its interior principle of symmetry is itself the principle of justice.[371]

Until recently, interestingly, literary critics—the custodians of
some of our most beautiful cultural inheritances—were among
those most likely to treat the category of the beautiful with maximum suspicion. Scarry, an English professor, argues that throughout

the 1980s and 1990s beauty was "banished" from conversation, except insofar as it was the subject of "political critique."[372] Suspicion, indeed, remains a default stance among many literary critics to this day, for at least two reasons. First, because conceptions of beauty determine what is most worthy of attention and care, they also determine what is least worthy of attention and care. Judgments like these are always a matter of politics, but with the beautiful we are invited to experience them as a matter of the natural. Second, cultural artifacts such as novels and "tragedies well-made"—or even treaties and international covenants—are able to naturalize certain views on what it is to be human precisely because their beauty, their aura of transcendence, makes us receive them uncritically. One way or another, they train individuals and communities to perceive and judge racial, sexual, gender, class, and national identity   in others and in themselves.

Joseph Slaughter points to a striking example. Analyzing UN debates over the proposed Universal Declaration of Human Rights, Slaughter gives particular focus to the arguments generated around Article 29: "Everyone has duties to the community in which alone the free and full development of his personality is possible." Fernand Dehousse, Belgium's delegate, objected to versions of the community-oriented language, citing Daniel Defoe's classic novel *Robinson Crusoe* in his effort to justify his position: man, the novel shows, does not need a community to freely develop his personality. Isolated, self-inventing, concerned with his own freedoms and possessions rather than with his duties to others, Dehousse's Crusoe is an embodiment of the negative model of liberal personhood so often criticized by communitarian scholars. With this high-profile invocation of Crusoe, we see the cultural training and biases that were responsible for the U.S. demotion of economic, social, and cultural rights over the next several decades. Indeed, scholars such as Slaughter see hints of the Western cultural imperialism that infuses the human rights regime. As Edward Said writes: "The prototypical modern realistic novel is *Robinson Crusoe,* and certainly not accidentally it is about a European who creates a fiefdom for himself on a distant, non-European island."[373]

Human rights as a rhetorical form is one of our great contemporary moral beauties. In a recent special issue of *PMLA (Publications of the Modern Language Association,* the flagship journal of literary criticism) on human rights and the humanities, Samera Esmeir explains why so many scholars are so quick to resist its allure. International human rights law, she argues, transforms "humanity into a juridical status, which precedes, rather than follows and describes, all humans." In other words, law aspires to call into existence and to constitute "a human who would otherwise remain nonhuman." It thereby risks "erasing all other humanities, not only in imposing its particular vision of humanity but also, and more crucially, in erasing their past existence before the law's intervention."[374] In a similar vein, Slaughter writes that international human rights are "necessary but suspicious vehicles" that "project a new universal, international citizen-subjectivity" through "monadic, self-sufficient Enlightenment individualism," "historically narrow, generic universalism," and "residual nationalism."[375]

Pheng Cheah emphasizes that such criticisms are not attempts to dismiss the valuable contribution of human rights discourse, but rather to understand its full complexity. Rights, Cheah argues, define who we are as actors within "global capitalism," thus suturing us into its inequalities. But they also provide our only way for mobilizing against these inequalities. Rights, he warns, are "violent gifts."[376]

I must confess that I found myself liking these sweet old men. When I feel ashamed of this, I tell myself: anybody would've liked them, if they sat with them, touched them, heard the sound of their voices, listened to their stories. Spending two long afternoons with Kaneko-san, for instance, I had the cliché reaction that people have in those situations: I was surprised he was so normal, so harmless. Waiting in front of his house for him the second day, I couldn't help grinning happily when I saw him arrive: scooting toward us on an old upright bicycle, gray hair messy in the breeze, legs pumping slow, intentional circles, wobbling at the end—for all the world reminding me of Kermit the Frog videos from my childhood.

When we began our interview, his wife remained nearby, close enough to watch over him (he had recently returned from the hospital) but generally staying out of our sight. He was nearly ninety, but he had an energy about him that felt young, almost boyish, like he couldn't stop from marveling at each moment he was alive. Like he couldn't believe he had survived. He recalled an intense moment when he expected to die while in prison camp in China. All the soldiers were called to the courthouse—they all suspected it was going to be a mass execution.

"This time at last, eh?" I thought. And then, they called out all the names. The judge, right? Called them out. And then, in the end, it was announced: "Immediate release." And for a moment, everyone was silent. Everybody was half unbelieving. And in the midst of that, little by little everybody started bursting out in tears. Wailed and cried, we did. We men in our thirties, men in their fifties—all of them yelled out, wailing, hugging each other, and cried. And then we, just like that, without going back into the prison camp at all—then we went into a famous restaurant. We entered the restaurant, and there was a farewell party. And we thought, we're getting all sorts of good things here. And then the translator, when he came, he went around to each table, and then I asked. "Why did China let us free?" And then, this is what he said. "You see, if we were to execute you, your father, your mother, they would cry, wouldn't they? The citizens of Japan would be angry, wouldn't they? China does not want war with Japan. We definitely don't want that. That's why we set you free."

Kaneko-san, like the others I met, is thankful to China. At first he thought they were being released as part of some negotiation for reparations. But when he realized they were simply being released, he couldn't believe it. He said it began a transformation in his soul, bringing him to support Communist China and to perceive the person he was before as a kind of devil. Prison camp in Siberia, where he had been the five previous years, had been very different. It was a brutal and humiliating time. He remembers it being too cold to go outside, so urinating in the canteen he had to drink from. He recalls slipping in the ice in the latrine and falling into the sewage pits, getting covered in icy shavings of feces and then running inside for warmth, only to have the shavings melt and begin stinking up the room. There was no medicine, he said. His friends died of pneumonia, diarrhea. He recalled being forced to clean the storeroom where they piled dead bodies in the winter, because the ground was frozen too hard for digging. They piled up like frozen fish. "The suffering of those five years," he said, "was far worse than any during the war."

What was perhaps just as difficult, when Kaneko-san returned to Japan after release from China, he was publicly shamed—not for the war crimes he committed, but for confessing to them. It was a painful payback for the years he had lost.

> [Angry] When we, who out of patriotism went to China and fought, return home—now, somehow or other, we've been brainwashed

and are under inspection. Have you ever heard such nonsense? . . .
That's right! When we go somewhere, you can count on the police
to come along behind. Everything—what month, what day, what
time—it's all written down! That's how it was then. Have you ever
heard such nonsense? However you think about it . . . You know?!
For His Majesty the Emperor, we gave our lives. Japan lost, then we
were shipped off, put to manual labor . . . When we come back,
"brainwashed"—this nonsense . . . No company would hire us. I
did go to a company and guess what? It was ended in two days.
Fired. Fired in two days.

Those willing to talk about what really happened—especially
those who publicly voiced support of Communist China—were
hated, ostracized, and threatened. Sakakura-san remembered being
at a meeting for veterans, where one of the speakers spent a significant amount of time denying that war crimes had been committed:
"Now he's saying there isn't anyone who ever did these things! And
I thought then that I would object, but then—since I was all alone,
you know . . . I just stayed quiet, and I just joined in . . ."

Later, Sakakura-san went on a trip with his soldier buddies. He
brought it up with them in the smaller group, thinking either they
would privately agree with him about what they had done or he
would teach them a lesson and shame them for denying it. "And
about these bad things I said, 'But you did all these things, didn't
ya?' I said. And he [referring to one of the other soldiers]—he
grabbed onto my sleeve, and he said, 'Listen to me. You say those
things, and you're done for.'"

Nobody wanted these things to be said. Men like Kaneko-san
and Sakakura-san were violating the collective decision to be silent
and to deny. And for that too they could not find forgiveness.

Once again, these are the common starting assumptions for thinking about storytelling and human rights. For listeners and bystanders, stories promote bonding and empathy, and empathy promotes helping behavior. For survivors, stories provide intelligibility and closure, and closure provides healing.

I want to focus for now on the former. As Richard Rorty frames it, we have experienced two centuries of moral progress largely because sad and sentimental stories, "repeated and varied over the centuries, have induced us, the rich, safe, powerful people, to tolerate, and even to cherish, powerless people—people whose appearance or habits or beliefs at first seemed an insult to our own moral identity, our sense of the limits of permissible human variation."[377] With each new story we hear, a previously hidden or invisible form of suffering is exposed: E. M. Forster's *A Passage to India* forever altered British views on colonialism; Harriet Beecher Stowe's *Uncle Tom's Cabin* mainstreamed what had formerly been the outlier movement of abolition. New stories like these teach us new sites of care, new sites of pain, and we instinctively respond to them. When we read Richardson's *Pamela,* as Lynn Hunt would put it, we learn pity for all Pamelas, fictional and corporeal. Or rather, we respond with pity as a biological mandate, as Virginia Woolf characterizes it in *Three Guineas:* we see photographs of the war dead and we feel a natural disgust that makes us oppose war. "Those photographs are not an argument; they are simply a crude statement of fact addressed to the eye. But the eye is connected with the brain; the brain with the nervous system . . . When we look at those photographs some fusion takes place within us; however different the education, the traditions behind us, our sensations are the same; and they are violent."[378]

Such moral theories of natural benevolence date back to the eighteenth century, when, according to Julie Stone Peters, figures like Francis Hutcheson and the Earl of Shaftesbury participated in the reformulation of Aristotelian catharsis as an "emotion-based social union through narrative identification." "Pity, generated by narrative," Peters writes, "was to serve as a mechanism for uniting humanity and stimulating charitable action through the sentimental bond."[379] And this mechanism was perceived to be part of our very physiology. Thomas Jefferson writes: "Nature hath implanted in our breasts a love of others, a sense of duty to them, a moral instinct, in short, which prompts us irresistibly to feel and to succor their distresses."[380] Theorizing a "sense of soul we may call the sympathetick," Francis Hutcheson asserts: "When we see or know the pain, distress or misery of any kind which another suffers, and turn our thoughts to it, we feel a strong sense of pity, and a great proneness to relieve, where no contrary passion withholds us."[381]

But we needn't go that far. Sympathy doesn't need to be natural, neurally programmed, or God-given to have force. We don't have to imagine that humans inherently tend toward the good. After all, satire and suspicion of moral theories of natural benevolence are also conspicuous in the eighteenth century, which is as much the age of de Sade as it is the age of humanitarianism. The French novelist Madame Riccoboni declared in 1769: "One would readily create unfortunates in order to taste the sweetness of feeling sorry for them"; and the protagonist of Françoise Vernes's *Voyageur sentimental* (1786) says, "A tear of sentiment, what sweeter reward."[382] Empathy and the altruism effect can have varied subterranean emotional sources. They can be contingent social constructs, artifacts of a particular society's way of socializing its subjects into collaborative prosocial behavior, and they can nonetheless still feel as implacable as biology in shaping the lives of those subjects. Stories train us how to act and how to feel; they help us create alternative, imaginary selves (more beautiful, more courageous, more empathetic, more tender) that we yearn to be more like. In that way human rights culture may operate according to the same deep and powerful principles of social behavior that drive brand loyalty or attachment to logos (principles easier to disdain than to transcend): *Yes, this is the kind of person I would like to be. This is how I'd like people to see me.* We don't have to be good to want to be good.

We are, after all, comprehensively self-centered creatures. Even our moments of deepest anguish over the fates of others can be emotional extensions of our unceasing self-regard. It is a brutal but basic psychological truth, for instance, that grief over the loss of loved ones involves no small portion of sorrow over our own hurtling mortality. Or, in like manner, that empathy for distant strangers requires first the cognitive work of transforming the strangers into people that appear related to or like us. One would have to be an impossible moral purist to lament such human self-care.[383] We don't have to care *only* for others to care for others. Caring for others can be complicated, multilayered—an expression, among other things, of our self-care, or even a strategy we adopt for enhancing our self-concept—and it still counts as caring for others. While they trouble me, I've never been fully convinced by arguments that claim that partially self-interested motivations negate the goodness of actions or irredeemably taint the goodness of the interior moral deliberations that produce them.

At the same time, however, the social fact of impure motivations has always made it easy to become cynical about the popularization of sentiment—and never more so than now, living as we do in the society of the spectacle. Ishmael Beah's memoir of child-soldiering, discussed earlier, was reviewed this way in *Time* magazine: Beah is "a rock star," the child soldier is "the most sexy category" of war victim, and the "weaponized child" is a "great scene setter" for a Hollywood with a "weapons-grade crush on Africa."[384]

The reaction this sort of thing provokes in us is not just about purism. There's something morally significant about the instinctive revulsion we feel when we see such narcissistic altruism, such care that is as much about the desires of the helper as the needs of the helped. It is caring by the bulk, caring that is defined not only by curiosity but by shallow curiosity, caring that can look at the other without seeing the particularity of the other. Stanley Cavell weighs the consequences: the humanitarian's intention "is to acknowledge the outcast as a human being; but his effect is to treat a human being as an outcast, as if the condition of outcastness defined a social role, a kind of sub-profession, suited for a certain kind of human being."[385] The narcissism behind this reduction of others often manifests itself in one of two ways: depth larceny or moral vanity. Consider each.

First, depth larceny. Eva Hoffman argues that some portion of the ostensibly empathetic and respectful social elevation of Holocaust survivors involves the petty desire of the comfortable for "existential grandeur." Survivors are "sent to suburban high schools, interviewed, begged for their tales from hell." This desire for the survivor is, in part, lurid interest (*We love those Holocaust stories*—one of Hoffman's students tells her—*they're so dramatic*). But it is also, writes Hoffman, a matter of "significance envy." We live lives of passivity, leisure, and spectacle; our art, our culture, our politics, even our psyches, writes Hoffman, "can be deconstructed nearly out of existence."[386] But the Holocaust cannot; it remains itself, a promise of authenticity. The encounter with the survivor thereby puts the listener (whose life may feel banal, mediated, low-stakes) close to the touch of history, close to choices that matter, close, finally, to "the real thing." " 'My friend was in Buchenwald,' a guest was overheard to say to another at a recent party. 'Oh,' retorted the other rather smugly, 'Our friend was in Auschwitz.'" How easily our empathy for the victim, Hoffman concludes, turns into "exploitation and the violation of the one thing that ought never be thus used: the pain and death of others."[387]

As bad as such underidentification is, however, the other extremes are little better. Overidentification, in which one has a desire, even need, to deeply and sincerely empathize, can lead to illusions of assimilating the other's experience, vicarious victimhood, or the feeling that one's own survival as witness is a kind of adequacy.[388] And anti-identification, in which one endows the survivor with sanctity and approaches him with awe, functions as self-protection, Dori Laub warns, a way "to keep him at a distance, to avoid the intimacy entailed in knowing."[389] But it isn't just that these various types of personal "memorialization" are morally distressing or narcissistic or callous at an individual level—it's that collectively they generate a "secondary amnesia," in which the Holocaust expands into "an increasingly empty referent, a *symbol* of historical horror, an allegory of the Real, the familiar catastrophe and a stand-in for authenticity and for history."[390]

Now consider moral vanity. At a dramatic rally in Edinburgh during the Make Poverty History campaign (an attempt to mobilize U.S. support for action against global poverty), Nairobi journalist John Kamau asked a Scottish university student if he thought the spectacle would make any difference. "Should I be hopeful?" Kamau asked. The student replied: "This is not only about you, it is about our humanity." In other words, the point of the campaign was as much about publicly becoming a certain kind of person as it was about actually bringing relief to those who were suffering. One teacher commented, "I feel proud for the first time," and another student declared: "This is very exciting. I want to be counted among those who stood up against world poverty."[391] Kate Nash comments on such reactions: "The creation of feeling for the suffering of distant people, which can generate a collective understanding of moral obligations to act to relieve that suffering, always risks degenerating into an emotionally indulgent admiration of one's own sensitivity, sincerity and strength of will."[392]

"It is one thing for a man to act out of his great love for Isolde," philosopher Bernard Williams writes, "another for him to do so out of a concern for his image of himself as a great Tristan."[393] But there is an important distinction to be made here between moral vanity and moral pride. It seems a deep confusion ethically, and pointless as a psychological matter, to lament moral pride: the feeling of satisfaction that comes from receiving approbation from others for virtuous behavior; the feeling of inner harmony we get when we act according to our identity-conferring moral commitments; and even the feelings of excitement and thrill that may come from immersing oneself in a righteous collective (Holocaust rescuer Hetty Voûte recalls her youthful work as part of the Nazi resistance with an almost joyful nostalgia[394]).

Moral vanity, or what Williams calls "moral self-indulgence," is a different matter. We are morally vain when our moral pride is no longer the consequence of our actions but the goal of them. Moral vanity is temporally prior. It implies, Williams writes, that a person has "substituted for a thought about what is needed, a thought which focuses disproportionately upon the expression of his own disposition, and that he derives pleasure from the thought that his disposition will have been expressed—rather than deriving pleasure, as the agent who is not self-indulgent may, from the thought of how things would be if he acts in a certain way, that way being (though he need not think this) the expression of his disposition."[395] This kind of moral vanity, writes Williams, is "a reversal at a line which I take to be fundamental to any morality or indeed sane life at all, between self-concern and other-concern."[396]

The central problem for Williams is the relative dominance of reflexivity in moral deliberation. "It is not the basic characteristic of a generous man's deliberations," Williams argues, "that they use the premiss 'I am a generous man.'"[397] And it is no defense to redescribe such self-regard (that is, taking the expression of one's own disposition as a motive for acting) as a matter of "integrity." Integrity is not, properly, a motive. It is not a virtue, and it is not something we defend, pursue, or display. Rather, Williams argues, when a person is said to "display integrity," it means that he is acting "from those dispositions and motives which are most deeply his, and has also the virtues that enable him to do that. Integrity does not enable him to do it, nor is it what he acts from when he does so."[398] A person with integrity "genuinely cares for something and has the characteristics necessary to live in the spirit of that."[399] A person who seeks integrity, by contrast, cares primarily for himself.

It is troubling to imagine the ostensibly generous man smiling to himself as he demonstrates his graciousness, to imagine Tristan secretly delighting in his self-image. But is their interior pleasure the only problem? Would it help to reimagine Williams's cases without such suspicious satisfaction? I don't think so. Let's imagine a more serious Kantian moral agent—let's call him Smith. Smith does not smile to himself. Smith draws bright lines around the problem of pleasing self-regard. He believes actions are morally worthy only when they are performed from the motive of duty. For Smith, people who perform moral actions out of self-interest (shopkeepers who are honest because it is good for business) or self-satisfying sympathy (people who "find an inner pleasure in spreading joy around them"[400]) are not performing actions of moral worth.[401] Smith totally excludes self-regard; only respect for the moral law suffices. Is Smith our ultimate answer to the queasy pleasure of benevolent behavior?

Perhaps—but many would say the price we pay for this solution is too high. When we see Smith acting from the motive of duty in Kant's strict way, we witness, finally, moral action untainted by pleasure.[402] But at the same time, we witness something just as alienating and repugnant as pleasure. Michael Stocker explains:

Suppose you are in the hospital, recovering from a long illness. You are very bored and restless and at loose ends when Smith comes in once again. You are now convinced more than ever that he is a fine fellow and a real friend—taking so much time to cheer you up, traveling all the way across town, and so on. You are so effusive with your praise and thanks that he protests that he always tries to do what he thinks is his duty, what he thinks will be best. You at first think he is engaging in a polite form of self-deprecation, relieving the moral burden. But the more you two speak, the more clear it becomes that he was telling the literal truth: that it is not essentially because of you that he came to see you, not because you are friends, but because he thought it was his duty, perhaps as a fellow Christian or Communist or whatever, or simply because he knows of no one more in need of cheering up and no one easier to cheer up.[403]

Surely none of us would like to be treated that way by a friend. If the problem for Williams was the self-reflexivity of moral deliberation, the problem for Stocker is the abstraction of the other in moral deliberation. What's wrong, in other words, isn't that Smith is taking pleasure in seeing himself as a moral person. It's that he is acting from the motive of moral duty, that he's *doing the right thing* instead of *visiting you*.

Together, Williams and Stocker reveal what is at stake in our intuition that there is something unworthy in the behavior of Kate Nash's morally callow, rally-going students. They are inauthentic—inauthentic in their relationship with those they are helping (the world's poor are duties rather than persons) and inauthentic in their relationship to themselves (they seek rather than have integrity).

But is it, in the end, really so bad to want to admire oneself as an altruist? Or to elicit in others the desire to admire themselves as altruists? Or to help others not because of who they are in particular but because one wishes to be helping somebody? Mightn't we argue in all these cases that what we are witnessing here is a version of James Waller's "escalating commitments," but pushing now toward care rather than injury? First, get them to wear bracelets and go to concerts; then, to give money; then, to collect signatures for petitions; then, to make ethical career choices; eventually, to become the kind of person who would disobey illegal orders, or take risks to rescue another. It would be a tragedy if our discomfort with morality-as-a-means became integrity fetishism, if it began interfering with our ability to endorse and amplify the psychological countertechniques to genocide. How important, in the end, is the difference between the appearing-altruist and the altruist, especially when "appearing" in this context means something more like "to come forth" than its etymologically later variant "to seem"?

So, to return to Hutcheson, Shaftesbury, and Jefferson: Is it true that we are drawn to stories of suffering because of our natural benevolence? Over the centuries, many theories have been offered to explain the seemingly paradoxical drive in humans to expose themselves to representations of violence, disease, or injury visited upon other humans. In his *Poetics,* Aristotle notes that "we take pleasure in contemplating the most precisely made images of things which in themselves we see with pain" because learning provides enjoyment.[404] David Hume argues that "sentiments of beauty" in art transform the passions of fear and pity into delightful movements of the soul.[405] In *Beyond the Pleasure Principle,* Freud explains the human impulse to repetitively return to moments of suffering by arguing that we acquire a feeling of control over traumatic events when we replay them in controlled frameworks. And literary critic Norman Holland uses psychoanalytic models of sexual desire, aggression, and fear to argue that readers derive through stories the gratification of managing repressed fantasies.[406]

It could also be argued that we are drawn to stories that provoke revulsion because it gives us pleasure to think of ourselves as the type of people who experience revulsion when witnessing violence.[407] Or that we are experiencing the complex pleasure of using the suffering of others as an emotional contrast object—the blissful relief that comes when, after interiorizing the pain of the other, we let go and return to our selves (the pleasure, in other words, of exhalation), combined with the satisfaction that comes from knowing not only that others have suffered like us, but that they have suffered *more* (achieving status-quo euphoria through downward social comparison).

Edmund Burke explains how "pain can be a cause of delight" through analogy. Just as regular physical excitation through labor is necessary for the pleasurably healthy functioning of our bodies, mental excitation through terror can be a mechanism for the healthy operation of our mental capacities.[408] Psychologist Marvin Zuckerman summarizes contemporary biosocial theories of sensation-seeking that argue that pleasure is produced by an optimal level of cognitive stimulation, and that repressed behaviors or danger encountered within protective frames are particularly stimulating as novelty.[409] Others argue for the intrinsically positive valence of "arousal jag" (that is, negative stimulation followed by relief).[410] Evolutionary accounts of social behavior point to the survival advantages enjoyed by creatures drawn to "gratifying and thrilling literary entertainment": works that elicit strong emotion help "humans refine their skills for obtaining and disseminating information about emotions and thus become better adapted to the mind-reading, mind-revealing, and mind-concealing requirements of their lives."[411]

Discussing the banality of being, Ralph Waldo Emerson writes: "There are moods in which we court suffering, in the hope that here, at least, we shall find reality, sharp peaks and edges of truth." Emerson is intellectually adjacent here to a broadly developed Romantic view, espoused in different ways by critics and philosophers ranging from Max Weber and Georges Bataille to Leslie Fiedler, which asserts that in secularizing societies characterized by disenchantment—and in modernizing societies increasingly dominated by wage-labor and, consequently, microregulation of body, behavior, and space—the encounter with evil and bodily violation substitutes for a lost spiritual clarity and transcendence, and the transgressions of crime and horror represent a form of liberation and an attractive Faustian heroism.[412] By contrast, it could be argued that depictions of terror captivate precisely because they present an anxiety-inducing challenge to ethical and social order only to ritualistically and satisfyingly banish it.[413]

Playing the historian's trump card, Karen Halttunen answers this question of anomalous attraction by inverting it. Why *wouldn't* we enjoy representations of suffering? She argues that the idea of an instinctive or natural revulsion from pain is a "distinctively modern" invention, a product of the eighteenth-century cult of sensibility.[414] (Sadistic pornography as a popular cultural form is also, therefore, a modern invention, she argues; the consequence of making pain a taboo was a dramatic increase in pain's role in pornography.)[415] Humans are and have always been, quite naturally, fascinated by pain. Only in the modern world are we trained to believe we are not attracted to the things we are attracted to.

If we defamiliarize the process and shift the perspective slightly, the leisure act of reading about the suffering of others looks like a deliberate exercise in schadenfreude rather than empathy. The reader picks up a novel knowing that the characters within will suffer pain, heartbreak, and exile; the reader savors it. And much the same could be said of the novelist. She creates characters of such complex imaginative layering that they feel real. She lives with them over time, invests them with deep personhood, often only to devise ingenious torments for them, often only to kill them. Even in the absence of gratuitous narrative affliction, writing needs heartlessness. The act of focus, for instance—creating secondary characters as ornaments to the principals who matter—is a kind of ruthlessness. Some people matter; others do not.

When we read fictions of suffering, we are, in part, feeding our need to see others suffer, whether in the mild form of downward social comparison, or the extreme form of reckless delight in destruction. This speculation isn't unlike arguments long made of comedy. We laugh as an expression of our superiority; we laugh as a way of simultaneously experiencing and denying our exhilaration over a moment's liberated cruelty.[416] *Don't worry, there is nothing serious in this, we can enjoy it.* If it isn't so hard for us to see that laughter can be pitiless, why not tears? Can't tears also serve as a distancing or defensive mechanism that reinforces the privilege and isolation of the subject?

But such cynicism is hard to accept. There is a deep satisfaction, a sorrowful joy, that comes from the experience of solidarity in suffering, from sharing one's grief and feeling the weight of another's. Sometimes I think it is a basic human need: for connectedness, for something beyond the existentially impoverished quality of most human interactions. To have that feeling *discredited*—that is difficult. And this is precisely why sympathy and empathy have long been sites of intense interrogation in literary studies—because they are fundamental to our capacity to live in community and with dignity, fundamental to the changes we seek in the world and to the meaning such striving gives our lives. They are attractive targets for scholars who seek to be heard because their centrality to being means we are, each time, freshly jolted by their deconstruction.

On a certain level, however, whether or not the distrustful account of sympathetic reading I've just offered is plausible doesn't matter. Human motivation in a deep sense is not only unknowable but also, quite possibly, unimportant. What matters is what these stories do. Do they make a difference? Do they promote helping behaviors? Most people working in human rights think they do. And so we tell the stories over and over.

But perhaps they don't make a difference. Scarry warns of the danger of relying upon "generous imaginings" for promoting social change. *Uncle Tom's Cabin* and *A Passage to India* are rare and perhaps misleading examples of the power of cosmopolitan imagining. "The human capacity to injure other people is very great," she writes, "precisely because our capacity to imagine other people is very small."[417] And anyway, perhaps empathy isn't so much like a muscle that can be trained as capital that can be overspent. We spend our empathy on war photographs, or on fictional people, caring anxiously for them and leaving nothing for those whose lives we can actually touch. Elsewhere Scarry warns: "There is always the danger that a fictional character's suffering (whether physical or psychological) will divert our attention away from the living sister or uncle who can be helped by our compassion in a way that the fictional character cannot be; there is also the danger that because artists so successfully express suffering, they may themselves collectively come to be thought of as the most authentic class of sufferers, and thus may inadvertently appropriate concern away from others in radical need of assistance."[418]

Perhaps, after a good fictional cry, we are burnt out emotionally and avoid empathy in the real world. Perhaps such weeping allows us to feel that we have already given enough of ourselves. Perhaps we have already sufficiently affirmed our self-concept, our sense of our own goodness, through our fictional distress, and so feel no need to do more to achieve personal equilibrium. What need for meaningful action when we have already done the job of caring? Rousseau expressed all these concerns in 1758:

> In giving our tears to these fictions, we have satisfied all the rights of humanity without having to give anything more of ourselves; whereas unfortunate people in person would require attention from us, relief, consolation, and work, which would involve us in their pains and would require at least the sacrifice of our indolence, from all of which we are quite content to be exempt. It could be said that our heart closes itself for fear of being touched at our expense. In the final accounting, when a man has gone to admire fine actions in stories and to cry for imaginary miseries, what more can be asked of him? Is he not satisfied with himself? Does he not applaud his fine soul? Has he not acquitted himself of all that he owes to virtue by the homage which has just rendered it? What more could one want of him? That he practice it himself? He has no role to play; he is no actor.[419]

Sentimental politics, Lauren Berlant writes, substitutes "changes in feeling" for "substantial social change."[420] This argument has been made especially sharply in examinations of U.S. racism. Jodi Melamed, for instance, asserts that multicultural, sympathy-based literary studies in U.S. colleges and universities socializes white students to perceive themselves as antiracist "by virtue of their antiracist feeling," even as they serve and benefit from the "new apartheid between haves and have-nots."[421] As Philip Fisher argues in his discussion of *Uncle Tom's Cabin*, the sentimental novel invokes "tears rather than revolt."[422] In the empathetic reading experience such works provide, he asserts, "the feeling of suffering becomes more important than actions against suffering."[423]

And perhaps it is not even the feeling of suffering we are having when we become emotionally caught up in such stories. Perhaps it is not even feeling, in the deep, internal way we think of "feeling." Perhaps it is something more on the surface, more exterior. In *The Claim of Reason*, Stanley Cavell distinguishes between the capacity for imagination and for imaginativeness. Imagination makes connections, sees relation; imaginativeness merely produces vivid imagery. Dickens, he explains, excelled in both capacities, but he also knew that even though he could get the "Pecksniffs and Murdles of the world to cry over the pictures he presented of poverty and the deaths of children," he couldn't make them see their personal connections to the suffering.[424]

Slavoj Žižek presses the argument to an extreme, theorizing something like an exteriorization of the self:

> This is how we should grasp the fundamental Lacanian proposition that psychoanalysis is not a psychology: the most intimate beliefs, even the most intimate emotions such as compassion, crying, sorrow, laughter, can be transferred, delegated to others without losing their sincerity. In his Seminar on *The Ethic of Psychoanalysis*, Lacan speaks of the role of the Chorus in classical tragedy: we, the spectators, came to the theatre worried, full of everyday problems, unable to adjust without reserve to the problems of the play, that is to feel the required fears and compassions—but no problem, there is the Chorus, who feels the sorrow and compassion instead of us—or, more precisely, we feel the required emotions through the medium of the Chorus: "You are then relieved of all worries, even if you do not feel anything, the Chorus will do so in your place."[425]

Using canned laughter as a model for all externally experienced feelings, Žižek concludes that we can do our "duty of compassion" and "accomplish our duty of mourning" without ever needing to do more than gaze drowsily and stupidly at a television screen.[426]

After all, what do these awful stories actually make us do? Here's Rousseau again:

> I hear it said that tragedy leads to pity through fear. So it does; but what is this pity? A fleeting and vain emotion which lasts no longer than the illusion which produced it; a vestige of natural sentiment soon stifled by the passions; a sterile pity which feeds on a few tears and which has never produced the slightest act of humanity. Thus, the sanguinary Sulla cried at the account of evils he had not himself committed. Thus, the tyrant of Phera hid himself at the theatre for fear of being seen groaning with Andromache and Priam, while he heard without emotions the cries of so many unfortunate victims slain daily by his orders.[427]

And even if pity generated by tragedy could truly affect us, could make us decide to take an action in the real world, the repertoire of actions available to us generally matter no more than pantomimes. Woolf writes: "To scribble a name on a sheet of paper is easy; to attend a meeting where pacific opinions are more or less rhetorically reiterated to people who already believe in them is also easy; and to write a cheque in support of those vaguely acceptable opinions, though not so easy, is a cheap way of quieting what may conveniently be called one's conscience."[428]

Some would argue that Rousseau and Woolf are wrong here—or rather, they're right about what they're measuring, but they're measuring the wrong kind of thing. As isolated acts frozen in time, none of the above (tears at the theater, petitions, rallies, checks) make much difference. But such acts are neither isolated nor temporally frozen. Each is part of a collective of similar actions that together make a difference. Each is also a point along an arc of time that might very well be tracking a path of moral evolution and escalating commitments.

Rousseau and Woolf might reply: Perhaps. But the problem isn't just that pity-inspired acts tend to be individually trifling. It's also that as parts of collectives of similar actions over arcs of time they are potentially pernicious. They are the product of narratives, and the worries about pity-inspiring victimization narratives—especially sensational narratives, and especially sensational narratives about racial others—are many. Over time they may solidify the notion of the victims as a separate category of persons; victims can feel pressured to adapt their stories and even self-conceptions to fit global narrative expectations; victimhood-as-identity undermines efforts by those in need to assert agency and even rights; image saturation can make it difficult to see victims as persons rather than patterns; and focus on extreme violence to the body distracts us from less theatrical forms of structural violence (harm through institutional denial of basic needs), thus thinning out efforts to imagine broader programs of social and economic justice.

These are major challenges for the contemporary human rights movement. A philosophical system built upon our mutual capacity to suffer pain is separated only by a thin line from a philosophical system that understands survivors exclusively through their experience of pain.

———

Commenting on an early draft of the previous section, a friend scribbled a note in the margins to me: "You were in a dark place when you wrote this, Jim!" Is such pessimism about sentimental human rights narration far-fetched, the product of mistaken ways of thinking?

For scholars of human rights and witnessing who seek positive theoretical models for the work they are doing, models that are as intellectually persuasive and emotionally compelling as the depressing criticisms just tracked, the work of Emmanuel Lévinas has been something of an existential answer. Lévinas's writing, his "ethics of alterity," is increasingly influential in literary and cultural studies today. At the heart of his philosophy is the metaphor of a face-to-face encounter with another person. The face of the other, Lévinas writes, makes ethical claims upon us, claims that do not simply elicit responses from us but instead *constitute* us. We come into being as particular persons in relation to others who, in the immediate face-to-face relationship, strike us both as infinitely foreign and irresistibly intimate—foreign because the other can never be assimilated or reduced to sameness; intimate because identity is, finally, intersubjective. In a sense, there is no self before and apart from its response to the other. "To respond to the face, to understand its meaning," Judith Butler explains, "means to be awake to what is precarious in another life or, rather, the precariousness of life itself." But this kind of understanding cannot be "an extrapolation from an understanding of my own precariousness to an understanding of another's precarious life." The face of the other, she writes, "calls me out of narcissism towards something finally more important."[429]

Kelly Oliver explains that such Lévinasian articulations of subjectivity and identity are an emerging corrective to what she believes is the still-dominant neo-Hegelian tendency to conceptualize relationships as struggles for recognition. "Rather than seeing others with the objectifying gaze of a self-sufficient subject examining, subordinating, or struggling with the other, we can see others with loving eyes that invite loving response." But, she asks: "What is love beyond domination? What is love beyond recognition?"[430] Lévinas writes: "Communication would be impossible if it should have to begin in the ego, a free subject, to whom every other would be only a limitation that invited war, domination, precaution and information. To communicate is indeed to open one-self, but the openness is not complete if it is on the watch for recognition. It is complete not in the opening to the spectacle of or the recognition of the other, but in becoming a responsibility for him."[431]

Lévinas is unique in the way he helps us to think theoretically about compassion and our ability to be present to one another, whether as listeners or as readers.[432] Another approach for those interested in "ethical criticism" can be found in the archives of 1990s literary and cultural studies—a moment sometimes referred to as the "ethical turn." Robert Eaglestone, in a rather sweeping but nonetheless useful and insightful way, summarizes ethical criticism then and now as comprising two camps: those, such as Nussbaum, who see literary texts as forms of clarifying "moral reasoning" that reflect and inform our lives and cultivate our ethical responsibilities; and those influenced by deconstruction, such as J. Hillis Miller, who argue that literature offers nothing like clear moral reasoning but rather an experience of "undecidability" that is ethical precisely insofar as it interrupts our relationship with confident ethical knowledge.[433]

Dorothy Hale is one example among many scholars who are currently working to integrate such theoretical work into the language and rhetoric of human rights. She takes the arguments in the preceding section about the cruelty of character-driven literature and turns them on their heads. Yes, she concedes, in fundamental ways the experience of a novel is the experience of violation. This is because we encounter characters in novels in much the same way we encounter other minds. They are so real to us that, on some level, we feel they have "autonomy," they "have a right to human rights." But instead they are trapped: by the author, by the plot, by our perceptions as readers, by aesthetic form itself. She writes:

"The all-too-visible incarceration of subjectivity by aesthetic form is decried as an abuse of representational power. The author who must more or less use a character for his or her expressive ends is felt to be exploitative. The reader who identifies with a character worries about emotional colonization. And the reader and author who feel only the aesthetic thrill of the character's fate carry the guilt of the voyeur."

This guilty pleasure, however, is precisely the starting point of a literary ethics. In novels, the argument goes, we encounter characters as simultaneously free persons and constrained aesthetic artifacts. They exceed our ways of knowing, and because this unsettles us, we seek to reduce them to limited things that we can understand. In this way, literature holds up a mirror to our own being in the world, allowing us to see—or rather, to experience—the way all of our human possibility "is produced in and through the operation of social constraint."[434] The encounter with the literary other is ethical knowledge because it helps us see ourselves as the other, to see how we, too, come into being through mutual vulnerability and constraint, to feel rather than simply know the debts we owe to one another. It is ethical knowledge because of what it starts, because it surprises and often confounds us, unsettles the certainties that we cling to and that limit us, opens us to difference and, ultimately, to the demands of what remains beyond us.

Sometimes I think that all the paradoxes of representation described in this book, all the ways it is impossible to get it right for others, are starting points in just this way.

———

The previous section brought me to the end of what I have to say about storytelling and ethics, the end of the long walkway I mentioned earlier. Now I want to say a word about the direction of scholarly writing today.

Mostly, scholars are comfortable not mattering. In fact, many would defend not mattering as a precious cultural resource. There should be, they argue, some space for the free play of creative thought, for meditations on the meaning of our world that are not restricted to the short-term concerns of our historical moment or crippled by instrumental thinking. *Studying poetry at a public university is all well and good, but how many jobs will it create for our state economy?* Defending irrelevance in the face of such attitudes echoes the call of the spiritual. Poetry, literary critic Paul Fry writes, is "the release from significance," "the disclosure of freedom through the underdetermination of meaning." Poetry, and the criticism that amplifies our experience of poetry, satisfies our deep need to experience *being* rather than *doing*. So when Fry urges fellow scholars away from historically engaged criticism toward conceptions of the aesthetic that suspend "our purposeful engagement with the world," he is calling for a disengagement which is, finally, ethical.[435]

This sort of argument comes in many forms. Making a case for the primacy of our physiological responses to aesthetic phenomenon, literary theorist Hans Ulrich Gumbrecht calls for us to rediscover in our research and teaching the "moments of intensity" that art brings, moments valuable precisely because "there is nothing edifying in [them], no message, nothing that we could really learn from them."[436] As Adorno writes, those who fret over "relevance" are simply unable "to listen patiently to a text whose language challenges signification and by its very distance from meaning revolts in advance against positivist subordination of meaning."[437] Relevance, in other words, manifests itself in many ways. What many call irrelevance is often the horizon of understanding.

Even among those scholars who see value in resisting relevance, however, a great many have found themselves since 2001 yearning for engagement. They seek a way to reconcile their scholastic pursuits and their moral identities, to relieve the felt pressure of internal contradiction.

The year 2001 is often identified as a moment of radical, sweeping change for world politics and U.S. culture. I generally find such characterizations unpersuasive. However, there are some claims about shifts in U.S. ethical self-conception since 2001 that seem to me undeniable and fundamental. As many have noted, even the vocabulary of the country has changed, bringing into common use unfamiliar words and phrases (ghost prisoner, black site, stress position, waterboarding) and bringing unfamiliar meanings to old words (preemption, rendition). There is, of course, no such thing as a pretorture U.S. past. Still, it is almost impossible to exaggerate the significance of the United States' *official* and *public* articulation of torture policy. Even in the Civil War, when the territorial integrity of the United States was in jeopardy, the U.S. government and military officially repudiated torture. In 1863, General Orders No. 100, better known as the "Lieber Code," affirmed the more than 300-year ban on torture in Anglo-American jurisprudence, declaring: "Military necessity does not admit of cruelty—that is, the infliction of suffering for the sake of suffering or for revenge, nor of maiming or wounding except in fight, nor of torture to extort confessions."[438]

Post-rendition, post-preemption, scholars across the humanities in the United States have begun asking, with an intensity not seen since the Vietnam War, "What is the point of what I'm doing? How does the knowledge I'm creating or disseminating relate to what's happening in the real world?" Many have come to believe that at this particular moment, the most pressing questions they must take up involve the United States' relationship to the contemporary human rights movement.

In my own discipline, literary and cultural studies, we have seen the burgeoning of a new subfield. A recent clustering of scholarly works focusing on literature and human rights includes Joseph Slaughter's *Human Rights, Inc.*; Elizabeth Anker's *Fictions of Dignity: Embodying Human Rights in World Literature;* Wendy Hesford's *Spectacular Rhetorics: Human Rights Visions, Recognitions, Feminisms;* Domna Stanton's special issue of *PMLA* on human rights; Kay Shaffer and Sidonie Smith's *Human Rights and Narrated Lives;* Thomas Keenan's work on media and human rights; Sophia McClennen's work to "bridge the disconnect between the humanities and human rights activism"[439]; my own *That the World May Know;* Elizabeth Swanson Goldberg's *Beyond Terror: Gender, Narrative, Human Rights;* and a subfield-defining monograph from Goldberg and Alexandra Schultheis Moore, *Theoretical Perspectives on Human Rights and Literature.* This is to say nothing of the many dissertations and forthcoming book manuscripts I've read by young literary scholars working in human rights, or the increasingly wide use in literary studies of rights-oriented works from related disciplines (including Lynn Hunt's *Inventing Human Rights,* Elaine Scarry's *The Body in Pain,* and Giorgio Agamben's *State of Exception*), or the conferences and faculty seminars in the past several years on human rights in the humanities (in London, New York, Beirut, Vancouver, Chicago, the Twin Cities, New Orleans, Providence, the National Humanities Center, and elsewhere), or the accelerated creation of human rights minors in liberal arts programs around the country, including my own Macalester College.

These academic trends represent change of a different kind from that of the Vietnam War era, the last time U.S. scholars felt the pressure of history so intensely. For young scholars then, the

aestheticism of the New Criticism seemed increasingly discon-
nected from the values and aspirations of the time. Catherine Gallagher and Stephen Greenblatt's characterization of the mid-1970s
discovery of anthropological criticism reveals how irrelevant for-
malist training had made them feel: "[Clifford Geertz's work re-
turned] our own professional skills to us as more important,
more vital and illuminating, than we had ourselves grasped." It
helped to "renew in us a sense of their value."[440] The new literary
historians were those who desired connection to "the lives real
men and women actually live," to "the everyday, the place where
things are actually done." Or, as Gallagher and Greenblatt write
with characteristic grace: "We wanted the touch of the real in
the way that in an earlier period people wanted the touch of the
transcendent."[441]

Scholars today are developing a new kind of affect toward the
real. Their projects might best be understood as therapeutic rather
than anthropologic. They seek less to touch the real than to recover from it. But if we are indeed experiencing a new therapeutic
turn, it is a strangely impersonal one, one deeply uncomfortable
with the place of the self. Global war puts scholars under obligations. First, to better understand our roles as public moral actors,
even as this project of self-understanding seems narcissistically inappropriate to the scale of the time. And second, to better understand the harm to others that we are implicated in, even as this
undertaking is experienced as voyeuristic, a pornography of abjection. Or, worse, even as it is experienced as a "gift" of generous
attention—not unlike the "gift" of humanitarianism itself, which
is certainly an act of care but also an act of power, a performance of
privilege that reinscribes hierarchy. "Though we laud charity as a
Christian virtue," Mary Douglas writes, "we know how much it
wounds."[442]

The critical study of human rights is the expression or, rather, the working out of such ethical impasses. In other words, human rights work allows therapeutic displacement. It allows one to experience self-preoccupation as an aspect of a purportedly universalizing institutional structure. It also allows one to perform one's private anxieties and needs as an aspect of orientation to the other. More generously, one might say that human rights work offers a secular substitute to the experience of redemption; namely, to be personally met by that which impersonally exceeds the self. Less generously, one might say that these splits between interior desire and public function are symptoms of, or parallels to, the perfidious contradictions of human rights in international politics. For instance, nations pursue essentially "private" interests through the rhetorical and institutional frame of the "public" good of human rights. Human rights are therefore an effective tool for mobilizing populations to disregard human rights, most notably in so-called "wars of liberation." Or, the human rights regime functions to absorb the externalities of, and therefore to act in concert with, the systems it acts against. As the argument goes, human rights work mitigates and therefore sustains the injustices of global neoliberalism just as it mitigates and therefore sustains the injustices of particular detention systems. The various births of human rights are understood less as emancipations from any given order than as refinements of them.

From Arendt to Žižek, scholars have argued that the idea of universal human rights has always depended upon and even produced a series of cruel and devastating exclusions. When we imagine the "man" in the "rights of man" or (today) the "human" in "human rights," we are always imagining a particular kind of human, a normal. Depending on the historical epoch, our definitions have excluded slaves, or women, or the stateless. It has therefore been argued that a universal rights regime is a regulatory regime not unlike—or rather shares the same epistemological grounds as—a globally ambitious, militarized state sovereignty. That is, the idea of rights is tied into the state's threatening capacity to define the very nature of the human.[443]

At the same time, however, it is conceded that human rights remain something we *cannot not want* (to borrow a phrase from Gayatri Chakravorty Spivak), and that even the most cynical invocations of rights open space for reappropriation and possibilities of genuine emancipation. As one scholar explains: "The projection of the normative egalitarian imaginary not only sets the terms and limits of universality's constituency, it makes possible nonhegemonic rearticulations of universality's compass."[444] In other words, when a system publicly prescribes what it means to be normal, it is constraining you but also, paradoxically, making it possible for you to creatively imagine more inclusive possibilities. It prompts liberation both because it has put before you a disguised command that can be undisguised, or a set of assumptions that can be deconstructed, and because even hypocritical or merely gestural uses of egalitarian rhetoric help to publicly legitimize egalitarian principles.

The ambivalence of U.S. scholars toward human rights is a mirror image of the U.S. government's ambivalence. For the former, human rights discourse is suspect because it is viewed as an extension of U.S. hegemony; for the latter, because it is viewed as an infringement upon it. The United States helped give birth to the United Nations and, through the sponsorship of Eleanor Roosevelt, the Universal Declaration of Human Rights. But it has also refused to ratify a range of crucial human rights treaties, including the Convention on Economic, Social, and Cultural Rights, the Convention on Discrimination against Women, and the Convention on the Rights of the Child. The vision of a fully realized international human rights movement is both the latest incarnation of American utopian promise and its dystopic nightmare.

———

I have one last story to share.

The first soldier I met in Japan was Kubotera-san. Even now, so many years later, my memory of that visit is very clear. As the interviews accumulated over time, details began to wash away: what each person's house was like, what they were wearing, who else was there. I can only reconstruct it now by looking back at my notes. But I still see Kubotera-san kneeling on a pillow in the center of that meticulously cleaned, elegantly simple, wood-plank room, frail hands folded on his thighs, head slightly bowed, spine effortlessly erect.

In some ways, it is not the content of the interview that remains most vivid. He described himself as somebody who killed children, and I had to ask him about that, and I had never done that before. But listening to somebody talk about how they killed a child is an unsettling experience in part because it doesn't feel unsettling enough. (It would take many months before I was able to have coherent emotions about that, and even then it manifested itself in curious ways.)

When we sat down together, he gave us small portions of peanuts to eat. He had harvested them, shelled and dried them, and roasted them for us. Later I learned that he had redone his paper walls in anticipation of our visit. We chatted awkwardly for a bit at first, looking for harmless topics. I learned that he was the oldest of eleven children raised on a farm, that he had no memories of studying or playing, because when he wasn't working in the field he needed to take care of his siblings. Our conversation was laced with his apologies: "We're country folk. We don't know much about things in the city. And we're old, besides, so all we can do is give you a country-style reception"; "And, well, my brain is a little old, and I tend to get Showa dates and AD dates mixed up." The way he held himself—Kubotera-san seemed resigned to being *less*. And he seemed, also, like he was prepared to receive something, something that, if tracked to its source, might have shadowed hope. It felt so wrong that I was the person talking to him—a literature professor from a small college in the Midwest, for God's sake. But we talked, for a long time.

It was our longest single interview session, in fact. We didn't understand, because it was the first one, what that would do to a person like him. We had so many questions we wanted to ask. We just kept asking. I shifted continually on the floor, aches gathering in my knees and shoulders. He remained so still, I didn't even realize he was in pain until he needed help rising at the end. It was hot, so he drank then, thirstily. There was something about that act—that simple release into his own need—that struck me. I realized later what it was. The small acts of self-care that we incessantly perform, that we don't even think of as self-care—adjusting our balance for comfort, fidgeting to release tension, scratching ourselves or rubbing our faces for relief or stimulation—he had done none of that.

The rain threatened that day, so I had brought my umbrella. After a lengthy goodbye, I realized I forgot it and darted back into the entryway to grab it. I forgot to take off my shoes. My interpreter threw herself onto her knees to brush her hands over where I had walked, apologizing.

Notes

Acknowledgments

Index

NOTES

Epigraphs

Page ix: Zbigniew Herbert, comment on "Why the Classics," in *The Poetry of Survival: Post-War Poets of Central and Eastern Europe,* ed. Daniel Weissbort (New York: St. Martin's Press, 1991), p. 334.

Page 71: Hetty Voûte, *The Heart Has Reasons: Holocaust Rescuers and Their Stories of Courage,* ed. Mark Klempner (Cleveland: Pilgrim Press, 2006), p. 24.

Page 71: Samuel Taylor Coleridge, "Fears in Solitude," in *The Poems of Samuel Taylor Coleridge,* ed. Ernest Hartley Coleridge (Oxford: Oxford University Press, 1924), p. 259.

Page 102: Nora Okja Keller, *Comfort Woman* (New York: Penguin, 1997), p. 62.

Page 115: Adam Smith, *The Theory of Moral Sentiments* (Indianapolis: Liberty Classics, 1976), p. 47.

1   Lincoln Li, *The Japanese Army in North China: 1937–1941* (Oxford: Oxford University Press, 1975), p. 21.

2   Michael Weiner, *Race and Migration in Imperial Japan* (London: Routledge, 1994), p. 30.

3   Brian Daizen Victoria, *Zen at War* (New York: Rowman & Littlefield, 2006), p. 91.

4   David Sanger, "Japanese Aide Apologizes for Calling Nanjing Massacre a Fabrication," *New York Times,* May 7, 1994.

5   "No Comfort" (editorial), *New York Times,* March 6, 2007.

6   Christopher Barnard, *Language, Ideology, and Japanese History Textbooks* (New York: RoutledgeCurzon, 2003), p. 17.

7   Higashinakano Shudo, *The Nanking Massacre: Fact versus Fiction, A Historian's Quest for the Truth,* trans. Sekai Shuppan (Tokyo: Sekai Shuppan, 2005), p. i.

8   Carolyn Dean comprehensively analyzes how pornography, as a concept applied to the representation of suffering, shapes contemporary understandings of the limits of compassion. See "Empathy, Pornography, and Suffering," *differences: A Journal of Feminist Cultural Studies* 14, no. 1 (2003): 88–124. See also Stéphane Audoin-Rouzeau, "Extreme

Violence in Combat and Wilful Blindness," *International Social Science Journal* 54 (December 2002): 491–497.

9   William Pfaff, "An Active French Role in the 1994 Genocide in Rwanda," *International Herald Tribune*, January 17, 1998, Opinion, p. 6.

10   Emmanuel Dongala, *Johnny Mad Dog* (New York: Picador, 2006), p. 147.

11   Susan Sontag, *Regarding the Pain of Others* (New York: Farrar, Straus and Giroux, 2003), p. 95.

12   Thomas Keenan, "Mobilizing Shame," *South Atlantic Quarterly* 103, no. 2/3 (Spring/Summer 2004): 435–449.

13   Cathy Caruth, "Trauma and Experience: Introduction," in *Trauma: Explorations in Memory*, ed. Cathy Caruth (Baltimore: Johns Hopkins University Press, 1995), p. 6.

14   See *The Critical Link 4: Professionalization of Interpreting in the Community*, ed. Cecelia Wadensjö, Birgitta Englund Dimitrova, and Anna-Lena Nilsson (Amsterdam: John Benjamins, 2007).

15   Hannah Arendt, *Eichmann in Jerusalem: A Report on the Banality of Evil* (New York: Penguin, 1994), pp. 288, 49, 287.

16   Stanley Milgram, "Some Conditions of Obedience and Disobedience to Authority," *Human Relations* 18 (February 1965): 67.

17   Ibid., p. 75.

18   Elaine Scarry, *The Body in Pain: The Making and the Unmaking of the World* (New York: Oxford University Press, 1985), p. 4.

19   Eva Hoffman, *After Such Knowledge: Memory, History, and the Legacy of the Holocaust* (New York: PublicAffairs, 2004), p. 7.

20   Ibid., p. 9.

21   Caruth, "Trauma and Experience," p. 5.

22   Cathy Caruth, "Recapturing the Past: Introduction," in Caruth, *Trauma: Explorations in Memory*, pp. 153–154.

23   Patricia Hampl, *I Could Tell You Stories* (New York: Norton, 1999), p. 73.

24   Hoffman, *After Such Knowledge*, p. 15.

25   Claude Lanzmann, "The Obscenity of Understanding: An Evening with Claude Lanzmann," in Caruth, *Trauma: Explorations in Memory*, p. 204.

26   David Eng and David Kazanjian, *Loss: The Politics of Mourning* (Berkeley: University of California Press, 2003), p. 9.

27   Marc Nichanian, "Between Genocide and Catastrophe," in Eng and Kazanjian, *Loss*, p. 133.

28   Ibid., p. 134.

29 Shoshana Felman, *The Juridical Unconscious: Trials and Traumas in the 20th Century* (Cambridge, MA: Harvard University Press, 2002), pp. 144–146. Felman contrasts literary and legal justice this way: "Literature is a dimension of concrete embodiment and a language of infinitude that, in contrast to the language of the law, encapsulates not closure but precisely what in a given legal case refuses to be closed and cannot be closed. It is to this refusal of the trauma to be closed that literature does justice" (8).

30 Allen Feldman, "Memory Theaters, Virtual Witnessing, and the Trauma-Aesthetic," *Biography* 27, no. 1 (Winter 2004): 169, 170, 166.

31 Hoffman, *After Such Knowledge*, p. 175.

32 Ibid., p. 176.

33 Maurice Blanchot, *The Writing of the Disaster,* trans. Ann Smock (Lincoln: University of Nebraska Press, 1995), p. 84.

34 Quoted in Ruth Franklin, *A Thousand Darknesses: Lies and Truths in Holocaust Fiction* (Oxford: Oxford University Press, 2007), p. 4.

35 Dominick LaCapra, *Writing History, Writing Trauma* (Baltimore: Johns Hopkins University Press, 2001), p. 93.

36 Alvin Rosenfeld, quoted in Franklin, *A Thousand Darknesses,* pp. 4, 6.

37 Philip Gourevitch, quoted in James Dawes, *That the World May Know: Bearing Witness to Atrocity* (Cambridge MA: Harvard University Press, 2007), p. 60.

38 Amy Hungerford, *The Holocaust of Texts: Genocide, Literature, and Personification* (Chicago: University of Chicago Press, 2003), p. 117. I have provided a shorthand account of a complex array of arguments about trauma. Please see Cathy Caruth, *Unclaimed Experience: Trauma, Narrative, and History* (Baltimore: Johns Hopkins University Press, 1996); LaCapra, *Writing History, Writing Trauma;* Ruth Leys, *Trauma: A Genealogy* (Chicago: University of Chicago Press, 2000); E. Ann Kaplan, *Trauma Culture: The Politics of Terror and Loss in Media and Literature* (New Brunswick, NJ: Rutgers University Press, 2005). See also Andrew Gross and Michael Hoffman, "Memory, Authority, and Identity: Holocaust Studies in Light of the Wilkomirski Debate"; Allen Feldman, "Memory Theaters, Virtual Witnessing, and the Trauma-Aesthetic"; and Kay Schaffer and Sidonie Smith, "Conjunctions: Life Narratives in the Field of Human Rights"—all in *Biography* 27, no. 1 (Winter 2004): 25–47, 163–202, and 1–24.

39 Charles T. Mathewes, *Evil and the Augustinian Tradition* (Cambridge: Cambridge University Press, 2001), p. 44.

40 See Claudia Card, *The Atrocity Paradigm: A Theory of Evil* (Oxford: Oxford University Press, 2002), p. 49.

41 Jean-Jacques Rousseau, *Politics and the Arts: Letter to M. D'Alembert on the Theater* (Glencoe, IL: Free Press, 1960), p. 23.

42 Arendt, *Eichmann in Jerusalem*, p. 276.

43 Hannah Arendt, *The Life of the Mind* (New York: Harcourt, 1978), p. 180.

44 Norman Podhoretz, quoted in Adam Kirsch, "Beware of Pity," *New Yorker*, January 12, 2009, p. 12. For more on the critical reception of Arendt's argument, see David Cesarani, *Becoming Eichmann: Rethinking the Life, Crimes, and Trial of a "Desk Murderer"* (Cambridge, MA: Da Capo Press, 2007), pp. 343–356. The argument against banality has resurged of late in a series of studies in philosophy and psychology. For a brief literature review, see S. Alexander Haslam and Stephen Reicher, "Beyond the Banality of Evil: Three Dynamics of an Interactionist Social Psychology of Tyranny," *Personality and Social Psychology Bulletin* 33, no. 5 (May 2007): 615–622.

45 Harold Rosenberg, "The Shadow of the Furies," *The New York Review of Books* 23, January 20, 1977, pp. 47–48.

46 Cesarani, *Becoming Eichmann*, p. 350.

47 Bernhard Schlink, *The Reader* (New York: Vintage, 1998), p. 157.

48 I borrow these questions from Donald Donham, who examines unflinchingly the personal queries put to scholars like me working with violence. See "Staring at Suffering: Violence as a Subject," in *States of Violence: Politics, Youth, and Memory in Contemporary Africa*, ed. Edna G. Bay and Donald Donham (Charlottesville: University of Virginia Press, 2006), pp. 16–34.

49 Sheldon Harris, *Factories of Death: Japanese Biological Warfare, 1932–45, and the American Cover-Up* (New York: Routledge, 1994), pp. 54, 59, 55.

50 Ivy Lee, "Probing the Issues of Reconciliation More Than Fifty Years after the Asia-Pacific War," in Peter Li, ed., *Japanese War Crimes: The Search for Justice* (New Brunswick, NJ: Transaction, 2003), pp. 24–25.

51 Harris, *Factories of Death*, pp. 61, 77–78.

52 Lee, "Probing the Issues of Reconciliation," p. 25.

53 Tsuneishi Keiichi, "Unit 731 and the Japanese Army's Biological Warfare Program," in *Japan's Wartime Medical Atrocities: Comparative Inquiries in Science, History, and Ethics*, ed. Jing-Bao Nie, Nanyan Guo, Mark Selden, and Arthur Kleinman (New York: Routledge, 2010), p. 28.

54 Daniel Barenblatt, *A Plague upon Humanity: The Hidden History of Japan's Biological Warfare Program* (New York: HarperPerennial, 2004), p. xii.
55 Ibid., p. 173.
56 Harris, *Factories of Death*, p. 67.
57 Barenblatt, *A Plague upon Humanity*, p. 60.
58 Harris, *Factories of Death*, pp. 49, 51.
59 Ibid., pp. 62, 70, 71, 65; Barenblatt, *A Plague upon Humanity*, pp. 55–56, 81.
60 Jing-Bao Nie, Mark Selden, and Arthur Kleinman, introduction to Nie, Guo, Selden, and Kleinman, *Japan's Wartime Medical Atrocities*, p. 5.
61 Barenblatt, *A Plague upon Humanity*, p. xiii.
62 Harris, *Factories of Death*, p. 44.
63 Barenblatt, *A Plague upon Humanity*, pp. xxiii, 234; Nie, Selden, and Kleinman, introduction to Nie, Guo, Selden, and Kleinman, *Japan's Wartime Medical Atrocities*, p. 5.
64 Harris, *Factories of Death*, p. 42; see also Yuki Tanaka, *Hidden Horrors: Japanese War Crimes in World War II* (Boulder, CO: Westview Press, 1996), p. 162.
65 Nie, Selden, and Kleinman, introduction to Nie, Guo, Selden, and Kleinman, *Japan's Wartime Medical Atrocities*, p. 7.
66 Harris, *Factories of Death*, p. 189.
67 Ibid., p. 207.
68 Ibid., p. 220.
69 Nanyan Guo, "Discovering Traces of Humanity: Taking Individual Responsibility for Medical Atrocities," in Nie, Guo, Selden, and Kleinman, *Japan's Wartime Medical Atrocities*, pp. 108–109.
70 Sigmund Freud, *Civilization and Its Discontents*, trans. Joan Riviere (New York: Jonathan Cape & Harrison Smith, 1930), pp. 85–86. For a fuller and more sophisticated explication of Freud's view of war, see Jean Bethke Elshtain, "Freud's Discourse of War/Politics," in *International/Intertextual Relations: Postmodern Readings of World Politics*, ed. James Der Derian and Michael J. Shapiro (Toronto: Lexington, 1989), pp. 49–68.
71 Barbara Ehrenreich, *Blood Rites: Origins and History of the Passions of War* (New York: Henry Holt, 1997), pp. 94–95.
72 Zygmunt Bauman, *Modernity and the Holocaust* (Ithaca, NY: Cornell University Press, 1990), p. 95.
73 See Daniel Chirot and Clark McCauley, *Why Not Kill Them All: The Logic and Prevention of Mass Political Murder* (Princeton, NJ: Princeton University Press, 2006), p. 142.

74 Ervin Staub, "The Roots of Evil: Social Conditions, Culture, Personality, and Basic Human Needs," *Personality and Social Psychology Review* 3, no. 3 (1999): 182–184.

75 Ben Kiernan, *Blood and Soil: A World History of Genocide and Extermination from Sparta to Darfur* (New Haven, CT: Yale University Press, 2007), p. 50.

76 For a history of the term, see Samantha Power, *"A Problem from Hell":American and the Age of Genocide* (New York: Basic, 2002), pp. 17–45.

77 I borrow the phrase from Staub, "The Roots of Evil," p. 184.

78 James Waller, *Becoming Evil: How Ordinary People Commit Genocide and Mass Killing* (Oxford: Oxford University Press, 2002), pp. 86–87. For studies of "the Nazi personality," see pp. 55–87. One study conducted by the U.S. Secret Service on perpetrators of school shootings found no way to distinguish the killers from the general population; see Elliot Aronson, "Reducing Hostility and Building Compassion: Lessons from the Jigsaw Classroom," in *The Social Psychology of Good and Evil*, ed. Arthur Miller (New York: Guilford Press, 2004), pp. 470–471. Relatedly, see also Roy F. Baumeister and W. Keith Campbell, "The Intrinsic Appeal of Evil: Sadism, Sensational Thrills, and Threatened Egotism," *Personality and Social Psychology Review* 3, no. 3 (1999): 210–221.

79 Christopher Browning, *Ordinary Men: Reserve Police Battalion 101 and the Final Solution in Poland* (New York: HarperPerennial, 1998).

80 Kiernan, *Blood and Soil*, pp. 37–38.

81 Staub, *The Roots of Evil: The Origins of Genocide and Other Group Violence* (Cambridge: Cambridge University Press, 1989), pp. 232–245.

82 Waller, *Becoming Evil*, pp. 153, 176.

83 Browning, *Ordinary Men*, p. 159.

84 Saburo Ienaga, quoted in Ehrenreich, *Blood Rites*, p. 213.

85 See Eriko Aoki, "Korean Children, Textbooks, and Educational Practices in Japanese Primary Schools," in *Koreans in Japan: Critical Voices from the Margin*, ed. Sonia Riang (London: Routledge, 2000), p. 162. See also Emiko Ohnuki-Tierney, *Kamikaze, Cherry Blossoms, and Nationalisms: The Militarization of Aesthetics in Japanese History* (Chicago: University of Chicago Press, 2002), p. 128.

86 Ohnuki-Tierney, *Kamikaze, Cherry Blossoms, and Nationalisms*, pp. 132, 137, 140.

87 Marcus Tullius Cicero, *The Speeches of Cicero: Pro T. Annio Milone*, trans. N. H. Watts (Cambridge, MA: Harvard University Press, 1953), p. 16.

88   International Committee of the Red Cross, *People on War Report: ICRC Worldwide Consultation on the Rules of War* (Geneva: ICRC, October 1999), pp. ix, xv, 13.

89   David Grossman, *On Killing: The Psychological Cost of Learning to Kill in War and Society* (Boston: Little, Brown, 1995), pp. 4, 1–16.

90   Arendt, *Eichmann in Jerusalem*, p. 106.

91   Reinhold Niebuhr, *Moral Man and Immoral Society: A Study in Ethics and Politics* (Louisville, KY: Westminster John Knox Press, 2001), pp. 272, 18.

92   Philip Zimbardo, *The Lucifer Effect: Understanding How Good People Turn Evil* (New York: Random House, 2007), pp. 299–307.

93   There are a range of terms and concepts for thinking about the way people attempt to maintain a unitary sense of identity despite the bewildering array of contradictions in their behavior, personalities, and values. These range from the commonplace to the clinical. Most familiar is the nonclinical use of the word "compartmentalize," which we use to explain our capacity to box up and put aside various negative behaviors, events, or aspects of self so as to experience and manage ourselves more comfortably in different contexts. This term is used to account for a range of behaviors, from the ordinary (thinking of oneself as honest while cheating on one's taxes) to the extreme (a soldier compartmentalizing his emotions so as to be able to function effectively). Compartmentalization is also a psychological term used to describe how we organize our sense of self. That is, do we tend to segregate our positive and negative beliefs about ourselves into different contextualized identities (the "me" here versus the "me" there) or do we integrate the positive and negative across contexts? See Carolyn Showers and Virgil Zeigler-Hill, "Compartmentalization and Integration: the Evaluative Organization of Contextualized Selves," *Journal of Personality* 75, no. 6 (December 2007): 1181–1204. Compartmentalization is also a clinical term related to dissociation. Together these terms refer to a trauma-related continuum of psychological phenomena characterized by a structural division of personality: that is, parts of the personality are "dissociated" or blocked off from one another. The range of disorders and symptoms dissociation encompasses is exceptionally broad. See Onno van der Hart, Ellert Nijenhuis, Kathy Steele, Daniel Brown, "Trauma-Related Dissociation: Conceptual Clarity Lost and Found," *Australian and New Zealand Journal of Psychiatry* 38, no. 11–12 (2004): 906–914; Richard Brown, "Different Types of 'Dissociation' Have Different Psychological Mechanisms,"

Journal of Trauma and Dissociation 7, no. 4 (2006): 7–28; Daphne Simeon, "Depersonalization Disorder: A Contemporary Overview," *CNS Drugs* 18, no. 6 (2004): 343–354. Within literature on PTSD alone, Emily Holmes and colleagues write, "we find the term 'dissociation' has been used as a 'catch-all' to cover the symptoms of depersonalization, derealization, amnesia, emotional numbing and flashbacks, where patients feel as if the trauma is happening again in the here-and-now"; see Emily A. Holmes, Richard J. Brown, Warren Mansell, R. Pasco Fearon, Elaine C. M. Hunter, Frank Frasquilho, and David A. Oakley, "Are There Two Qualitatively Distinct Forms of Dissociation? A Review and Some Clinical Implications," *Clinical Psychology Review* 25 (January 2005): 1–23. Finally, in his study of Nazi doctors at Auschwitz, Robert Jay Lifton developed the notion of "doubling," which postulates an adaptive strategy of creating two connected yet autonomous selves for two incompatible environments: the loving home and the unspeakable Auschwitz; see Lifton, *The Nazi Doctors: Medical Killing and the Psychology of Genocide* (New York: Basic, 1986). In his crisp explanation and critique of Lifton, James Waller raises the important question of how such concerns about the coherence of the self should be revised in light of the "postmodern" view of the self as inherently fragmentary and multiple rather than unified and coherent; see Waller, *Becoming Evil*, pp. 111–123.

94   Arthur Applbaum, *Ethics for Adversaries: The Morality of Roles in Public and Professional Life* (Princeton, NJ: Princeton University Press, 1999), pp. 39, 105, 34. Applbaum, I should emphasize, rejects this defense of lawyering, insisting that, whatever else they are, lawyers are also liars.

95   A British soldier, quoted in Brian Glover, *Humanity: A Moral History of the 20th Century* (New Haven, CT: Yale University Press, 2001), p. 52.

96   Lifton, *The Nazi Doctors*, pp. 435–436. See also Arendt, *Eichmann in Jerusalem*, p. 106.

97   See, for instance, Ben Lieberman, "Nationalist Narratives, Violence between Neighbours and Ethnic Cleansing in Bosnia-Hercegovina: A Case of Cognitive Dissonance?" *Journal of Genocide Research* 8, no. 3 (September 2006): 300–301.

98   Tim O'Brien, "How to Tell a True War Story," in *The Things They Carried* (Boston: Houghton Mifflin, 1990), p. 88.

99   Richard J. Bernstein, *Hannah Arendt and the Jewish Question* (Cambridge, MA: MIT Press, 1996), pp. 177–178.

100 Zimbardo, *The Lucifer Effect*, p. 80.

101 Ibid., p. 104.

102 Ibid., p. 156.

103 Simone de Beauvoir, *The Ethics of Ambiguity*, trans. Bernard Frechtman (New York: Citadel Press, 1994), p. 36.

104 John Glenn Gray, *The Warriors: Reflections on Men in Battle* (New York: Harper, 1970), p. 181.

105 Glover, *Humanity*, p. 362.

106 On trauma and tragedy, see Hoffman, *After Such Knowledge*, p. 41. Lifton offers this crisp analysis of "totalistic ideology":

> It puts forward its own claim to immortality and exclusive truth in specific psychological manipulations of the environment I have delineated elsewhere: milieu control (of all communication); mystical manipulation (continuous efforts at behavior control from above while maintaining the appearance of spontaneity from below); demand for purity (constant accusations of guilt and shame in the name of an unrealizable ideal of absolute devotion and self-sacrifice); the cult of confession (ritual self-exposure to the totalistic "owner" of every self); the sacred science (combining deification of the Word with the claim of equally absolute secular scientific authority); loading of the language (into definitive, thought-terminating solutions for the most complex human problems); doctrine over person (so that the evidence of individual experience must be subsumed to or negated by the idea system); and the dispensing of existence (the ultimate and inevitable line drawn between those with the right to exist and those who possess no such right). (Lifton, *The Nazi Doctors*, p. 472)

> The contemporary self, Lifton argues, may be especially vulnerable to the lure of a genocidal ideology, to its promise that one can conquer one's own death by killing others. "I have in mind such characteristics as exacerbated meaning-hunger due to one's loss of symbolic moorings, to confusion about the endless images of possibility to which one is exposed, along with one's intensified struggles with death anxiety having to do with nuclear-weapons imagery of annihilation or even extinction" (Lifton, *The Nazi Doctors*, p. 499).

107 Eric H. Erikson, "Ontogeny of Ritualization in Man," *Philosophical Transactions of the Royal Society, London* B251 (1966): 340, 346, 337–349.

108 Lifton, *Thought Reform and the Psychology of Totalism* (New York: Norton, 1961), p. 425.

109 Weiner, *Race and Migration*, p. 13.

110 Ibid., p. 19.

111 Ibid., pp. 15–16.

112 Ibid., p. 12.

113 Ibid., pp. 24, 30.

114 Ibid., p. 27.

115 Ibid., pp. 30–31.

116 Aoki, "Korean Children, Textbooks, and Educational Practices," p. 158.

117 Norimitsu Onishi, "Ugly Images of Asian Rivals Become Bestsellers in Japan," *New York Times*, November 19, 2005.

118 While many studies suggest that violence against civilians in wartime is counterproductive to ultimate war goals, recent research on civil wars shows how such "irrational" terroristic violence can in fact deliberately serve "rational" war aims. See, for instance, Alexander B. Downes, "Desperate Times, Desperate Measures: The Causes of Civilian Victimization in War," *International Security* 30, no. 4 (Spring 2006): 152–195; Jean-Paul Azam and Anke Hoeffler, "Violence against Civilians in Civil Wars: Looting or Terror?" *Journal of Peace Research* 39, no. 4 (2002): 461–485; Stathis N. Kalyvas, "Wanton and Senseless? The Logic of Massacres in Algeria," *Rationality and Society* 11, no. 3 (1999): 243–285.

119 De Beauvoir, *The Ethics of Ambiguity*, p. 101.

120 Jonathan Shay, *Achilles in Vietnam: Combat Trauma and the Undoing of Character* (New York: Simon & Schuster, 1994), p. 80.

121 Jean Améry, *At the Mind's Limits: Contemplations by a Survivor on Auschwitz and Its Realities*, trans. Sidney Rosenfeld and Stella P. Rosenfeld (New York: Schocken, 1986), pp. 26, 28.

122 On bystanders generally, see Staub, *The Roots of Evil*, pp. 87–88.

123 Power, *"A Problem from Hell,"* p. xviii.

124 Thomas Hobbes, *Leviathan* (Oxford: Basil Blackwell, 1960), p. 81.

125 Thucydides, *The Peloponnesian War* (New York: Random House, 1951), p. 334.

126 Chirot and McCauley, *Why Not Kill Them All?*, p. 36.

127 Samuel Taylor Coleridge, "Fears in Solitude," in *The Poems of Samuel Taylor Coleridge*, ed. Ernest Hartley Coleridge (Oxford: Oxford University Press, 1924), p. 260.

128 Gregory Sieminski, "The Art of Naming Operations," *Parameters* (Autumn 1995): 81–98.

129 Christian Davenport, "In Choosing Its Battle Names, the Military Must Know Its Target Audience," *Washington Post,* March 20, 2010, p. A01.
130 Sieminski, "The Art of Naming Operations," pp. 81–98.
131 Weiner, *Race and Migration in Imperial Japan,* p. 189.
132 Marguerite Feitlowitz, *A Lexicon of Terror: Argentina and the Legacies of Torture* (Oxford: Oxford University Press, 1998), p. 61.
133 Jacobo Timerman, *Prisoner without a Name, Cell without a Number,* trans. Toby Talbot (Madison: University of Wisconsin Press, 1981), p. 51.
134 Lifton, *Thought Reform,* pp. 429, 425.
135 Arendt, *Eichmann in Jerusalem,* pp. 85, 105. For more on fascism's damage to language, see George Steiner, *Language and Silence* (New York: Atheneum, 1977), pp. 95–109; George Orwell, "Politics and the English Language," in *The Orwell Reader: Fiction, Essays, and Reportage* (New York: Harvest, 1956), pp. 355–366, 363.
136 Hannah Arendt, "Lying in Politics," in *Crises of the Republic* (San Diego: Harcourt Brace Jovanovich, 1972), p. 20.
137 Claude Lanzmann, *Shoah: The Complete Text of the Acclaimed Holocaust Film* (New York: Da Capo Press, 1995), p. 145.
138 Ibid., pp. 3, 4, 9, 39, 40, 45, 63, 127, 129, 136, 183. On the difficulty of representing the Holocaust, see Gertrud Koch, trans. Jamie Daniel and Miriam Hansen, "The Aesthetic Transformation of the Image of the Unimaginable: Notes on Claude Lanzmann's *Shoah,*" *October,* no. 48 (Spring 1989): 15–24.
139 Albert Bandura, "Moral Disengagement in the Perpetration of Inhumanities," *Personality and Social Psychology Review* 3, no. 3 (1999): 196.
140 See Donald T. Campbell, "Systematic Error on the Part of Human Links in Communication Systems," *Information and Control* 1 (1958): 334–369.
141 For a comprehensive review, see Roy F. Baumeister, Ellen Bratslavsky, Catrin Finkenauer, and Kathleen D. Vohs, "Bad Is Stronger Than Good," *Review of General Psychology* 5, no. 4 (2001): 323–370.
142 See Jennifer Crocker, Shawna Lee, and Lora Park, "The Pursuit of Self-Esteem: Implications for Good and Evil," in Miller, *The Social Psychology of Good and Evil,* p. 278.
143 Glover, *Humanity,* p. 60.
144 William Broyles Jr., "Why Men Love War," *Esquire,* November 1984, p. 56.
145 Gray, *The Warriors,* pp. 51, 57.
146 Baumeister and Campbell, "The Intrinsic Appeal of Evil," p. 213.

147 Browning, *Ordinary Men*, p. 69.

148 Ibid., p. 161.

149 Baumeister and Campbell, "The Intrinsic Appeal of Evil," p. 214.

150 David Philipps, *Lethal Warriors: When the New Band of Brothers Came Home* (New York: Palgrave, 2010), p. 76.

151 Browning, *Ordinary Men*, p. 68.

152 Zimbardo, *The Lucifer Effect*, p. 300.

153 Timerman, *Prisoner without a Name*, pp. 37–38.

154 Ibid., p. 40.

155 William Schulz, *In Our Own Best Interests: How Defending Human Rights Benefits Us All* (Boston: Beacon, 2002), p. 25.

156 Baumeister and Campbell, "The Intrinsic Appeal of Evil," pp. 215–216.

157 James Jones, *The Thin Red Line* (New York: Scribner, 1962), p. 198.

158 A Soviet soldier, quoted in Glover, *Humanity*, p. 55.

159 Rollo May, *Power and Innocence: A Search for the Sources of Violence* (New York: Norton, 1972), p. 167.

160 Christopher Hedges, *War Is a Force That Gives Us Meaning* (New York: PublicAffairs, 2002), p. 101.

161 Ibid., p. 99.

162 Ibid., p. 103.

163 Peggy Reeves Sanday, *Fraternity Gang Rape: Sex, Brotherhood, and Privilege on Campus* (New York: New York University Press, 1990), p. 171.

164 Paul Fussell, *The Great War and Modern Memory* (New York: Oxford University Press, 1975), p. 90.

165 A French soldier, quoted in Michael Walzer, *Just and Unjust Wars: A Moral Argument with Historical Illustrations* (New York: Basic, 1977), p. 316.

166 Jonathan Shay, *Odysseus in America: Combat Trauma and the Trials of Homecoming* (New York: Scribner, 2002), p. 211.

167 Gray, *The Warriors*, pp. 50–51.

168 Hedges, *War Is a Force*, p. 3.

169 Wendy Hesford, *Spectacular Rhetorics: Human Rights Visions, Recognitions, Feminisms* (Durham, NC: Duke University Press, 2011), pp. 94–96. Wendy Brown's work is discussed in this section of *Spectacular Rhetorics*, and the final quotation I have used is Brown, cited in *Spectacular Rhetorics*.

170 Norimitsu Onishi, "In Japan, a Historian Stands by Proof of Wartime Sex Slavery," *New York Times*, March 31, 2007.

171 Honda Katsuichi, *The Nanjing Massacre: A Japanese Journalist Confronts Japan's National Shame* (New York: Eastgate, 1999), p. xx.

172 Tanaka, *Hidden Horrors*, pp. 95, 100, 99.

173 Ibid., p. 103.

174 Catherine MacKinnon, "Rape, Genocide, and Women's Human Rights," in *Mass Rape: The War against Women in Bosnia-Herzegovina*, ed. Alexandra Stiglmayer (Lincoln: University of Nebraska Press, 1994), pp. 188, 189.

175 Ian Buruma, *The Wages of Guilt* (New York: Farrar, Straus, Giroux, 1994), p. 194.

176 Elisabeth Jean Wood, "Armed Groups and Sexual Violence: When Is Wartime Rape Rare?" *Politics and Society* 37, no. 1 (March 2009): 131–162.

177 Maria Eriksson Baaz and Maria Stern, "Why Do Soldiers Rape? Masculinity, Violence, and Sexuality in the Armed Forces in the Congo (DRC)," *International Studies Quarterly* 53 (2009): 498.

178 Wood, "Armed Groups and Sexual Violence," p. 135.

179 Baaz and Stern, "Why Do Soldiers Rape?" p. 497.

180 Martha Huggins, Mika Haritos-Fatouros, and Philip Zimbardo, *Violence Workers: Police Torturers and Murderers Reconstruct Brazilian Atrocities* (Berkeley: University of California Press, 2002), p. 86.

181 A Vietnam veteran, quoted in Tanaka, *Hidden Horrors*, p. 106.

182 Sandra Whitworth, "Militarized Masculinity and Post-Traumatic Stress Disorder," in *Rethinking the Man Question: Sex, Gender and Violence in International Relations*, ed. Jane L. Parpart and Marysia Zalewski (London: Zed, 2008), p. 118.

183 Nancy Chodorow, *The Reproduction of Mothering: Psychoanalysis and the Sociology of Gender* (Berkeley: University of California Press, 1978), pp. 62, 181.

184 Freud, quoted in Chodorow, *The Reproduction of Mothering*, p. 182.

185 Jessica Benjamin, *The Bonds of Love: Psychoanalysis, Feminism, and the Problem of Domination* (New York: Pantheon, 1988), p. 77.

186 Susan Griffin, *Pornography and Silence: Culture's Revenge against Nature* (New York: Harper & Row, 1981), p. 92.

187 Pierre Bourdieu, *Masculine Domination*, trans. Richard Nice (Stanford, CA: Stanford University Press, 2001), p. 52.

188 For those with interest, an excellent starting point is Kelly Oliver's explanation of Lévinas on paternal love; see Oliver, *Family Values: Subjects between Nature and Culture* (New York: Routledge, 1997), pp. 195–214.

189 Ibid., pp. 2, 101, 2. See also her *Womanizing Nietzsche: Philosophy's Relation to the "Feminine"* (New York: Routledge, 1995).

190 Ruth Seifert, "War and Rape: A Preliminary Analysis," in *Mass Rape: The War against Women in Bosnia-Herzegovina,* ed. Alexandra Stiglmayer (Lincoln: University of Nebraska Press, 1994), pp. 63–64.

191 Susan Brownmiller, "Making Female Bodies the Battlefield," in Stiglmayer, *Mass Rape,* p. 181.

192 Human Rights Watch, *The Human Rights Watch Global Report on Women's Human Rights* (New York: Human Rights Watch, 1995), p. 2.

193 Nora Okja Keller, *Comfort Woman* (New York: Penguin, 1997), p. 71.

194 Will Durant, *Lessons of History* (New York: Simon & Schuster, 1960), p. 81.

195 Glover, *Humanity,* p. 47.

196 P. W. Singer, *Children at War* (Berkeley: University of California Press, 2006), pp. 5–6, 29.

197 Fyodor Dostoyevsky, *The Brothers Karamazov,* trans. Constance Garnett (New York: Norton, 2011), p. 209.

198 Thomas Hardy, "Nature's Questioning," in *Thomas Hardy: Selected Poems,* ed. Tim Armstrong (London: Pearson Longman, 2009), p. 58.

199 Thomas Hardy, "Hap," in *Thomas Hardy: Selected Poems,* pp. 42–43.

200 Ha Jin, *Nanjing Requiem* (New York: Pantheon, 2011), p. 68.

201 J. L. Mackie, "Evil and Omnipotence," *Mind* 64, no. 254 (April 1955): 200.

202 Susan Nieman, *Evil in Modern Thought: An Alternative History of Philosophy* (Princeton, NJ: Princeton University Press, 2002), p. 119.

203 David Hume, *Principal Writings on Religion, Including Dialogues Concerning Natural Religion and the Natural History of Religion* (Oxford: Oxford University Press, 2008), p. 100, pt. 10.

204 Ibid., pp. 107–108, pt. 11.

205 See Alvin Plantinga, *The Nature of Necessity* (Oxford: Clarendon Press, 1974), pp. 165–196. See also Plantinga, *God, Freedom, and Evil* (Grand Rapids, MI: Eerdmans, 1974), pp. 49–50.

206 Alexander Pope, "An Essay on Man," in *The Poems of Alexander Pope,* ed. John Butt (New Haven, CT: Yale University Press, 1963), pp. 510, 514–515.

207 On Pope's health, see George Rousseau, "Medicine and the Body," in *The Cambridge Companion to Alexander Pope,* ed. Pat Rogers (Cambridge: Cambridge University Press, 2008), pp. 210–212.

208 C. S. Lewis, *The Problem of Pain* (New York: Macmillan, 1962), p. 83.

209 Ibid., p. 67.

210 Augustine, quoted in Plantinga, *God, Freedom, and Evil,* p. 27.

211 See Adams, *Horrendous Evils.*

212 See John Hick, *Evil and the God of Love* (San Francisco: Harper & Row, 1978).

213 John Keats, *Letters of John Keats,* ed. Robert Gittings (Oxford: Oxford University Press, 1970), p. 249.

214 Adams, *Horrendous Evils,* p. 39.

215 Albert Camus, *The Plague,* trans. Stuart Gilbert (New York: Vintage, 1991), p. 98.

216 Nieman, *Evil in Modern Thought,* p. 70.

217 Mackie, "Evil and Omnipotence," p. 210.

218 Hume, *Dialogues,* p. 102, pt. 10.

219 Ibid., p. 98, pt. 10.

220 David Benatar, *Better Never to Have Been: The Harm of Coming into Existence* (Oxford: Oxford University Press, 2006), pp. 30, 102.

221 On the latter, see Christina Maslach, "Negative Emotional Biasing of Unexplained Arousal," *Journal of Personality and Social Psychology* 37, no. 6 (June 1979): 953–969; and Gary Marshall and Philip Zimbardo, "Affective Consequences of Inadequately Explained Physiological Arousal," *Journal of Personality and Social Psychology* 37, no. 6 (June 1979): 970–988.

222 See Baumeister et al., "Bad Is Stronger Than Good," pp. 323–370.

223 Terry Eagleton, *On Evil* (New Haven, CT: Yale University Press, 2010), pp. 60–61.

224 Human Security Centre, *Human Security Report 2005: War and Peace in the 21st Century* (New York: Oxford University Press, 2005), http://www.hsrgroup.org/human-security-reports/2005/text.aspx.

225 Maria Stephan and Erica Chenoweth, "Why Civil Resistance Works: The Strategic Logic of Nonviolent Conflict," *International Security* 33, no. 1 (Summer 2008): 7–44.

226 See Shelley E. Taylor, "Asymmetrical Effects of Positive and Negative Events: The Mobilization-Minimization Hypothesis," *Psychological Bulletin* 110, no. 1 (1991): 67–85. See also Theresa Glomb, Devasheesh P. Bhave, Andrew G. Miner, and Melanie Wall, "Doing Good, Feeling Good: Examining the Role of Organizational Citizenship Behaviors in Changing Mood," *Personnel Psychology* 64 (2001): 191–223.

227 William James, *The Will to Believe and Other Essays in Popular Philosophy* (New York: Dover, 1956), pp. 24–25.

228 Jane Allyn Piliavin and Hong-Wen Charng, "Altruism: A Review of Recent Theory and Research," *Annual Review of Sociology* 16 (1990): 30, 27–65.

229 Arie Nadler, "Inter-Group Helping Relations as Power Relations: Maintaining or Challenging Social Dominance between Groups through Helping," *Journal of Social Issues* 58, no. 3 (2002): 490.

230 Howard Margolis, *Selfishness, Altruism, and Rationality: A Theory of Social Choice* (Cambridge: Cambridge University Press, 1982), p. 22.

231 Richard McElreath and Robert Boyd, *Mathematical Models of Social Evolution: A Guide for the Perplexed* (Chicago: University of Chicago Press, 2007), p. 82.

232 Robert Wright, *The Moral Animal: Evolutionary Psychology and Everyday Life* (New York: Pantheon, 1994), p. 174.

233 Richard Dawkins, quoted in Matt Ridley, *The Origins of Virtue: Human Instincts and the Evolution of Cooperation* (New York: Viking Penguin, 1997), p. 19.

234 George Williams, quoted in Ridley, *The Origins of Virtue*, p. 18.

235 E. O. Wilson, *The Social Conquest of Earth* (New York: Liveright, 2012), pp. 184, 247, 250. Relatedly, see Jung-Kyoo Choi and Samuel Bowles, "The Coevolution of Parochial Altruism and War," *Science* 318 (26 October 2007): 636. See also Piliavin and Charng, "Altruism: A Review of Recent Theory and Research"; Margolis, *Selfishness, Altruism, and Rationality;* and C. Daniel Batson, *The Altruism Question: Toward a Social-Psychological Answer* (Hillsdale, NJ: Erlbaum, 1991).

236 Batson, *The Altruism Question*, p. 127; C. Daniel Batson, Nadia Ahmad, and E. L. Stocks, "Benefits and Liabilities of Empathy-Induced Altruism," in Miller, *The Social Psychology of Good and Evil*, p. 362.

237 Kristin R. Monroe, Michael C. Barton, and Ute Klingemann, "Altruism and the Theory of Rational Action: Rescuers of Jews in Nazi Europe," *Ethics* 101 (October 1990): 115.

238 Hoffman, *After Such Knowledge*, p. 213.

239 Amartya Sen, "Rational Fools: A Critique of the Behavioral Foundations of Economic Theory," *Philosophy and Public Affairs* 6, no. 4 (Summer 1977): 317, 322–323, 336.

240 Robert Rowthorn, "Ethics and Economics: An Economist's View," in *Economics and Ethics?* ed. Peter Groenewegen (London: Routledge, 1996), p. 16.

241 Elinor Ostrom, *Governing the Commons: The Evolution of Institutions for Collective Action* (Cambridge: Cambridge University Press, 1990).

242 See Mark Levine, Clare Cassidy, Gemma Brazier, and Stephen Reicher, "Self-Categorization and Bystander Non-Intervention: Two Experimental Studies," *Journal of Applied Social Psychology* 32, no. 7 (2002): 1452–1463.

243 See Muzafer Sherif, O. J. Harvey, B. Jack White, William R. Hood, Carolyn W. Sherif, *The Robbers Cave Experiment: Intergroup Conflict and Cooperation* (Middletown, CT: Wesleyan University Press, 1988).

244 Batson et al., "Benefits and Liabilities," p. 374.

245 See, for instance, Oliver Kim and Mark Walker, "The Free Rider Problem: Experimental Evidence," *Public Choice* 43 (1984): 3–24.

246 Elinor Ostrom and Oliver E. Williamson (2009 Nobel laureates in Economic Sciences), interview by Adam Smith, December 6, 2009, http://www.nobelprize.org/.

247 Arendt, *Eichmann in Jerusalem*, p. 131.

248 Piliavin and Charng, "Altruism," p. 35.

249 Jan Egeland, quoted in Lena Khor, *Human Rights Discourse in a Global Network: Books beyond Borders* (Burlington, VT: Ashgate, forthcoming). Khor analyzes the way NGOs operate within certain storytelling conventions, complete with heroes, villains, and magical solutions for overcoming misfortune. Crisis stories that can't be made to fit such templates often fail to "take" in the media and public imagination. But succeeding in the media by conforming to conventions means that information is damaged. "In such situations," Lena Khor writes, "complexities in crises are simplified, critical differences between crises participants are blurred, vital historical precedents are overlooked because these [media and human rights] industries refuse to find or use other ways to tell crisis stories."

The consequences can be devastating. Consider media response to the refugee crisis in Goma after the Rwandan genocide in 1994. Heroes (aid workers) saving victims (Hutu refugees) from misfortune (war homelessness) and bad nature (cholera epidemic). It was "great TV," as one cameraman said—just an irresistible story. And it meant that the world worked with earnest benevolence to provide material aid and organizational structure to fleeing Hutu genocidaires who were rearming to continue their fight. See Philip Gourevitch, *We Wish to Inform You That Tomorrow We Will Be Killed with Our Families: Stories from Rwanda* (New York: Picador, 1998), p. 163.

250 Samuel P. Oliner and Pearl M. Oliner, *The Altruistic Personality: Rescuers of Jews in Nazi Europe* (New York: Free Press, 1988), pp. 135–136.

251 See Jerry M. Burger, "Self-Concept Clarity and the Foot-in-the-Door Procedure," *Basic and Applied Social Psychology* 25, no. 1 (2003): 79–86.

252 Piliavin and Charng, "Altruism," p. 43.

253 Eva Fogelman, *Conscience and Courage: Rescuers of Jews during the Holocaust* (New York: Doubleday, 1994), p. 162.

254 Elliot Aronson, "Reducing Hostility and Building Compassion: Lessons from the Jigsaw Classroom," in Miller, *The Social Psychology of Good and Evil*, p. 482.

255 Oliner and Oliner, *The Altruistic Personality*, p. 149.

256 Batson et al., "Benefits and Liabilities," pp. 365–366.

257 Steven Prentice-Dunn and Ronald Rogers, "Deindividuation and the Self-Regulation of Behavior," in *Psychology of Group Influence*, ed. Paul Paulus (Hillsdale, NJ: Erlbaum, 1989), p. 100.

258 Thomas Ashby Wills and Jodi Resco, "Social Support and Behavior toward Others: Some Paradoxes and Some Directions," in Miller, *The Social Psychology of Good and Evil*, p. 425.

259 Oliner and Oliner, *The Altruistic Personality*, pp. 184–185, 177.

260 Piliavin and Charng, "Altruism," p. 31.

261 Ibid., p. 33. See Perry London, "The Rescuers: Motivational Hypotheses about Christians Who Saved Jews from the Nazis," in *Altruism and Helping Behavior: Social Psychological Studies of Some Antecedents and Consequences*, ed. J. Macaulay and L. Berkowitz (New York: Academic Press, 1970), pp. 241–250.

262 Mark Osiel, *Obeying Orders: Atrocity, Military Discipline and the Law of War* (New Brunswick, NJ: Transaction, 1999), p. 178.

263 Ibid., pp. 181–182.

264 Ibid., p. 192.

265 Ibid., p. 197.

266 Ibid., p. 35.

267 Ibid., p. 23.

268 Jacques Semelin, *Purify and Destroy: The Political Uses of Massacre and Genocide*, trans. Cynthia Schoch (New York: Columbia University Press, 2007), p. 252.

269 The best starting point for thinking about freedom, determinism, and blame remains P. F. Strawson, "Freedom and Resentment," *Proceedings of the British Academy* 48 (1962): 1–25.

270 Hannah Arendt, *The Human Condition* (Chicago: University of Chicago Press, 1958), p. 241.

271 Alan Schrift, introduction to *Modernity and the Problem of Evil*, ed. Alan Schrift (Bloomington: Indiana University Press, 2005), pp. 1–2; Jennifer L. Geddes, introduction to *Evil after Postmodernism: Histories, Narratives,*

and Ethics, ed. Jennifer L. Geddes (New York: Routledge, 2001), p. 1; Card, *The Atrocity Paradigm,* p. 28.

272 Friedrich Nietzsche, *Beyond Good and Evil,* trans. R. J. Hollingdale (New York: Penguin, 1990), §201, p. 123.

273 Card, *The Atrocity Paradigm,* p. 28.

274 See, for instance, ibid., p. 3; Adam Morton, *On Evil* (New York: Routledge, 2004), p. 57; Marcus Singer, "The Concept of Evil," *Philosophy* 79, no. 308 (April 2004): 196; Paul Thompson, "The Evolutionary Biology of Evil," *The Monist* 85, no. 2 (2002): 246.

275 Eagleton, *On Evil,* p. 16.

276 Ibid., p. 127.

277 Saint Augustine, *Confessions,* trans. R. S. Pine-Coffin (New York: Penguin, 1961), pp. 47–48 (bk. 2, ch. 4).

278 Augustine, *City of God,* trans. Marcus Dods (New York: Modern Library, 1950), p. 387 (bk. 12, chap. 7).

279 Eagleton, *On Evil,* p. 61.

280 See Norma Field, "War and Apology: Japan, Asia, the Fiftieth, and After," *positions* 5, no. 1 (1997): 1; see also Barnard, *Language, Ideology, and Japanese History Textbooks,* pp. 4–5.

281 Field, "War and Apology," p. 2.

282 Ibid., p. 12.

283 N. Muira, cited in Barnard, *Language, Ideology, and Japanese History Textbooks,* p. 5. Thomas Cushman argues that national apologies can be empty rituals that leave intact "the very social structures and cultural logic of *realpolitik* that created the possibilities for genocide to occur in the first place." Thomas Cushman, "Genocidal Rupture and Performative Repair in Global Civil Society: Reconsidering the Discourse of Apology," in *The Religious in Responses to Mass Atrocity: Interdisciplinary Perspectives,* ed. Thomas Brudholm and Thomas Cushman (Cambridge: Cambridge University Press, 2009), p. 218.

284 Field, "War and Apology," p. 11.

285 Ibid., p. 25.

286 Ibid., pp. 25–26.

287 Barnard, *Language, Ideology, and Japanese History Textbooks,* p. 58.

288 Ibid., p. 61.

289 Ibid., p. 71.

290 Lifton offers a few ideas about the cultural concept of confession in China; see his *Thought Reform,* pp. 390–398.

291 Michel Foucault, *The History of Sexuality*, vol. 1, trans. Robert Hurley (New York: Penguin, 1978), pp. 61–62.

292 Leigh Payne, *Unsettling Accounts: Neither Truth Nor Reconciliation in Confessions of State Violence* (Durham, NC: Duke University Press, 2008), p. 19.

293 Ibid., p. 18.

294 Ibid., p. 19.

295 Ibid., pp. 58, 61.

296 Ibid., p. 72.

297 Ibid., pp. 73–74.

298 Ibid., p. 28.

299 Ibid., p. 29.

300 Ibid., p. 30.

301 Renée Epelbaum, quoted in Feitlowitz, *A Lexicon of Terror*, p. 20.

302 Simon Wiesenthal, *The Sunflower: On the Possibilities and Limits of Forgiveness* (New York: Schocken, 1997), p. 28.

303 Ibid., pp. 53–54.

304 Cynthia Ozick, "The Symposium," in Wiesenthal, *The Sunflower*, pp. 205, 208, 210.

305 Hampl, *I Could Tell You Stories*, p. 73.

306 Wole Soyinka, *The Burden of Memory, the Muse of Forgiveness* (Oxford: Oxford University Press, 1999), p. 33.

307 Pumla Gobodo-Madikizela, *A Human Being Died That Night: A South African Story of Forgiveness* (Boston: Houghton Mifflin, 2003), pp. 117–118.

308 A leader in the underground women's movement in East Germany, cited in Molly Andrews, "Truth-Telling, Justice, and Forgiveness: A Study of East Germany's 'Truth Commission,'" *International Journal of Politics, Culture and Society* 13, no. 1 (Fall 1999): 110.

309 Joe Mozingo, "Coming to Terms with Sadism," *Los Angeles Times*, December 15, 2010.

310 Kay Schaffer and Sidonie Smith, *Human Rights and Narrated Lives: The Ethics of Recognition* (New York: Palgrave Macmillan, 2004), pp. 175–176.

311 Susie Linfield, *The Cruel Radiance: Photography and Political Violence* (Chicago: University of Chicago Press, 2010), p. 45.

312 Patricia Yeager, "Consuming Trauma; or, the Pleasures of Merely Circulating," in *Extremities: Trauma, Testimony, and Community*, ed. Nancy K. Miller and Jason Tougaw (Chicago: University of Illinois Press, 2002), p. 47.

313 Peace Boat is a Japan-based nongovernmental organization that focuses on human rights and environmentalism, using chartered passenger ships to create opportunities for international dialogue, education, and media outreach. A group of university students launched the first Peace Boat voyage in 1983. Frustrated by government censorship over Japanese war crimes, the students sought opportunities to interact with those in neighboring countries who could offer firsthand accounts of Japanese aggression.

314 Payne, *Unsettling Accounts*, p. 19.

315 Barnard, *Language, Ideology, and Japanese History Textbooks*, pp. 3–4.

316 John Beverley, *Testimonio: On the Politics of Truth* (Minneapolis: University of Minnesota Press, 2004), p. 31.

317 Ibid., p. 30.

318 "The Stanford Mind," Review & Outlook, *Wall Street Journal*, December 22, 1988, p. A14.

319 Beverley, *Testimonio*, p. 73.

320 David Horowitz, "I, Rigoberta Menchú, Liar," *Salon*, January 11, 1999.

321 Beverley, *Testimonio*, pp. 92–93.

322 Doris Sommer, *Proceed with Caution, When Engaged by Minority Writing in the Americas* (Cambridge, MA: Harvard University Press, 1999), pp. 116, 120.

323 Shoshana Felman and Dori Laub, *Testimony: Crises of Witnessing in Literature, Psychoanalysis, and History* (New York: Routledge, 1992), p. 60.

324 Lifton, *Thought Reform*, p. 15.

325 Mao Tse-tung, quoted in ibid., pp. 13–14.

326 Eugene Kinkead, *In Every War but One* (New York: Norton, 1959), pp. 87–88.

327 Ibid., pp. 87–88.

328 Edgar H. Schein, "Some Observations on Chinese Methods of Handling Prisoners of War," *Public Opinion Quarterly* 20, no. 1 (Spring 1956): 322.

329 Kinkead, *In Every War but One*, p. 137.

330 Schein, "Some Observations on Chinese Methods of Handling Prisoners of War," pp. 326, 325.

331 Kinkead, *In Every War but One*, p. 138.

332 Lifton, *Thought Reform*, p. 423.

333 Ibid., p. 75.

334 Peter Brooks, *Troubling Confessions: Speaking Guilt in Law and Literature* (Chicago: University of Chicago Press, 2000), p. 22.

335 Scarry, *The Body in Pain*, pp. 133, 136.

336 Patrick Deer, "The Ends of War and the Limits of War Culture," *Social Text* 25, no. 291 (Summer 2007): 2.

337 Patrick Coy, Lynn Woehrle, and Gregory Maney, "Discursive Legacies: The U.S. Peace Movement and 'Support the Troops,'" *Social Problems* 55, no. 2 (2008): 180.

338 See Donald Anderson, *When War Becomes Personal: Soldiers' Accounts from the Civil War to Iraq* (Iowa City: University of Iowa Press, 2008), p. xi.

339 Buruma, *The Wages of Guilt,* p. 31.

340 Naomi Klein, *The Shock Doctrine: The Rise of Disaster Capitalism* (New York: Metropolitan, 2007), pp. 329, 339, 326.

341 Ibid., pp. 380, 349, 337.

342 John Dower, *Cultures of War: Pearl Harbor/Hiroshima/9-11/Iraq* (New York: Norton, 2010), pp. 396–397.

343 Ibid., p. 414.

344 Joseph Stiglitz and Linda Bilmes, "The Three Trillion Dollar War," *Times of London,* February 23, 2008.

345 John Dos Passos, *Nineteen Nineteen* (New York: Signet Classic, 1969), p. 341; see also p. 147.

346 Anthony Swofford, *Jarhead* (New York: Scribner, 2003), p. 11.

347 J. M. Coetzee, "Into the Dark Chamber: The Novelist and South Africa," *New York Times,* January 12, 1986.

348 Tanaka, *Hidden Horrors,* pp. 27–28.

349 See, for instance, Kenneth Roth's interview by Charlie Rose, July 13, 2005, www.charlierose.com.

350 Commander from Battle of Algiers, quoted in Darius Rejali, *Torture and Democracy* (Princeton, NJ: Princeton University Press, 2007), p. 488 (brackets in original).

351 Rejali, *Torture and Democracy,* p. 489.

352 Ibid., p. 24.

353 Ibid., pp. 483, 492.

354 Bauman, *Modernity and the Holocaust,* p. xi.

355 I have taken this characterization from Franklin, *A Thousand Darknesses,* p. 13.

356 William Pfaff, "An Active French Role," p. 6.

357 Soyinka, *The Burden of Memory, the Muse of Forgiveness,* pp. 38–39.

358 Lynn Hunt, *Inventing Human Rights: A History* (New York: Norton, 2007), pp. 45–46.

359 Ibid., p. 39.

360 Margaret Cohen, *The Sentimental Education of the Novel* (Princeton, NJ: Princeton University Press, 1999), pp. 145, 161.

361 Lynn Festa, "Sentimental Bonds and Revolutionary Characters: Richardson's *Pamela* in England and France," in *The Literary Channel: The Inter-National Invention of the Novel* (Princeton, NJ: Princeton University Press, 2002), pp. 85, 91.

362 Friedrich Schiller, *On the Aesthetic Education of Man* (Oxford: Clarendon Press, 1967), p. 215.

363 Ludwig Wittgenstein, *Tractatus Logico-Philosophicus* (New York: Humanities Press, 1961), p. 147 (6.421). For commentary on this enigmatic statement, see Robert Eaglestone, "One and the Same? Ethics, Aesthetics, and Truth," *Poetics Today* 25, no. 4 (Winter 2004): 595–608.

364 William Wordsworth, preface to "Lyrical Ballads," in *The Norton Anthology of English Literature,* ed. M. H. Abrams, 5th ed., vol. 2 (New York: Norton, 1986), pp. 166–167.

365 Helen Vendler, "The Ocean, the Bird, and the Scholar: How the Arts Help Us to Live," *New Republic,* July 19, 2004, p. 29.

366 Elaine Scarry, *On Beauty and Being Just* (Princeton, NJ: Princeton University Press, 1999), p. 107.

367 Marcia Mueder Eaton, *Merit, Aesthetic and Ethical* (New York: Oxford University Press, 2001), p. 18. On past disregard of beauty in philosophy, see, for instance, Jane Forsey, "The Disenfranchisement of Philosophical Aesthetics," *Journal of the History of Ideas* 64, no. 4 (October 2003): 581–597.

368 Martha C. Nussbaum, *Love's Knowledge: Essays on Philosophy and Literature* (New York: Oxford University Press, 1990), p. 15.

369 Martha Nussbaum, *Cultivating Humanity: A Classical Defense of Reform in Liberal Education* (Cambridge, MA: Harvard University Press, 1997), p. 87.

370 See Martha C. Nussbaum, *Women and Human Development: The Capabilities Approach* (New York: Cambridge University Press, 2000), pp. 70–79. See also Amartya Sen, *Inequality Re-examined* (Cambridge, MA: Harvard University Press, 1992).

371 On the form of the Universal Declaration, see Mary Ann Glendon, *A World Made New: Eleanor Roosevelt and the Universal Declaration of Human Rights* (New York: Random House, 2001), p. 174. On symmetry as the principle of justice, see Scarry, *On Beauty and Being Just*.

372 Ibid., pp. 57–58.

373 Edward Said, *Culture and Imperialism* (New York: Vintage, 1994), p. xii.

374 Samera Esmeir, "On Making Dehumanization Possible," *PMLA* 121, no. 5 (October 2006): 1544, 1547.

375 Joseph Slaughter, *Human Rights, Inc.: The World Novel, Narrative Form, and International Law* (New York: Fordham University Press, 2007), p. 33.

376 Pheng Cheah, *Inhuman Conditions: On Cosmopolitanism and Human Rights* (Cambridge, MA: Harvard University Press, 2006), p. 172.

377 Richard Rorty, "Human Rights, Rationality, and Sentimentality," *Yale Review* 81, no. 4 (October 1993): 1–20.

378 Virginia Woolf, *Three Guineas* (New York: Harcourt, Brace and Company, 1938), p. 15.

379 Julie Stone Peters, "'Literature,' the 'Rights of Man,' and Narratives of Atrocity: Historical Backgrounds to the Culture of Testimony," *Yale Journal of Law and the Humanities* 17 (Summer 2005): 272.

380 Thomas Jefferson, quoted in Peters, "'Literature,' the 'Rights of Man,' and Narratives of Atrocity," pp. 260–261.

381 Francis Hutcheson, quoted in Halttunen, *Murder Most Foul*, p. 63.

382 Madame Riccoboni and Françoise Vernes, respectively quoted in Luc Boltanski, *Distant Suffering: Morality, Media and Politics*, trans. Graham Burchell (Cambridge: Cambridge University Press, 1999), p. 101.

383 It shouldn't make a difference to us, Peter Singer writes, "whether the person I can help is the neighbor's child ten yards from me or a Bengali whose name I shall never know, ten thousand miles away." But it generally does. We are able to purchase tickets for the opera with astonishing poise, even as children around the world are, at the very moment of our purchase, starving to death for want of that ticket money—the moral equivalent, Peter Unger argues by way of Singer, of walking past a shallow pond as a child drowns, unwilling to help because we don't wish to muddy our clothes. Distance, for humans, is a moral fact—lamented when it involves our capacity to dismiss distant suffering, but experienced as the essence of human meaning when it involves our capacity for supererogatory sacrifice for our children, for our beloved ones, for those we hold close. See Peter Singer, "Famine, Affluence, and Morality," *Philosophy and Public Affairs* 1, no. 3 (Spring 1972): 231–232.

384 Belinda Luscombe, "Pop Culture Finds Lost Boys," *Time*, February 12, 2007, pp. 62–64.

385 Stanley Cavell, *The Claim of Reason* (New York: Oxford University Press, 1979), pp. 436–437.

386 Hoffman, *After Such Knowledge,* pp. 60, 154, 173, 175.

387 Ibid., pp. 172–174.

388 See LaCapra, *Writing History, Writing Trauma,* pp. 211, 47, 98, 102; Hesford, *Spectacular Rhetorics,* p. 98.

389 Dori Laub, "Bearing Witness, or the Vicissitudes of Listening," in Felman and Laub, *Testimony,* p. 72.

390 Hoffman, *After Such Knowledge,* p. 177.

391 John Kamau and Oliver Burkeman, "Trading Places," *Guardian,* July 4, 2005.

392 Kate Nash, *The Cultural Politics of Human Rights: Comparing the US and UK* (Cambridge: Cambridge University Press, 2009), p. 153.

393 Bernard Williams, *Moral Luck* (Cambridge: Cambridge University Press, 1981), p. 45.

394 Hetty Voûte, *The Heart Has Reasons: Holocaust Rescuers and Their Stories of Courage,* ed. Mark Klempner (Cleveland: Pilgrim Press, 2006), pp. 19–44.

395 Williams, *Moral Luck,* p. 47.

396 Ibid., p. 47.

397 Ibid., p. 48.

398 Ibid., p. 49.

399 Ibid., p. 49.

400 Immanuel Kant, "Grounding for the Metaphysics of Morals," in *Ethical Philosophy: Grounding for the Metaphysics of Morals* and *Metaphysical Principles of Virtue,* 2nd ed., trans. James Ellington (Indianapolis: Hackett, 1994), §398, p. 11.

401 For Kant, to act entirely from benevolent motives is to act in accord with duty rather than for the sake of duty. Kant is not opposed to this; he just thinks it is not what makes an action morally worthy. At best, he argues, we have an indirect duty to cultivate our capacity for sympathy, as a sort of moral backup mechanism. Kant writes that compassion is "one of the impulses placed in us by nature for effecting what the representation of duty might not accomplish by itself." Immanuel Kant, "The Metaphysics of Morals," in *Ethical Philosophy,* §35, p. 122. Relatedly, see Martin Gunderson's "Seeking Perfection: A Kantian Look at Human Genetic Engineering," *Theoretical Medicine and Bioethics* 28, no. 2 (2007): 87–102.

402 There has, naturally, been a great deal of discussion about what constitutes a proper moral agent in Kant's sense. For a defense of the motive of duty, with special reference to the "overdetermination of actions," see

Barbara Herman, "On the Value of Acting from the Motive of Duty," *Philosophical Review* 90, no. 3 (July 1981): 359–382; Marcia Baron, "The Alleged Moral Repugnance of Acting from Duty," *Journal of Philosophy* 81, no. 4 (April 1984): 197–220.

403 Michael Stocker, "The Schizophrenia of Modern Ethical Theories," *Journal of Philosophy* 73, no. 14 (August 1976): 462.

404 Aristotle, *Poetics*, trans. Seth Benardete and Michael Davis (South Bend, IN: St. Augustine's Press, 2002), ch. iv, pp. 8–9.

405 David Hume, "Of Tragedy," in *On the Standard of Taste and Other Essays,* ed. John W. Lenz (1757; repr., Indianapolis: Bobbs-Merrill, 1965), p. 32.

406 See Norman Holland, *The Dynamics of Literary Response* (New York: Oxford University Press, 1968), pp. 281–307.

407 Noël Carroll, *The Philosophy of Horror* (New York: Routledge, 1990), p. 193.

408 Edmund Burke, *A Philosophical Enquiry into the Origin of Our Ideas of the Sublime and Beautiful* (1757; repr., New York: Oxford University Press, 1990), pp. 122–123.

409 Marvin Zuckerman, *Behavioral Expressions and Biosocial Bases of Sensation Seeking* (Cambridge: Cambridge University Press, 1994).

410 William Brewer, "The Nature of Narrative Suspense and the Problem of Rereading," in *Suspense: Conceptualizations, Theoretical Analyses, and Empirical Explorations,* ed. Peter Vorderer, Hans J. Wulff, and Mike Friedrichsen (Mahwah, NJ: Erlbaum, 1996), p. 108.

411 Paul Hernadi, "Why Is Literature: A Coevolutionary Perspective on Imaginative Worldmaking," *Poetics Today* 23, no. 1 (Spring 2002): 33.

412 See, for instance, David Stewart, "Cultural Work, City Crime, Reading, Pleasure," *American Literary History* 9, no. 4 (Winter 1997): 676–701.

413 John Mitchell Mason, *Mercy Remembered in Wrath* (New York: Buel, 1795), p. 6. See also Carroll, *The Philosophy of Horror,* p. 199.

414 Karen Halttunen, *Murder Most Foul: The Killer and the American Gothic Imagination* (Cambridge, MA: Harvard University Press, 1998), p. 63.

415 Ibid., 69.

416 For a range of such views, from Hobbes to Freud, see Michael Billig, *Laughter and Ridicule: Toward a Social Critique of Humour* (London: Sage, 2005).

417 Elaine Scarry, "The Difficulty of Imagining Other People," in *For Love of Country?* ed. Martha Nussbaum and Joshua Cohen (Boston: Beacon Press, 2002), p. 103.

418 Scarry, *The Body in Pain*, p. 11.

419 Rousseau, *Politics and the Arts*, p. 25.

420 Lauren Berlant, "The Subject of True Feeling: Pain, Privacy, and Politics," in *Cultural Pluralism, Identity Politics, and the Law*, ed. Austin Sarat and Thomas Kearns (Ann Arbor: University of Michigan Press, 1999), p. 54.

421 Jodi Melamed, *Represent and Destroy: Rationalizing Violence in the New Racial Capitalism* (Minneapolis: University of Minnesota Press, 2011), pp. 36–37.

422 Philip Fisher, *Hard Facts: Setting and Form in the American Novel* (Oxford: Oxford University Press, 1987), p. 108.

423 Ibid., p. 110. On the way "liberal guilt" in the face of victimization can be counterproductive to improving conditions in the world, see Julie Ellison, *Cato's Tears and the Making of Anglo-American Emotion* (Chicago: University of Chicago Press, 1999), pp. 178–181, 183–184.

424 Cavell, *The Claim of Reason*, p. 354.

425 Slavoj Žižek, *The Sublime Object of Ideology* (London: Verso, 1989), pp. 34–35.

426 Ibid., pp. 34–35.

427 Rousseau, *Politics and the Arts*, p. 24.

428 Woolf, *Three Guineas*, p. 16.

429 Judith Butler, *Precarious Life: The Powers of Mourning and Violence* (New York: Verso, 2004), p. 134.

430 See Kelly Oliver, *Witnessing: Beyond Recognition* (Minneapolis: University of Minnesota Press, 2001), p. 19.

431 Emmanuel Lévinas, *Otherwise Than Being: Or, Beyond Essence*, trans. Alphonso Lingis (Hague: Nijhoff, 1981), p. 119.

432 Elizabeth Anker, I should note, offers important cautions about deconstructive/Lévinasian ethics. Anker argues that the emphasis on the "exemplary" in such work "ends up writing off actual, proximate, and commonplace scenes of decision-making wherein 'impossible' unannounced alterity is not at issue," and that "the concentration on alterity has at times produced a fetishization of that condition and a sublime fascination with victimization that inadvertently covers over . . . material disparities." See her *Fictions of Dignity: Embodying Human Rights in World Literature* (Ithaca, NY: Cornell University Press, 2012), p. 12.

433 Robert Eaglestone, "One and the Same? Ethics, Aesthetics, and Truth," *Poetics Today* 25, no. 4 (Winter 2004): 602–605.

434 Dorothy Hale, "Aesthetics and the New Ethics: Theorizing the Novel in the Twenty-First Century," *PMLA* 124, no. 3 (1999): 903.

435 Paul Fry, *A Defense of Poetry: Reflections on the Occasion of Writing* (Stanford, CA: Stanford University Press, 1995), pp. 204, 4, 55.

436 Hans Ulrich Gumbrecht, *Production of Presence: What Meaning Cannot Convey* (Stanford, CA: Stanford University Press, 2004), pp. 98, 103.

437 T. W. Adorno, "Commitment," in *Aesthetics and Politics,* trans. Francis McDonagh (London: New Left Books, 1977), p. 179.

438 Richard Shelly Hartigan, ed., *Lieber's Code and the Law of War* (Chicago: Precedent, 1983), p. 48.

439 Sophia McClennen, "The Humanities, Human Rights, and the Comparative Imagination," *CLCWeb: Comparative Literature and Culture* 9, no. 1 (2007): 14.

440 Catherine Gallagher and Stephen Greenblatt, *Practicing New Historicism* (Chicago: University of Chicago Press, 2000), p. 20.

441 Ibid., pp. 21, 48, 31.

442 Mary Douglas, quoted in R. L. Stirrat and Heiko Henkel, "The Development Gift: The Problem of Reciprocity in the NGO World," *Annals of the American Academy of Political and Social Science* 554, no. 1 (1997): 73.

443 See Ian Baucom, *Specters of the Atlantic: Finance Capital, Slavery, and the Philosophy of History* (Durham, NC: Duke University Press, 2005).

444 Slaughter, *Human Rights, Inc.,* p. 5.

ACKNOWLEDGMENTS

Several paragraphs in this manuscript were previously published as portions of the following essays: "The Gulf Wars and the US Peace Movement," *American Literary History* 21 (Summer 2009): 418–428; "Human Rights in Literary Studies," *Human Rights Quarterly* 31 (May 2009): 394–409; and "Fictional Feeling: Philosophy, Cognitive Science, and the American Gothic," *American Literature* 76 (September 2004): 437–466. I am grateful for permission to reprint.

INDEX